Scaling Up, Scaling Down

Scaling Up, Scaling Down

Overcoming Malnutrition in Developing Countries

Edited by

Thomas J. Marchione

Gordon and Breach Publishers

Australia   Canada   China   France   Germany   India
Japan   Luxembourg   Malaysia   The Netherlands
Russia   Singapore   Switzerland

TX
360.5
.S32
1999

Amsteldijk 166
1st Floor
1079 LH Amsterdam
The Netherlands

British Library Cataloguing in Publication Data

Scaling up, scaling down : overcoming malnutrition in
    developing countries
    1. Malnutrition – Developing countries 2. Nutrition –
    Developing countries 3. Malnutrition – Government policy –
    Developing countries
    I. Marchione, Thomas
    616.3'9'0091724

    ISBN 90-5700-547-6

CONTENTS

FOREWORD

On the eve of the twenty-first century, new optimism, new commitment and a new sense of challenge have entered into global development. Widespread achievement in improving access to basic health, primary education, clean water, basic sanitation and family planning—and in reducing poverty more generally over the last two decades—has created new hope that further progress is possible and at an accelerated rate. The global conferences of the 1990s, attended by many heads of state, have ensured visibility and new commitments to a series of specific goals for spreading these achievements in all regions of the world.

Nutritional advance has both contributed to and benefited from this record of achievement and growing optimism. Since 1980, the prevalence of stunted and underweight children has been substantially reduced in Asia, Latin America, the Caribbean, the Middle East and North Africa—achieving rates of reduction of seven to nine percent per decade in the prevalence of stunting in each region. Only in Sub-Saharan Africa has undernutrition been stagnant: the tragic accompaniment of poor economic and social performance, reinforced by falling export prices, declining international assistance and rising debt.

Stunting and underweight reflect the general inadequacy of protein, energy and micronutrients in the diets of children, along with underlying failures in health and family care. In the early 1990s, this general malnutrition continued to be causally associated with more than half of the 12 million young children who die each year in the developing regions of the world.

In addition to this albeit uneven progress in combating general malnutrition, dramatic advances have been achieved in tackling iodine and vitamin A deficiency. Since 1990, some 60 countries have taken steps to iodate all salt produced within their borders and require all imported salt to meet international requirements for iodation. The result has been a dramatic decline in iodine deficiency: prevalence has been halved and an estimated 12 million children have been saved from severe mental retardation. Rapid and significant reductions in vitamin A deficiency have also been made by incorporating vitamin capsules into the public health regime for young children, along with other health actions.

The nutrition challenge confronting us in the twenty-first century is to advance these gains. Commitments to accelerate action in tackling nutritional problems are at the heart of this important, positive and energizing volume. Part I outlines the challenge. Parts II to IV deal with the supportive actions that must be taken, analyzed within the important and stimulating framework of "scaling up from the grassroots" and "scaling down from the summit." The summit consists of the governments of developing countries together with the groups that play the critical international role in nutrition—donors, universities, international intergovernmental and nongovernmental organizations.

The approach of the volume is analytical: to encourage a "culture of inquiry" and analysis, not to present a cookbook of predetermined recipes. Moreover, the inquiry is focused on the practical questions of what to do and how, rather than on the relatively over-addressed questions of why nutrition problems occur. There are case studies covering Vietnam, Haiti, Togo and Bangladesh, as well as numerous references to actual experience in outlining and analyzing approaches that have and have not succeeded.

The concepts of scaling up and scaling down are the hallmarks of the volume. Often, scaling up is used in "development speak" to mean little more than to ensure that an approach is carried on at a scale sufficient to cover a district or a country, not merely a community. Thomas Marchione and his fellow authors go much further. They make it clear that it is the *quality* of the relationship between the grassroots and the summit that is important for scaling up to ensure that the summit is listening and learning and is playing its necessary role in supporting and responding. Marchione and colleagues emphasize that the success or failure of most nutritional efforts at grassroots depends on the broader context, including scaling down by the summit—the nature of the responses and support the summit gives to the grassroots. Such support must cover a wide range of forms— ultimately the creation of an enabling environment that encourages local action; with employment and income opportunities for small and landless farmers: pro-poor growth policies; ready access to cost-effective technologies; and open, fair and dynamic markets, nationally and internationally.

All this underlines the need for effective partnership with the large number of groups involved directly and indirectly in nutrition, and with those engaged in economic and social programming and policy making. The many issues addressed in this book should help provide both the perspective and specifics by which to improve such partnerships.

Reading this book makes clear that the task of reducing and ending malnutrition is a challenging but achievable goal. It is the conviction of Marchione that in the last few years we have entered a new development era, one that "provides a new array of opportunities and constraints for addressing the world's nutrition problems." This new era has been created in part by the end of the Cold War, by ending competition with socialist and non-aligned economic alternatives. Other changes have brought new opportunities and growing emphasis on commitment to human rights, including the right to food and nutrition; the increase in the number of democratic governments; the rising importance of civil society and new knowledge and experience of participatory techniques. Marchione warns about some negative developments: the decline in development assistance, the vicissitudes of market forces, and the reluctance of private investors to offset these trends by increasing support to poorer countries. Most troubling of all are the large number of civil conflicts and complex emergencies, which are so clearly related to the worst of the nutritional situations.

Notwithstanding these constraints, progress and new and important opportunities ultimately depend on how people and leaders respond to them to improve nutrition worldwide. This is the challenge that deserves our support. This volume makes a major contribution by defining the tasks and encouraging the commitments needed.

Richard Jolly
Chairman, UN Nutrition Council
ACC Sub-Committee on Nutrition

PREFACE

At the end of the twentieth century many countries in the Third World face persistent problems of malnutrition and hunger that have preoccupied practitioners, researchers and policy-makers for at least fifty years. Of special concern to the authors in this book is the chronic malnutrition of children under five years of age, particularly the general malnutrition that affects their ability to maintain international standards of growth. In the early 1990s, general malnutrition was affecting an estimated one-third of children in developing countries, mostly in south Asia and Sub-Saharan Africa.

This malnutrition causes dramatically increased death rates from infectious diseases each year, including an estimated six and one-half million deaths in 1995 and increased lifetime disability for many more. The health equation is simple: improved nutrition equals improved health, life rather than death for millions of people. How to get from here to there is the question. This book's principal focus is on programs addressing this chronic malnutrition problem of young children, with strong secondary emphasis on the broader global problems of food and nutrition. Chapter 1, for example, reviews the status and trends of world food supply, food poverty, micronutrient malnutrition and the transient hunger connected to civil war and natural disaster. Chapter 9 is devoted to a vitamin A antiblindness program, and in chapter 13 steps are advocated to break the intergenerational relationships of malnutrition through more attention to women's nutrition.

In the half-century since World War II, nutritionists have developed a sophisticated understanding of the complex interrelationships between food production, consumption, nutrition and hunger. Considerable research and theorizing by nutritionists, anthropologists, geographers and economists have also been devoted to measuring and building conceptual models of the societal causes of food insecurity and malnutrition. These models converge on a key goal of policy and programming: nutrition security, the sustainable achievement by individuals of nutrition adequate for maintaining health, growth and productive participation in society.

The widely known UNICEF model of underlying and basic causes of poor nutrition is supported by the authors in this volume: household food insecurity, poor access to health amenities and inappropriate caring behavior are all linked to basic failures in the prevailing political, social and economic systems. This dovetails with the conceptual models of hunger and food insecurity that have been elaborated and accepted by other development organizations and by academics. This book begins with an analysis of food supply (global and national food availability), food poverty (access to food by households) and food deprivation (utilization of food in household and in the human body).

The volume includes examples of projects and programs designed to bring about nutritional security and to overcome malnutrition through sustainable community-focused programs. Using these examples, the authors provide insights into the profession of twentieth-century practitioners: international nutrition and community nutrition, and what leading nutritionists have begun to call "public nutrition," i.e., nutrition problems of populations and the public policies and programs needed to address them. It contains program analysis and proscriptions relevant to government and non-governmental organizations designing, managing and evaluating food and nutrition programs. The book seeks in part to address the concerns of those who have alleged that scientific nutritionists in the last quarter of this century have neglected research and training on practical solutions.

Key to the practical solutions of the world's malnutrition problems is the quality of the relationship between the "grassroots" and the development "summit." Peter Uvin, in chapter 5, identifies the grassroots as communities, community-based organizations and local government agencies closest to the malnutrition problem in developing countries. The "summit" is described as foreign-assistance donors, universities, international organizations and international non-governmental organizations in developed countries and central governments in developing countries. A dynamic partnership that builds successful nutrition programs involves "scaling up" on the part of the grassroots and "scaling down" on the part of the summit. Again extending from Uvin, scaling goes beyond the notion of increasing or decreasing program sizes or amounts of resources. It is a more advanced way of thinking about what is often referred to as the "bottom-up" and "top-down" approaches to development. In this book scaling up involves strengthening local capacities to sustain nutritional security: building on useful elements in the existing local culture (cultural scaling up); expanding the size and spread (quantitative scaling up); increasing technical scope (functional scaling up); increasing human and financial sustainability (organizational scaling up); and influencing program priorities and policies of the summit (political scaling up). Scaling down refers to methods and capacities by which the summit nurtures and complements local grassroots development. As local capacities are scaled up, summit control over decisions and functions is scaled down. The accountability of the summit to the grassroots is strengthened.

Advocacy of these ideas is not new, but changes in the development environment in the last quarter of the twentieth century, particularly the ending of the Cold War, are new and highly compatible with it. The new environment presents needs and opportunities that require highly participatory and sensitive approaches to local needs and capacities for development. We have entered a new development era demanding a new public nutrition practice.

The proportion of the world's people living under governments with formal commitments to democratic governance grew to historic highs in the 1990s. Since 1975, non-governmental organizations working in the fields of development and humanitarian assistance are more numerous, active and likely to be heard in the corridors of power than ever before. Also unprecedented in human history is the growing consensus on the universal human rights that underpin nutritional security: economic rights, especially the human rights of individuals to food and to be free from hunger, and civil and political rights, especially human rights for women and children. All of this is facilitated by information technologies that are reaching every corner of the planet.

Yet this is a time of instability in state institutions and economic policies that had since World War II framed the quest to overcome hunger in poor countries. While economic liberalization has brought prosperity and promise to many in the developing world, globalization of finance and trade are treating food more and more like any other commodity and less and less like the unique life-giving substance that all people have a right to obtain.

In this new environment, practitioners in partnership with Third World communities are challenged to devise programs that sustainably reduce malnutrition. These chapters illustrate answers to these questions: What types of information are needed? What roles must partners play and what capacities must they have? What is the mix of skills and concerns that produces practitioners who can plan and implement successful nutrition security programs?

The book is divided into four parts. Part I (chapters 1–4), presents the range of food, malnutrition and hunger problems, and considers how well we are equipped to meet them in the new development era. In chapter 1, Uvin reviews problems we face after the end of the Cold War. Using the

World Hunger Program categories of food supply, food poverty and food deprivation, he analyzes the trends and prospects of world food production, food stocks and food assistance, general malnutrition (based on children underweight for age), and micronutrient deficiencies. David Pelletier (chapter 2) presents his meta-analysis of the relationship of child malnutrition to greatly increased risk of child mortality. His results imply a new development paradigm that is built on broad-based equitable development, grassroots capacity-building and empowerment of communities, rather than selective interventions targeted at high-risk individuals.

Chapters 3 and 4 consider changes in the practice of nutrition. Levinson and McLachlan give a short history of international nutrition after World War II, reviewing the shifts from top-down, pre-formulated multi-sectoral solutions determined by summit institutions to bottom-up programming sensitive to local contexts, needs and conditions. They caution against isolated interventions and question how far devolution can go. In chapter 4, Marchione derives six dimensions of the professional culture of public nutrition and describes how practice must shift in the new development era. Nutrition problem analysis must shift in the direction of greater employment of human rights norms, better understanding of macro-economic and political forces as causes, and more attention to indigenous knowledge as expert knowledge. Programming must trend toward local participation and flexible, adaptive process models rather than "blueprint" programming. It must link sectors horizontally with full knowledge of local needs, and more attention must be placed on local financial sustainability.

Chapters 5–9 (part II) contain one meta-analysis and four case studies of grassroots nutrition and health programs that have scaled-up along the dimensions of culture, quantity, function, organization and power. Peter Uvin (chapter 5) analyzes the growth of ten Third World NGOs who were winners of Alan Shawn Feinstein World Hunger Awards from 1986 to 1996. From the vantage point of political science, Uvin defines key terms: the summit, grassroots, scaling-up and scaling-down, which with some adaptation became the conceptual pillars of this book. Although the missions of the grassroots non-governmental organizations he describes are more typically aimed at elimination of poverty generally than at improving food or nutrition conditions specifically, the lessons he derives on how organizations grow in complexity, size and power are invaluable to nutrition programmers. Similarly, he reviews examples of scaling down resulting from political pressures from grassroots organizations.

Chapters 6 and 7 are premised on the concept of positive deviance: the assumption that some of the most appropriate knowledge and practices for good nutrition pre-exist among those poor mothers who know best how to raise healthy children. Programs then can be derived from scaling up these cultural elements. In chapter 6, Jerry and Monique Sternin and David Marsh present a dramatic illustration of how an international NGO, Save the Children, working with the full cooperation of the Vietnamese government, solved a desperate child malnutrition problem in Than Hoe Province near Hanoi, and widely scaled it up through the creation of a Living University. Gretchen Berggren et al. (chapter 7) review the cost-effective outcome of 30 years of community-based nutrition education programming through the Albert Schweitzer Hospital in the Artibonite Valley in central Haiti.

Chapter 8 evaluates the rehabilitation of government health centers in Togo's central district. Kasa Pangu et al. trace methods of organizationally scaling up district health centers, with the help of donor funding. Evidence is presented on the details of involving communities, raising local revenue through user fees, and negotiating equity policies, while significantly improving health service utilization rates.

This section ends with Ted Greiner and M. A. Mannan (chapter 9) evaluating how the World International Foundation cost-effectively improved consumption of vitamin A-rich vegetables among millions of extremely poor people in several districts in northern Bangladesh. They analyze the evolution of this program over nearly a decade, as it scaled up functionally, quantitatively and politically, while struggling with its summit partnerships and staff problems.

Part III (chapters 10–12) reviews methods and approaches for cost-effectively gathering critical information for nutritional security program design and evaluation. The section begins with Ellen Messer's overview of participatory and rapid methods that have been developed by anthropologists and other social scientists for quickly learning relevant parts of local cultures and community environments, and involving local people. Messer raises challenges and questions for summit practitioners in health and nutrition regarding their willingness to risk using these methods not only to extract information but to empower communities to solve their own problems.

In chapter 11 Timothy Frankenberger and Katherine McCaston, CARE food security advisors, outline the method of rapid food and livelihood security assessment. This method emerged from the field of applied anthropology and farming systems research. CARE finds it well suited to summit and grassroots interaction for diagnosing livelihood and nutrition security, while building local capacity to use the method. McLachlan and Levinson (chapter 12) illustrate, through a South African school feeding program, a new analytical tool called program constraints assessment. This method shapes interventions to fit existing institutional settings by identifying local policy and institutional constraints, while strengthening local abilities to analyze and solve problems.

Chapters 13 and 14 (part IV) present overviews of capacities needed by the summit to best facilitate scaling up. Micheline Beaudry begins the section by outlining nutritional problems and needs from the worldwide vantage point of UNICEF. She analyzes how governments must respect local communities and involve them in the programming process, how basic causes must be better analyzed, and she presents evidence supporting the need to reform nutrition research and academic training to respond to the demand for better programming. Chapter 14 is the editor's review of the entire book, presenting conclusions and lessons for summit practitioners on programming, research, advocacy and training appropriate for a new era of nutrition practice.

This volume evolved from ideas first developed in 1995 during my six months as an associate research professor in World Hunger at Brown University, Providence, Rhode Island, while on leave from the United States Agency for International Development. Seven of the chapters began as presentations at sessions of the Eighth Annual Hunger Research Briefing and Exchange in Providence. This book, therefore, is not intended to be consistent with the official views and policies of the United States government.

I wish to acknowledge the encouragement of colleagues at the Alan Shawn Feinstein World Hunger Program at the Watson Institute for International Studies, especially the specific contributions to this book by Peter Uvin and Ellen Messer. I am very grateful to Gerry Gold for the benefit of his wisdom and text editing. Thanks also to Matthew Marchione for his careful work on the many figures.

Most of all, thanks to my family for their forbearance through the process of editing this book on evenings, weekends and holidays. The redeeming hope is that this effort will encourage those at the development summit that hunger and malnutrition indeed can be overcome, and a new era of respect and partnership can be forged with those working so hard and creatively at the grassroots.

CONTRIBUTORS

KOMLAN AFLAGAH holds a master's degree in public health from the Institute of Tropical Medicine in Antwerp, Belgium. He worked as district medical officer in the central region of Togo before becoming director of primary health care at the Ministry of Health in Togo.

MICHELINE BEAUDRY is professor of community and international nutrition at Université Laval in Québec City, Canada. She is former chief of the Nutrition Section at UNICEF Headquarters in New York City. Her international experience has focused mainly upon Latin America and the Caribbean and after 1980, especially in Nicaragua, where she developed and directed a cooperation program between the University in Canada and several institutions in Nicaragua from 1980 to 1991.

GRETCHEN G. BERGGREN, a pediatrician, is maternal and child health consultant for the World Relief Corporation. Berggren was assistant professor/lecturer at Harvard University's School of Public Health, Department of Population and International Health, from 1968 to 1993. She is former director of community-based health information systems for the Albert Schweitzer Hospital in Deschapelles, Haiti, as well as former maternal and child health consultant with Save the Children. She also assisted Warren Berggren in development of the Hearth or "Foyer" method of nutritional rehabilitation, and participated in its adaptation to projects in Vietnam and Bangladesh.

WARREN L. BERGGREN, a public health physician, is director of the child survival program at the World Relief Corporation. He was formerly director of maternal and child health at the Albert Schweitzer Hospital, where he supervised nutritional rehabilitation of more than 8,000 children in hearths operated by the hospital. Berggren is former director of Save the Children's international primary health care program, and former associate professor of tropical public health and population sciences at Harvard University's School of Public Health.

ERVE BOTTEX is currently coordinator of AIDS-related community services in White Plains, New York. He is also a master's degree candidate in public health at the New York Medical College. From 1993 to 1996, Bottex was director of community health at the Albert Schweitzer Hospital.

BARTON R. BURKHALTER is technical officer with the Academy for Educational Development, assigned to the BASICS child-survival project in Washington, DC. He is former research professor of family and community medicine at the University of Arizona, former professor of urban and regional planning at the University of Michigan, and former director of the Center for International Health Information at the International Science and Technology Institute.

TIMOTHY R. FRANKENBERGER, an anthropologist, is senior food security advisor for the partnership and livelihood security unit of CARE International. Prior to CARE, Frankenberger worked for eight years as a farming systems research specialist with the Office of Arid Lands Studies at the University of Arizona.

TED GREINER is senior lecturer in international nutrition at the Unit for International Child Health at Uppsala University Medical School, Sweden. He has been a nutrition consultant to Sida for twelve years. Greiner specializes in program planning and management/evaluation of micronutrient and infant-feeding issues.

M. KABA is a district medical officer in the Ministry of Health, in the central region of Togo.

F. JAMES LEVINSON is director of the International Food and Nutrition Center at Tufts University. He is former director of the MIT International Nutrition Planning Program and the United States Agency for International Development's office of nutrition in Washington, DC. For the past thirty-two years, Levinson has been an active participant in nutrition-project design, monitoring and evaluation, as well as program-driven research in Asia, Africa and Latin America.

M. A. MANNAN is founder and former project director of the Nutritional Blindness Prevention Program for the World International Foundation in Bangladesh. Previously, Mannan was an official in that country's Ministry of Education.

THOMAS J. MARCHIONE, an anthropologist, is employed at the United States Agency for International Development, where he advises on food security and nutrition. Previously, he served as social scientist with the UN at the Caribbean Food and Nutrition Institute and directed the Great Lakes Project on U.S. industrial unemployment. Marchione has been a research professor at Brown University's World Hunger Program and the Institute for Nutrition Research in Oslo, Norway. His research focuses on the relationship of nutrition to national development and human rights.

DAVID R. MARSH, a pediatrician, entered international health after five years with the United States Indian Health Service and six years practicing with a health maintenance organization. He taught and practiced epidemiology at the Aga Khan University College of Medicine in Karachi for five years. Currently, Marsh has been with Save the Children for three years as a child survival specialist and epidemiologist.

M. KATHERINE McCASTON, an anthropologist, is the deputy livelihood security advisor for the partnership and livelihood security unit of CARE International. McCaston has directed field research in Latin America and Africa, and has coordinated project design and proposal development efforts in Angola, Ethiopia, Honduras, Kenya and Togo. She is currently a PhD candidate at the University of Arizona.

MILLA McLACHLAN is nutrition advisor for the Human Development Network at the World Bank. Previously, she was senior policy analyst at the Development Bank of Southern Africa, where she coordinated research on poverty issues and nutrition. McLachlan has contributed to the planning of national nutrition programs, such as an analysis of nutrition-relevant policies for a national report on poverty and inequality in South Africa.

ELLEN MESSER is associate professor (research) and former director of the World Hunger Program at the Watson Institute of International Studies, Brown University, Providence, Rhode Island. Messer, with Peter Uvin, is co-author and co-editor of *The Hunger Report* (World Hunger Program, 1993, 1995). Her research focuses upon issues of women and food (particularly in Mexico), the ecology and politics of world hunger, agrobiotechnology, and United States and international food and nutrition policy.

ROBERT S. NORTHRUP, a public health physician, is a technical officer for the BASICS Project, where he is currently working on public-private sector linkages for child survival. Northrup has been on the faculties of the University of Hawaii, University of Alabama, Brown University, Johns Hopkins University, and Gadjah Mada University in Indonesia.

KASA ASILA PANGU is regional advisor for health at UNICEF in Nairobi, Kenya. Previously he was senior advisor in health-systems development at UNICEF, New York City. Pangu is former technical adviser to the Minister of Health in Zaire, former associate professor at the Institute of Tropical Medicine in Antwerp, Belgium, and was coordinator of a primary health care project in Togo before joining UNICEF.

DAVID L. PELLETIER is associate professor of nutrition policy in the Division of Nutritional Sciences at Cornell University, Ithaca, New York. His interests involve causes and consequences of nutrition problems in developing and developed countries, and in the integration of technical, institutional and indigenous knowledge in policy and program development. His primary geographic foci have been in Sub-Saharan Africa and the United States.

JERRY STERNIN has twenty years of development experience as a Peace Corps volunteer and director in Nepal, the Philippines, Rwanda and Mauritania, and as Save the Children director in Bangladesh, the Philippines, Vietnam and Egypt.

MONIQUE STERNIN has worked in development in Bangladesh and Vietnam. She was responsible for creating a child-stimulation program at the International Center for Diarrheal Disease Research–Bangladesh in Dhaka, and developed, along with Jerry Sternin, a Nutrition Education Rehabilitation Program in Vietnam that reaches over one million people.

EL HADJI TAIROU holds a master's degree in public health from the Institute of Tropical Medicine in Antwerp, Belgium. He worked as a district medical officer before becoming regional director of health in the Ministry of Health, in the central region of Togo.

S. TCHEDRE is a district medical officer and social assistant in the Ministry of Health, in the central region of Togo.

PETER UVIN is associate professor (research) at the Watson Institute of International Studies at Brown University, Providence, Rhode Island. He is editor of the World Hunger Program's *The Hunger Report*, and has written extensively about issues of food, hunger, development aid and grassroots organizations. His work experience is primarily in francophone Africa; he has written articles about Burundi and Rwanda.

I   Malnutrition and Hunger: The Challenge

CHAPTER 1

Eliminating Hunger after the End of the Cold War: Progress and Constraints

Peter Uvin

In this chapter, three distinct but related concepts will be used to estimate the numbers of people affected by hunger and to analyze the global food situation: food shortage, food poverty, and food deprivation.[1] Each concept focuses on different aspects of the phenomenon of hunger and different levels of aggregation involved in its study.

Food shortage occurs when total food supplies within a geographic area—the world as a whole, or regions, or countries—are insufficient to meet the needs of the population living within that area. *Food poverty* refers to the situation in which households cannot obtain enough food to meet the needs of all their members. *Food deprivation* refers to inadequate individual consumption or absorption of food energy or of specific nutrients, the form of malnutrition known as undernutrition.

The overlay and the interplay between these three faces of hunger allows us to get a grasp of the key factors that underlie hunger: factors related to policy, distribution, culture, and economics. At the international level, the end of the Cold War has produced major changes in some of these,

1

and this has affected the different faces of hunger. Some of the changes have been positive, creating opportunity and willingness for governments and international organizations to modify policies in favor of the hungry and the poor. Others have been negative, producing disincentives and conflicting priorities for investing in overcoming hunger (on these matters, see Marchione 1996).

FOOD SHORTAGE

Global Food Supply

Global food supply data allow us to answer the question: "is there enough food in the world to provide all human beings with an adequate diet?" The answer is "yes" (Table 1.1). If we compute the global food supply in terms of calories and divide that number by the world's population (assuming an average per capita caloric requirement of 2350 kcal/day), there has been enough food to feed approximately 20% more people than the actual world population every year since the mid-1970s.

The picture changes, however, if we "improve" the diet of the world's population, allowing for 25% of the calories to come from animal products,

Table 1.1. Population Potentially Supported by the Current World Food Production

Year	Basic Diet		Full but Healthy Diet	
	Percentage of Actual World Population	Billion People	Percentage of Actual World Population	Billion People
1985	120.0	5.8	60.0	2.9
1986	120.3	5.9	60.2	3.0
1987	119.0	6.0	59.5	3.0
1988	119.4	6.1	59.7	3.1
1989	122.4	6.2	61.2	3.1
1990	124.0	6.3	62.0	3.2
1991	122.9	6.4	61.4	3.2
1992	124.0	6.5	62.0	3.3
1993	122.9	6.6	61.5	3.3
1994	122.3	6.7	61.1	3.4

Source: These data are extrapolations of a data series developed by Kates, Chen et al. 1988 in the first Hunger Report published by the World Hunger Program. They are based on FAO production and UN population data.

and creating a richer and more varied diet that includes vegetables, fruits and oils—basically a "full-but-healthy" diet, still less rich in meats and fats than the average North American diet. We now find that, with an improved diet, throughout this period, only approximately 60% of the world's population could be fed with existing food production.

Preliminary data indicate that total world *cereal* production fell by 2.7% in 1995/6 and rose by 9% in 1996/7 (*FAO Food Outlook*, Sept. 1996). If total food production followed this trend, this would *grosso modo* translate into a 5% and 2.5% per capita loss respectively for the basic and full-but healthy diets in 1995/6, and a major 7% and 3.5% gain respectively for 1996/7.

Another indicator used to assess global adequacy of food supplies is whether in a single year there are adequate carryover food stocks in the world should the following year be calamitous (Table 1.2). The only data available are for cereals, and they show that up to the middle of the 1990s cereal carryover stocks have fluctuated around 20% of world cereal consumption, but with a significant decline beginning in 1993/94. Since 1995/96, world cereal stocks have fallen for the first time in more than a decade below the 17–18% which the FAO secretariat considers the minimum necessary to safeguard world food security (FAO Food Outlook, June 1993). It is important to note that this decline in world cereal stocks is almost solely explainable by changes in developed country stocks (with US stocks being the lowest since 1973). Developing country cereal stocks remained largely stable throughout this period.

In short, the world produces enough food to feed its entire population on a basic diet, and has sufficient stocks to protect itself against disasters. However, the margins seem to be slim: world food production is only sufficient to cover diets that are close to vegetarian, and serious improvement in diets could not be achieved with current world food production levels.

Table 1.2. Cereal Carryover Stocks, Million Tons

	1991/92	1992/93	1993/94	1994/95	1995/96	1996/97 forecast
All cereals of which	336	381	339	312	266	282
Developed countries	175	214	170	153	108	127
Developing countries	162	167	169	158	158	155
Stocks as % of World Cereal Consumption	19	22	19	18	15	15

Source: Food Outlook, July–Aug. 1997.

Similarly, stocks are low and their stabilizing impact on prices is disappearing. The data clearly show slightly worsening trends from 1993 onwards.

Does this mean that the world is incapable of feeding more people a better diet? Or even worse, that the world is running out of food, having achieved its natural limits? The answer is a definite no. Current world production and stock levels are the outcome more of changeable government policies than of unmovable natural constraints. The observed recent decline in world food production, for example, is almost entirely due to the effects, and now the reversal, of rich country protectionist policies: first acreage reduction programs, and then decreases in agricultural subsidies in the United States and European Community. There is no reason to assume that the world could not produce significantly more food than it produced in the last few years, if provided with the incentives and the opportunity. Of concern is that investments in agriculture have markedly dropped from the mid-1980s to the mid-1990s (USDA 1997).

The world food production system is currently in a phase of profound realignment. During the latest General Agreement of Tariffs and Trade (GATT) round of negotiations, the rich countries agreed to a fundamental, albeit still limited, reorientation of the global food production and trade system. Rich countries are committed to decrease their farm subsidies by a set percentage, and their food exports by an even higher percentage. The 1996 U.S. Farm Bill goes a long way in that direction, as have recent EC changes in farm policy.

As a result, the world food system is evolving towards a different equilibrium, with food production and stocks declining in the European Community, the United States, and some other food subsidizing countries. This has begun to put an upward pressure on world food prices—a situation from which, according to standard economic wisdom, the Third World as a whole is likely to benefit in the medium to long run. Indeed, as world food prices rise, food production in the Third World should increase, as should Third World food exports: local farmers would not suffer anymore from artificially low-priced, subsidized, import competition, and would thus be able to increase their own production. According to the FAO (1995c), for example, for the developing countries as a whole, average per capita food supplies are projected to rise by 8% by the year 2010 (see USDA 1996c).

This quite positive picture looks different if one disaggregates to the level of individual countries or specific groups within countries—especially the poor and the hungry. How will food importing nations fare? How about Sub-Saharan Africa which according to all calculations will lose in the process? And how about net food-consuming groups, even in food-exporting countries? It is quite clear that "agricultural trade liberalization and declining producer support in developed countries may actually decrease the welfare of low income population groups in developing nations—especially those groups from food importing nations" (Meyers 1995; FAO 1995b). Hence, the effects of the GATT liberalization on hunger in many Third World countries are unclear, and may well be negative. A parallel process relates to the impact of the transition of most former Eastern European and USSR economies from socialism to capitalism: it is predicted that all the Central and East European countries will become net food exporters by 2005 (USDA 1996a).

National Food Shortages

Although global food supplies are adequate, many countries are vulnerable to national food shortages. Such countries are unable to meet their food needs either through their own production or through commercial food imports. Focusing on 66 countries that are potential food aid recipients, USDA (1997) reported a gap of over 8 million metric tons based on status quo or historical trends in national food consumption and 15 million metric tons based on theoretical food energy requirements. From 1997 to 2007 this gap is projected to grow to nearly 18 million tons for status quo needs and 24 million tons for nutritional needs: some 40 countries will continue to need food assistance. The majority of these countries are in sub-Saharan Africa, which will account for most of the projected global shortage. This is particularly troubling considering the emerging food aid situation discussed further in this section. On the other hand, the 1997 gap amounts to not more than 3–6% of the world's carryover stocks for that year and much less than 1% of the world's food production. Most of the food deprivation and undernutrition of people is not explained by this gap.

As can be seen from Table 1.3, the number of countries suffering from acute food shortages according to FAO's Global Information and Early Warning System increased greatly from 1992 onward, but seems to have dropped in 1996. These figures include a substantial number of recently created countries, in the Commonwealth of Independent States (Armenia, Azerbaijan, Georgia, Tajikistan), in Eastern Europe (Bosnia-Herzegovina, Macedonia) and in Africa (Eritrea). In 1994 the exceptional shortfalls coincided with civil war in five out of six European countries and in nine out of fifteen African ones (Eritrea and Ethiopia, although at peace now, can be said to suffer from the effects of decades of war). Food shortages in Haiti and Afghanistan were also coincident with war or civil unrest there. In Iraq, they related to the effects of past war and current sanctions (see also

Table 1.3. Number of Countries with Food Shortage or Famine, 1986–1997

Year	No.	Year	No.
1986	11	1992	27
1987	10	1993	24
1988	16	1994	25
1989	15	1995	25
1990	18	1996	21
1991	19	1997	29

Source: Derived from Foodcrops and Shortages, all issues 1985 to 1997: the list includes all countries that suffered from food shortages more than 8 months during the calendar year.

IFRCRCS 1995). In 1995 war or the effects of recent warfare were similarly related to food shortage in 20 out of 25 countries; the figures for 1996 were 18 out of 21. The few countries where long-term food shortage did not coincide with conflict were the People's Democratic Republic of Korea, Malawi, Nepal, Lesotho, Mongolia, and Zaire (The Democratic Republic of Congo).

Hence, "man-made disasters," the consequence of war or civil unrest, are by far the main causes of acute food shortages in the post-Cold War period. Throughout the 1990s they constituted more than half of all emergencies, more than half of which were in Sub-Saharan Africa. At the beginning of the 1990s, with the Cold War over, it was widely thought that the total eradication of man-made (if not all) famine was possible, even imminent. Yet, there was a resurgence of brutal ethnic conflicts throughout the world, and especially in Africa (Figure 1.1).

This increase in brutal civil wars is triggered by the end of the Cold War. The end of superpower competition and the disintegration of the Soviet empire took the lid off a large number of potentially explosive situations. Combinations of poverty, past discrimination, long-standing animosities, and populist politicians, provided fertile grounds for extremism and violence. In the absence of strong central states and with the withdrawal of international military support from many leaders, many new (Georgia, Bosnia, etc.) or not-so-new (Somalia, Liberia, Rwanda, etc.) states soon became immersed in violence and civil war. Many suffered a total disintegration of central authority. In the resulting protracted wars, food has been widely used as a weapon, with the warring parties destroying each other's access to food, and seeking to hinder international attempts at providing food, even to non-combatants (Messer 1994, 1996).

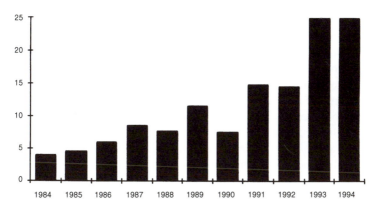

Figure 1.1. WFP relief operations for man-made disasters by number of beneficiaries (millions), 1984–1994. (*Source*: WFP 1994:24; 1995:19.)

Refugees and Internally Displaced Persons

Refugees and internally displaced people are among the world's most food insecure people. Refugees are defined as people who have been driven across international borders as a result of war or civil strife. Their assets and sources of income disappear, often overnight. As a result, their entitlement set collapses, in the worst cases to below starvation level. Data by the U.S. Committee for Refugees (USCR) indicate that at the end of 1992, approximately 19 million persons were refugees. This figure decreased to 16.3 million in 1993, remained stagnant in 1994, and continued to decrease slightly in 1995 (USCR 1994; USCR 1995; US Mission to the UN 1996). In addition, in 1993 at least 26 million people forced out of their homes and regions remained within the borders of their own countries (USCR 1995; ACC/SCN 1994).

International Responses to Famines and Refugee Situations

The world community, together with the governments involved, is increasingly capable of rapid response, adapting humanitarian aid to local realities, drawing on local or regional food supplies (triangular food aid), and minimizing negative consequences of emergencies on long-term development. This trend towards faster and more adapted international responses to emergencies had begun long before the end of the Cold War. It is rather linked to the increasingly widespread acceptance of a worldwide norm against starvation. It can be said, however, that the end of the Cold War has accelerated this trend, allowing for the development of stronger notions of humanitarian intervention, as well as the use of the military in humanitarian operations (Minear and Weiss 1995). On the other hand, the rise in the number and the severity of civil wars has put severe strains on the international humanitarian system.

All these changes have had both positive and negative effects on development prospects. On the positive side, much starvation has been averted as a result of timely (and even not so timely) international action. Using various methods, Steve Hansch (1995) of the Refugee Policy Group has recently attempted to quantify the number of worldwide deaths due to starvation. His conclusion is that "starvation deaths during the 1990s will range from 150,000 to 200,000 per year, with a likely value for 1995 of 250,000" (Hansch 1995:1). This figure is still unacceptably high, but constitutes a continuation of a declining trend that began in the 1950s. On the negative side, the need to intervene throughout the world with humanitarian aid has constituted an enormous diversion of development resources. This is manifested most clearly in the realm of food aid, to which we now turn.

Food Aid

Three trends have shaped recent food aid: an increase in the proportion of food aid devoted to humanitarian disasters; an increase in the share of food aid that went to the Newly Independent Countries; and a decline in overall levels of food aid since 1994. The first two of these trends began in the early 1990s and they are the direct result of the end of the Cold War. The third trend started in 1994 and results primarily from US domestic politics.

First, the proportion of food aid devoted to emergencies compared to other (project and structural) uses has greatly increased (see Table 1.4, with data on cereal food aid, which accounts for the vast majority of food aid shipments). Globally, the share of relief food aid in global food aid has climbed from approx. 20% in the beginning of the 1990s to more than 30% in 1992 and 1994. In 1994, the WFP found itself for the first time in its thirty year history in the position of providing more relief food aid than any other type of aid. Note that non-food humanitarian assistance presents the same picture: from 1971 to 1990, its value doubled every 4 or 5 years, from US$ 80 million to US$ 1 billion; between 1990 and 1993, it tripled to US$ 3.2 billion (IFRCRCS 1995).

Second, from 1991/92 onwards, the share of food aid that went to the "Economies in Transition" (the remains of the disintegration of the Soviet Union and its Eastern European allies) increased greatly, at the expense of the poorest and neediest African and Asian countries (Table 1.5). In parallel, the proportion of global food aid going to Low-Income Food-Deficit

Table 1.4. Global Cereal Food Aid by Type, 1988–1996

Year	Total MTs (000)	Relief (%)	Project (%)	Structural (%)
1988	13,153	22	27	51
1989	10,727	20	23	56
1990	12,458	20	20	60
1991	11,991	27	23	50
1992	13,402	33	17	50
1993	15,020	25	15	60
1994	10,700	34	22	44
1995	9,500	34	26	40
1996	7,700			

Source: WFP, Food Aid Monitor, June 1995:28; WFP, 1996:51; the 1996 food aid figure is a forecast from Food Outlook, Sept. 1996:2.

Countries (LIFDCs) declined from 1991 to 1994, reaching 65% in 1993/4, its lowest level in more than 20 years (Uvin 1994a). Donors have always maintained that food aid to the former East bloc would not be at the expense of aid to "traditional" recipients. The data in Table 5, however, document that this promise has not been kept. The great increase in food aid to Eastern Europe and the former Soviet Union (WFP 1996) seems to have been at the expense of the poorest, food-deficit countries. From 1994/5, these trends seem to have been halted, though. Food aid to the Economies in Transition fell, while the proportion of the LIFDCS increased again to its historical high levels. The interpretation of the latter trend is rendered difficult, however, as the two categories overlap: since January 1, 1995, nine CIS republics and 3 Eastern European countries (Albania, Macedonia and Romania) have been reclassified as LIFDCs. Together, they accounted for approximately 1,4 million tons of food aid in 1993/4 (FAO 1995a).

In 1995 a third shift suddenly occurred, namely a dramatic 25% decline in world food aid donations. This trend continued in 1996 (USDA 1996b; WFP 1996). The major reason for this rapid decline in world food aid shipments was the United States decision, taken in April 1995, to unilaterally reduce its Food Aid Convention (FAC) commitments. This had widespread ramifications because the U.S. Government has for many decades been the world's largest food aid donor through its Public Law 480 program.

As an immediate result, US food aid plummeted from a high of 8.5 million tons in 1993/94 to 4.3 million tons in 1994/95 (see FAO *Food Outlook*, April 1996: Table A.14; USDA, 1996b), accounting for more than the

Table 1.5. Cereal Food Aid Shipments by Region, 1986–1996

	(1) World, 1000 tons	(2) LIFDCs, 1000 tons	(3) LIFDCs as Percentage of World	(4) Economies in Transition, 1000 tons	(5) Economies in Transition as Percentage of World	(6) Emergency Food Aid as a Percentage of Total
1986/87	12552	11603	92	1	0	
1987/88	13609	12164	89	0	0	
1988/89	11326	9728	86	0	0	25
1989/90	11315	7979	71	1582	14	22
1990/91	12356	9799	79	1342	11	25
1991/92	13086	11000	84	1927	15	27
1992/93	15184	11073	73	4390	29	32
1993/94	12633	8226	65	4696	37	28
1994/95	9187	7944	86	1774	19	31
1995/96	7700	6000	86			

Source: Food Outlook, March–April 1996. LIFDCs are Low Income Food Deficit Countries.

observed decline in world food aid (meaning that other countries partly compensated). This reduction by the U.S. Government is extremely unfortunate. First, it implies a significant weakening of the international food aid regime, created by the United States in the first place. Indeed, the FAC was created in 1967, on the initiative of the United States, to promote burden sharing in the food aid field. It set up a system of minimum quotas for food aid for all rich countries, thus marking the beginning of the systematic involvement of all the world's rich countries in food aid. Up to the 1995 action by the U.S. Government, the FAC had an excellent track record which had almost never been violated by its members, even in years of bad harvest. Second, reduction in food aid took place exactly when world food prices were rising and projected demand for food aid was also rising, thus increasing poor, food-deficit countries' need for support (USDA 1995; USDA 1996d). These cutbacks hurt the low-income food-deficit countries although the "economies in transition" group took the single largest total cut (by approximately 60%).

FOOD POVERTY

Food poverty is the inability of households to obtain sufficient food to meet the nutritional needs of their members due to inadequate income, poor access to productive resources, inability to benefit from private or public food transfers, or lack of other entitlements to food. In this section, we present estimates of numbers of people living in households that cannot afford to provide their members the dietary energy (calories) they require.

In 1992, in preparation for the International Conference on Nutrition, the FAO produced estimates for the number of food-poor households in the world, including, for the first time, China and the other Asian communist countries. These data have become more or less generally accepted and reproduced by all international organizations.

According to these data, reproduced in Table 1.6, the absolute number of the food poor in the world began to decline after 1975, from 976 to 786 million persons in 1990. The picture that emerges, then, is more positive than generally assumed. The incidence of hunger in the world has declined significantly, and fewer people are undernourished now than fifteen years ago, not withstanding the addition of approximately 1.1 billion persons to the Third World's population. In 1996, FAO increased the 1990–1992 figures slightly to 840 million, but projected a continued major decline to 680 million by the year 2010. Table 1.6 shows that this decline has not been evenly spread across the world. It is primarily in the Near East and North Africa,

Table 1.6. The Percentages and Absolute Numbers of Chronically Malnourished (Underfed) by Region

Year	Sub-Saharan Africa	Near East & North Africa	Middle America	South America	South Asia	East Asia	China	All
Percent by Regions								
1970	35	23	24	17	34	35	46	36
1975	37	17	20	15	34	32	40	33
1980	36	10	15	12	30	22	22	26
1990	37	5	14	13	24	17	16	20
Numbers (millions) by Region								
1970	94	32	21	32	255	101	406	942
1975	112	26	21	32	289	101	395	976
1980	128	15	18	29	285	78	290	846
1990	175	12	20	38	277	74	189	786

Source: ACC/SCN 1992:105.

East Asia, and China that great improvements have been made. The worst trend is observed in Sub-Saharan Africa, where by 2010, one-third of the population is projected to be food insecure (FAO 1996).

Finally, a worrisome increase in food poverty can be detected in Eastern Europe. Economic change, as well as warfare in some countries, has provoked a "deterioration of unparalleled proportions in human welfare throughout most of the region" (Crossette 1994). UNICEF has documented that poverty, disease, malnutrition, and infant mortality are on the rise (UNICEF 1996). The same seems to hold for the former Soviet Union, where the same factors—economic change and civil strife—are provoking a massive contraction of incomes and entitlements, aggravated by the collapse of public health and social safety mechanisms.

FOOD DEPRIVATION

Food deprivation results from the inability of individuals to obtain sufficient food to meet their nutritional needs. This can be due either to overall food shortage, to household food poverty, or to the existence of a special need that is not satisfied. The latter most often applies to pregnant and lactating women, sick persons, children, and the elderly. Here, we will briefly present the available data for childhood undernutrition and for micronutrient deficiency. Childhood malnutrition data reflect disease and care as much as food availability. (See the next chapter by Pelletier and the discussion in chapter 13 by Beaudry.)

Childhood Undernutrition

In 1995, 157.6 million children under five years of age—29.3% of all children in that age group—were underweight, somewhat down from 168 million twenty years earlier (Table 1.7). This trend constitutes an improvement over past estimates: 1993 data, for example, predicted both higher proportions and higher absolute figures (ACC/SCN 1993; Uvin 1994a; Uvin 1994b; Uvin 1996). Note that part of the reason is actually that population growth has been slower than expected in most of the world during the last decade. On the other hand, Table 1.7 clearly indicates that the rate of improvement has been slowing down significantly during the 1990s, from a decline of 0.7% a year before 1990 to less than 0.3% in the first half of the 1990s. Note also that IFPRI (1997) data put the total number of underweight malnourished children in 1993 at a higher 180 million; their prediction for 2010 is 150 million—a decline from 33% to 25% of the world's children.

Table 1.7. Prevalences and Trends of Underweight (<2 SD Weight-for-Age) Children (0–60 months) by Region and Year

Region	Year				Trends in Percentage Points per Year	
	1975	1985	1990	1995	1985–1990	1990–1995
Sub-Saharan Africa	31.4	25.8	28.0	27.2	0.44	−0.16
Near East & North Africa	19.8	13.0	9.9	9.6	−0.62	−0.06
South Asia	67.7	55.3	50.1	48.8	−1.04	−0.26
East Asia	43.6	39.8	34.2	32.4	−1.12	−0.36
China	26.1	22.7	17.8	15.0	−0.98	−0.56
Middle America	19.3	18.1	15.3	15.2	−0.56	−0.18
South America	15.7	9.8	8.9	8.4	−0.18	−0.10
World	41.6	34.3	30.7	29.3	−0.72	−0.28
Absolute number of children	168	164	161	158[a]		

[a] Due to population new estimations of the population of children under five years of age, this number was revised upward by the World Health Organization to 167 million (WHO 1998). However, prevalence remained at approximately 30% of children in developing countries. See the text for other estimates.
Source: ACC/SCN 1992:67; ACC/SCN 1997:9.

At the 1990 World Summit for Children the international community agreed on a set of specific, quantifiable goals which included halving child malnutrition in all developing countries by the year 2000. At the current rate these targets will not be met. While during the years 1985–1990 the global rate of decline was about half the one needed to achieve the above target, progress has slowed during the first five years of the 1990s. According to the ACC/SCN (1997) update on the matter, "the 1990–1995 rate has slipped, globally and in most regions, to less than one fifth of that necessary." In 1996 at the World Food Summit in Rome the international community adopted the less ambitious objective of reducing the number of undernourished people in the world to half their present level by the year 2015. At current rates, even this target may well not be met.

Micronutrient Deficiencies

During the last decade, there has been an increased interest in micronutrient deficiencies—so-called hidden hunger. The reasons for that include the new scientific understanding that micronutrient deficiencies affect more people and have much more serious consequences than previously thought, as well as the experience that prevention or treatment of such deficiencies can be achieved at low cost (Maxwell and Frankenberger 1992; UNICEF 1992). According to Reutlinger (1993), another reason is that measures that deal with these kinds of malnutrition have the capacity to "reduce human suffering yet do not threaten the existing economic and political structures." Indeed, the reduction of micronutrient deficiencies is the kind of technical intervention that easily mobilizes medical doctors, public health specialists, planners and donors all over the world, is devoid of political risks, and provides relatively cheap and fast results.

The World Health Organization publishes data on the incidence of micronutrient deficiencies (WHO 1991); unfortunately, it uses different (and unusual) regional distinctions, making comparison with the previous tables difficult. Moreover, these WHO data are not historic, hence trends can only be conjectured with extreme difficulty.

As a consequence of iodine deficiency, 29% of the world's population is at risk of goiter, while 12% displays clinical manifestations. Iodine deficiency is usually highly localized, occurring especially in mountainous regions far from the sea. As a result, these data distort reality: for most countries, pockets of deficiency exist, with prevalences of goiter as high as 50% and full cretinism at 1–5%, while the rest of the population is much less affected (ACC/SCN 1987).

Iodine deficiency can be avoided by salt iodization at the low cost of 5 US cents per person per year. At the 1990 World Summit for Children most of the world's countries pledged to iodize at least 95% of all salt supplies by the end of the year 1995. In 1994, 58 countries, home to almost 60% of the developing world's children, are on track to achieve that goal. Another 32 countries could achieve the 1990 goal with an accelerated effort (UNICEF 1996; UNICEF 1994). Trends in iodine deficiency are negative in the former USSR and Eastern Europe, however (Crossette 1994).

Important progress has been made since the beginning of the 1990s in the eradication of vitamin A deficiency. According to figures presented by the World Bank, vitamin A availability per person is up in all developing regions except Africa (World Bank 1994; see too ACC/SCN 1993). Moreover, governments have increasingly resorted to vitamin A supplementation in health care centers or fortification of sugar to solve the problem (Ralte 1996). According to UNICEF, "of the 67 nations concerned [for which data are available], 35 are likely to come close to eliminating the problem by the end of 1995. Approximately two-thirds of the children at risk live in these countries" (UNICEF 1996; UNICEF 1994).

Iron deficiency is the most prevalent form of macronutrient malnutrition. Iron deficiency anemia touches approximately half of all premenopausal women and up to 79% of all pregnant women, primarily in Africa and South Asia (ACC/SCN 1993). Its prevalence has probably increased rather than decreased (Millman et al. 1991). This surge is due both to the improved quality of the reporting and to the fact that the availability of iron in most of the world's regions has decreased or stagnated. Indeed, other data show that iron availability per person is down in all developing regions except the Near East (World Bank 1994; ACC/SCN 1993). At the same time, in most countries government commitment to iron deficiency eradication seems to be much weaker and few public health programs have begun to address the problem seriously (UNICEF 1996).

CONCLUSION

This article has described various trends that impact on world hunger. On the negative side, the great increase in the number and the brutality of civil wars throughout the world—including in regions where there had been none for decades—has created immeasurable suffering, displacement, loss of life, and hunger. There seems to be little good news here: whenever one civil war ends (Mozambique, for example), another one erupts (Cambodia and the two Congos, for example). The international community has not found the mechanisms to cope with these crises. Innovative practices of humanitarian intervention and peacemaking have largely faltered, for they were too politically and financially costly. Food aid is declining rather than increasing (although its emergency content has gone up precisely to face these man-made disasters) and is still used politically by some donors.

On the positive side, policies that affect childhood malnutrition and some of the micronutrient deficiencies have gone further than would have been expected even a decade ago. Significant progress has been made during the last decade by governments and the international community in recognizing the importance of all childhood malnutrition and micronutrient deficiencies, and in designing and implementing programs to combat them. Public health interventions to reduce most micronutrient deficiencies have greatly expanded throughout the world with beneficial results. Worldwide, some kind of consensus has emerged around the need (and the capacity) of governments to invest in human resources. This new consensus constitutes a counter-reaction to the neglect of social considerations during the 5–10 years that structural adjustment monopolized the development agenda of the major institutions. Under pressure to focus on more than macro-economic variables, major donors, foremost the World Bank and USAID, have turned to investments in children and malnutrition to restore a balance.

At the uncertain side, we find the transition of most former Eastern European and USSR economies from socialism to capitalism. In the short run this has certainly led to rises in malnutrition in some of these countries as agricultural production fell, together with import capacity, and public health outlays declined. In the longer term, however, it is quite likely that the adoption of more modern and efficient production methods in the European economy will bring about increased food production—if civil wars and rising inequality do not wipe out these gains.

Another unclear trend can be found in the globalization of the world's economies—a trend that seems to have been strengthened by the end of the Cold War. In the absence of the usual ideological and strategic divisions, there is little choice left for individual states but to insert themselves in the global liberal financial, economic, and commercial order. From the world-wide application of structural adjustment to the massive extension of the GATT rules of free trade into agriculture, services, and intellectual property rights, all countries are becoming full competitors in the global market-place. According to the ideology of economic liberalism, this can only lead to the greatest benefit for the greatest numbers. But many people fear both the short-term and long-term impacts of these trends on the livelihoods of the poor throughout the world. The evidence is contradictory and the trends we observe until now (e.g. a decrease in world food production, for example, especially in the rich countries) will not necessarily last. It is certain that these trends will be crucial to shape food poverty and food shortage in all regions of the world. Given the prevailing distribution of political and economic power in the world, there seems to be little reason for many of the world's poor to rejoice. Political struggles, including those waged by countless NGOs throughout the world, will be the prime determinants of the poor's capacity to benefit from these economic trends (see also, Marchione 1996 and Ch. 4).

NOTES

1. The three aspects of hunger (food shortage, food poverty, and food deprivation), developed in conjunction with the World Hunger Program at Brown University, are quite similar to concepts of food insecurity (food availability, food access, and food utilization) commonly used by development agencies, such as the World Bank. However, most do not use the term, food utilization, except USAID. See Ch. 4 for a brief discussion. Moreover, although child malnutrition indicators are used to suggest food deprivation, the author recognizes that undernutrition in individuals involves interactions of food deprivations with the other two underlying causes in the UNICEF conceptual framework: poor health and poor care (see Chs. 2 and 13).

REFERENCES

ACC/SCN (Administrative Committee on Coordination/Sub-Committee on Nutrition)
(1987)   First Report on the World Nutrition Situation. Geneva: ACC/SCN.
ACC/SCN
(1992)   Second Report on the World Nutrition Situation; Volume 1 Global and Regional Results. Geneva: ACC/SCN.
ACC/SCN
(1993)   Second Report on the World Nutrition Situation; Volume II Country Trends Methods and Statistics. Geneva: ACC/SCN.
ACC/SCN
(1994)   Update on the Nutrition Situation. Geneva: ACC/SCN.
ACC/SCN
(1997)   "Update on the Nutrition Situation 1996. Summary of the Results for the Third Report on the World Nutrition Situation." SCN News 14 (July 1997): 7–9.
Crossette, B.
(1994)   "U.N. Study Finds a Free Eastern Europe Poorer and Less Healthy." New York Times, October 7: A13.

FAO (Food and Agricultural Organization of the United Nations)
   (1993–1996)   *Food Outlook* (*1993–7*). Rome: FAO Global Information and
      Early Warning System on Food and Agriculture.

FAO
   (1995a)   *Foodcrops and Shortages*. January/February. Rome: FAO Global
      Information and Early Warning System on Food and Agriculture.

FAO
   (1995b)   *Impact of the Uruguay Round on Agriculture*. Committee on
      Commodity Problems, Sixtieth Session, 3–7 April 1995, Item 5 of the
      Provisional Agenda. Rome: FAO.

FAO
   (1995c)   *World Agriculture: Towards 2010 Study*. New York: John Wiley & Sons.

FAO
   (1996)   *Food, Agriculture, and Food Security: Development since the World
      Food Conference and Prospects*. FAO World Food Summit Technical
      Background Document 1, Rome: FAO.

FAO/WHO
   (1992)   *Nutrition and Development—a Global Assessment*. Rome: FAO, WHO.

Hansch, S.
   (1995)   *Quantifying Deaths due to Starvation*. Washington: Refugee Policy
      Group.

IFPRI (International Food Policy Research Institute)
   (1997)   *The World Food Situation: Recent Developments, Emerging Issues, and
      Long-Term Prospects*. Washington: IFPRI.

IFRCRCS (International Federation of Red Cross and Red Crescent Societies)
   (1995)   *World Disasters Report 1995*. Dordrecht: Martinus Nijhoff.

Kates, R., Chen, R., Downing, T.E., Kasperson, J.X., Messer, E., and Millman, S.R.
   (1988)   *The Hunger Report 1988*. Providence, R.I.: World Hunger Program.

Marchione, T.
   (1996)   "The right to food in the post-Cold War era." *Food Policy* **21**(1):
      83–102.

Maxwell, S. and Frankenberger, T.
   (1992)   *Household Food Security: Concepts, Indicators, Measurements*. New
      York: UNICEF/IFAD.

Messer, E.
   (1994)   "Food Wars: Hunger as a Weapon in 1993." In *The Hunger Report
      1993*, ed. P. Uvin. Yverdon: Gordon & Breach.

Messer, E.
   (1996)   "Food Wars: Hunger as a Weapon of War in 1994." In *The Hunger
      Report 1995*, eds. E. Messer and P. Uvin. Amsterdam: Gordon &
      Breach.

MDIS
(1993)   *Global Prevalence of Iodine Deficiency Disorders.* Geneva: WHO
         Micronutrient Deficiency Information System. MDIS Working Paper
         No. 1.

Meyers, W.
(1995)   *Presentation Abstract.* Panel on "Global Food Security Trends, Trade
         Liberalization: The Changing Diet of the Poor" at the 8th Annual
         Hunger Research Briefing and Exchange. Providence, RI: Brown
         University, World Hunger Program.

Millman, S. R.
(1991)   *The Hunger Report: Update 1991.* Providence, R.I.: Brown University,
         World Hunger Program.

Minear, L. and Weiss, T.
(1995)   *Mercy under Fire: War and the Global Humanitarian Community.*
         Boulder, CO: Westview.

Ralte, A. L.
(1996)   "Progress in Overcoming Micronutrient Deficiencies: 1989–1994."
         In *The Hunger Report 1995*, eds. E. Messer and P. Uvin. Amsterdam:
         Gordon & Breach.

Reutlinger, S.
(1993)   *Addressing Hunger: An Historical Perspective of International
         Initiatives.* Background paper prepared for the World Bank conference
         on Overcoming Global Hunger, November 29–December 1, 1993.
         Washington: World Bank.

UNICEF (United Nations Children's Fund)
(1992)   *Nutrition Progress Report 1992.* New York: UNICEF.

UNICEF
(1994)   *The Progress of Nations.* London: Burgess of Abingdon.

UNICEF
(1996)   *State of the World's Children. 1996.* Oxford: Oxford University Press.

USCR (U.S. Committee for Refugees)
(1994)   *World Refugee Survey 1994.* Washington: U.S. Committee for
         Refugees.

USCR
(1995)   *World Refugee Survey 1995.* Washington: U.S. Committee for
         Refugees.

USDA (U.S. Department of Agriculture)
(1995)   *World Food Aid Needs and Availabilities.* GFA-7. Washington: USDA
         Economic Research Service.

USDA
(1996a) *International Agriculture and Trade, Europe Update.* WRS-96-S2.
         Washington: USDA Economic Research Service.

USDA
(1996b) *Food Aid Needs and Availabilities. Projections for 2005.* Commercial Agriculture Division, no. 9523. Washington: USDA Economic Research Service.

USDA
(1996c) *The U.S. Contribution to World Food Security. The U.S. Position Paper prepared for the World Food Summit.* Washington: USDA, Foreign Agricultural Service.

USDA
(1996d) *Long Term Projections for International Agriculture to 2005.* Commercial Agriculture Division, no. 9612. Washington: USDA Economic Research Service.

USDA
(1997) *Food Security Assessment.* Situation and Outlook Series. International Agriculture and Trade Reports, Washington DC: United States Department of Agriculture, Economic Research Service.

US Mission to the UN
(1996) *Global Humanitarian Emergencies, 1996.* Washington: U.S. Department of State.

Uvin, P.
(1994a) "The State of World Hunger." In *Hunger Report 1993,* ed. P. Uvin. New York: Gordon & Breach.

Uvin, P.
(1994b) *The International Organization of Hunger.* London: Kegan Paul.

Uvin, P.
(1996) "The State of World Hunger." In *Hunger Report 1995,* eds. E. Messer and P. Uvin. New York: Gordon & Breach.

World Bank
(1994) *Enriching Lives: Overcoming Vitamin and Mineral Malnutrition in Developing Countries.* Washington: World Bank.

WFP
(1994) *Annual Report 1993.* Rome: WFP.

WFP
(1990–1996) *Food Aid Monitor.* Rome: International Food Aid Information System.

WFP
(1996) *"World Food Aid Trends."* The Food Aid Monitor **26**: July 22.

WHO (World Health Organization)
(1991) *National Strategies for Overcoming Micronutrient Malnutrition.* EB 89/27 Geneva: WHO.

WHO
(1998) *Global Database on Child Growth and Malnutrition.* Geneva: WHO.

CHAPTER 2

Nutritional Status: The Master Key to Child Survival[1]

David L. Pelletier

The reduction of child mortality may be one of the most commonly stated objectives of health and development policy in developing countries (Taylor and Ramalingaswami 1993). During the past several decades, the primary instruments used to pursue this objective have been selective health interventions such as immunization, oral rehydration therapy, antibiotics and curative care (Huffman and Steel 1995; Walsh and Warren 1979). Some of these interventions have reached high levels of coverage and are responsible, in part, for the marked reduction in child mortality seen in many countries (World Bank 1993). Notwithstanding this general trend towards progress, child mortality rates remain high, and the coverage of selective health interventions remains low, in the rural or difficult-to-reach populations within countries, notably in Sub-Saharan Africa (Murray and Lopez 1994; Murray et al. 1994).

The post-World War II period during which this progress was made, albeit at an uneven rate across countries, was characterized by an unprecedented expansion in public health technology, international and bilateral development assistance, and health infrastructure development within low-income countries. The convergence of these forces created the necessary conditions for extending preventive and curative health services to a much larger proportion of the populations, facilitated by the fact that these health services were provided on a free or low-cost basis in most countries during most of this period (World Bank 1993). As discussed in other chapters in this volume, there is evidence and concern that these conditions may not be maintained, let alone expanded, in the post-Cold War period.

For decades, it has been known that the impact of infectious diseases on child mortality depends upon the individual's nutritional status. In 1968, Scrimshaw and colleagues documented the synergistic relationship between malnutrition and infection in one of the landmark publications in the recent history of nutritional sciences (Scrimshaw et al. 1968). Drawing together extensive evidence from biomedical research, clinical research and clinical practice, this synthesis formalized the "vicious cycle" view of malnutrition and infection which is now widely accepted in scientific and applied circles. Stated simply, this view holds that malnutrition adversely affects an individual's ability to resist and/or respond to infection, and infection adversely affects the individual's ability to utilize energy and nutrients from the diet. As illustrated best by the case of measles (Morley 1973), this physiological synergism can have devastating consequences for the individual.

Despite the broad recognition and acceptance of the malnutrition–morbidity synergism for over two decades, the implications of the malnutrition–infection synergism have yet to be reflected in policies designed to improve child survival in developing countries. Instead, the dominant approach to reducing child mortality has relied upon the selective health interventions mentioned above. The changes taking place during the post-Cold War period raise questions about the continued efficacy, sustainability and equity of curative care interventions, and they offer an opportunity to re-examine the potential role of nutritional improvement as a more sustainable and equitable approach in the future.

In order to assist this re-examination of the potential role of nutrition, this chapter addresses the following questions: (1) Does the relationship between malnutrition and mortality differ across diverse populations? (2) Is the effect of malnutrition on the risk of death limited to severe malnutrition, or is it also present in mild-to-moderate malnutrition? (3) Do malnutrition and infection have multiplicative effects on mortality at the population level, as would be predicted by theory? (4) Is it possible to estimate the percent of child deaths due to malnutrition, in order to decide on the most appropriate mix of intervention strategies on a global, country and community basis? and (5) Does malnutrition have similar effects on many infectious diseases, or are its effects confined to the well-defined examples of measles and diarrhea?

Answers to these questions are now forthcoming from a synthesis and re-analysis of epidemiologic studies conducted over the past two decades. Each question is taken up below after a description of the studies used in the meta-analysis.

DESCRIPTION OF STUDIES

A computer-assisted search of the literature, complemented by bibliographic branching, generated 28 reports of research meeting the basic criteria for this meta-analysis. These criteria are that the studies were community-based in developing countries, rather than hospital-based; they employed prospective methods to relate child mortality to indicators of nutritional status; they used anthropometric methods to indicate nutritional status; and the target population was preschool children under age five. The list of 28 reports is believed to be complete with respect to studies meeting these criteria.

The 28 reports actually refer to 21 separate studies, representing populations in 10 different countries. There is a clear bias in favor of Bangladesh (14 reports based on seven different studies). There are 10 reports from Africa (from Guinea-Bissau, Senegal, Zaire, Uganda, Tanzania and Malawi), three from Asia outside of Bangladesh (India, Indonesia and Papua New Guinea) and no reports from Latin America. All reports used one or more of the following anthropometric indicators: weight-for-age, height-for-age, weight-for-height and mid-upper arm circumference. Further details on this sample of studies, methods and findings are available in the full report (Pelletier 1994).

Consistency Across Populations

The earliest of the prospective studies took place in India (Keilmann and McCord 1978), Bangladesh (Sommer and Loewenstein 1975; Chen et al. 1980) and Papua New Guinea (Heywood 1982) and established the basic finding that the risk of mortality is inversely related to anthropometric indicators of nutritional status. The generalizability of this finding was first called into question by the findings from Kasongo, Zaire (Kasongo Project Team 1983). That study found no association between anthropometric indicators and subsequent mortality, and led to some discussion about possible population-specific relationships (Kasongo Project Team 1983; Bairagi 1985), a notion that continues to this day (Ewbank and Gribble 1993).

When the Kasongo study is examined in light of the entire set of prospective studies, it appears that the negative results are more likely due to methodological reasons. This is because more recent studies in Africa have all found the expected inverse relationship between nutritional status and mortality, including studies in Guinea-Bissau (Smedman et al. 1987), Senegal (Briend and Bari 1989), Uganda (Vella et al. 1993, 1994), Tanzania (Yambi 1988) and Malawi (Lindskog et al. 1988; Pelletier et al. 1994b). This is also confirmed in a recent study from a different region of Zaire itself (Van Den Broeck et al. 1993). Close inspection of the Kasongo report (Kasongo Project Team 1983) reveals that mortality was grossly underenumerated (only about 20% of the expected number of deaths were enumerated) and the anthropometric measurements were "obtained under conditions that are similar to operational conditions of screening in clinics" (Kasongo Project Team 1983). Thus, the overwhelming body of evidence supports the notion that the fundamental inverse relationship between nutritional status and mortality is consistent across populations. In fact, a surprising degree of consistency is observed even in the details of the relationship, as revealed by a subset of studies described in the following section.

MILD-TO-MODERATE MALNUTRITION

The perception that mild-to-moderate malnutrition (MMM) may have no consequences for child mortality was created in large part by the early findings from Chen et al. (1980) and the ensuing discussion. Empirically, those investigators observed elevated mortality among children with severe weight deficits (weight-for-age below 65% of the international reference) but no consistent relationship above that threshold. Commenting on this finding, Trowbridge and Sommer (1981) presented results based on mid-upper arm circumference (MUAC) from an earlier Bangladesh study. Those results showed a sharp increase in mortality among the severely malnourished (MUAC below 12.0 cms), with a more modest elevation among those children with moderate deficits (12–12.9 cms). Since then, many studies have confirmed the characteristic exponential relationship between mortality and anthropometric indicators (Pelletier 1994), which seemingly supports the concept that anthropometric deficits are only a serious concern at the extremes of the distribution. This has reinforced the notions of adaptation to malnutrition (Lipton 1983) and small-but-healthy (Seckler 1982), and it seems to reinforce the widespread practice of screening for severe malnutrition in many supplementary feeding programs.

With this historical perspective, it is of great interest to note that the results of Chen et al. have not been replicated by prospective studies since that time, including studies in the same area of Bangladesh, other areas of Bangladesh, other Asian countries, and several African countries.

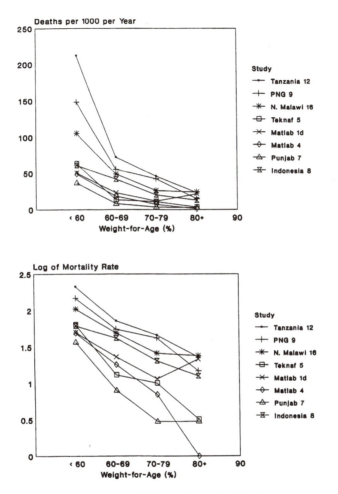

Figure 2.1. Relationship between child mortality and weight-for-age as a percentage of international median. (*Source*: Pelletier 1994.)

Figure 2.1 shows the results from seven other studies that employed similar methodologies and that can be compared in detail with those from Chen et al.[2] The top panel depicts mortality in natural units, and the bottom panel depicts the log (base ten) of mortality. The dominant impression from the top panel is, indeed, the marked elevation in mortality below 60% weight-for-age, especially in Tanzania, Papua New Guinea and Malawi which have high mortality rates at any given weight-for-age. However, the figure also reveals a clear elevation in mortality even at moderate (60–69%

weight-for-age) and mild (70–79% weight-for-age) anthropometric deficits. The bottom panel, using the log scale, merely accentuates this observation. It is interesting that the MUAC results of Trowbridge and Sommer (1981) fit this pattern exactly, but at the time they were interpreted as confirmation of a threshold effect as seen by Chen et al.

These figures suggest, first, that the Chen et al. (1980) study produced unusual results, for inexplicable reasons. They also reveal a clear elevation in mortality among those children with mild-to-moderate malnutrition that is remarkably consistent across populations, albeit not as marked as that seen in severe malnutrition. It is important to note that the modest elevation in mortality associated with mild-to-moderate malnutrition results in a lower screening efficiency for this group, and one that is probably unacceptably low in practical settings. However, it still has relevance for broader policy formulation in light of the much higher prevalence of mild-to-moderate malnutrition as compared to severe malnutrition. This is highlighted by the quantitative estimates of malnutrition's effect provided below.

Although the accumulated results of malnutrition–mortality relationships are striking for their consistency, it can be hypothesized that this association is simply or largely due to statistical confounding. According to this hypothesis, malnutrition and mortality may co-occur in the same households simply because both are associated with poverty, or low socioeconomic status (SES). It may be, for instance, that the malnutrition in those households is caused by poor nutrient intake and high disease exposure, whereas mortality may be caused by low immunization rates or inappropriate treatment of illness. Another possibility is that low weight-for-age is a byproduct of high disease exposure, and appears associated with mortality for this reason, but actually plays no causal role in mortality. Several studies have examined the possibility of confounding. As reviewed elsewhere (Pelletier 1994), all of them have found that a significant association between malnutrition and mortality persists even after controlling for confounding through various statistical techniques.

THE MULTIPLICATIVE EFFECTS OF MALNUTRITION AND MORBIDITY

The foregoing sections suggest that the effects of malnutrition on mortality are consistent across populations, are found in mild-to-moderate malnutrition as well as severe malnutrition, and are not simply due to confounding by socioeconomic factors or intercurrent illness. The eight studies represented in Figure 2.1 are important for another reason. These results provide confirmation that the physiological synergism described by Scrimshaw

(1968) does have multiplicative effects on mortality at the population level, as described below.

As shown earlier for six of these studies (Pelletier et al. 1993), a simple specification of the synergism between malnutrition and morbidity is that exposure to disease is constant within any given population, but the fatality rate per exposure varies with the degree of malnutrition. If this is so, then the risk of death for an individual child is related to the product (not the sum) of the probability of exposure to disease and the probability of being malnourished (i.e., it is a multiplicative model rather than an additive model). At the population level, it follows that the mortality rate should be related to the product of the burden of disease (exposure) and the prevalence of malnutrition. Note that one indicator of the burden of disease in a given population is simply the mortality rate among the well-nourished, because some proportion of well-nourished children will die of infectious diseases at some "baseline" rate that is determined by the types of diseases present and the health care available for treating them.

The data shown in Figure 2.1 (especially the lower panel) conform precisely to this theoretical model of synergism. It shows that populations with high "baseline mortality" (mortality among the relatively well-nourished, reflecting the population's burden of disease) have a systematically higher "response" to malnutrition.[3] For instance, the population in Punjab, India had the lowest level of baseline mortality (2.8/1000/year) and experienced an "increase" of 34/1000/year in going from >80% weight-for-age to <60% weight-for-age. By contrast, Iringa, Tanzania had the highest baseline mortality (23/1000/year) and experienced an "increase" of 189/1000/year in going from >80% weight-for-age to <60% weight-for-age. Under an additive model, Tanzania would have experienced roughly the same number of excess deaths as India (34/1000/year) in going from the well-nourished category to the severely malnourished category. The parallelism in the eight lines reveals that there is a consistent tendency across the eight studies, in which the mortality response to malnutrition is proportional to the baseline mortality level. This is formally tested and confirmed in Pelletier et al. (1993) and Pelletier et al. (1994a).

The above results and the inferences drawn from them are important because the samples sizes in the only controlled intervention trial were not adequate for testing the multiplicative effects of malnutrition and morbidity (Keilmann and McCord 1978). Thus, the present results provide the only evidence currently available for testing this hypothesis.

These observations have important implications for conceptualizing the relationships among malnutrition, morbidity and mortality, classifying causes of death, and planning actions to improve health and survival in developing countries. Specifically, malnutrition should not be viewed as a cause of death on its own; rather, malnutrition acts as a potentiator of existing infectious diseases, with the degree of potentiation proportional to the severity of malnutrition. Consequently, it is meaningless to ascribe a certain number of deaths to malnutrition alone, and it is grossly misleading to ascribe a certain number of deaths to infectious diseases alone, the latter being a particularly common practice. In developing countries with high rates of malnutrition, the excessive number of deaths ascribed to diarrhea, acute respiratory infection (ARI), measles, and other common infections places primacy on the proximate and clinically obvious cause, while ignoring the potentiating effects that severe and (less obviously) mild-to-moderate malnutrition has on those diseases. For example, the 1993 World Development Report ascribes only 2.4% of DALYs lost[4] to protein-energy malnutrition, as compared to 63% for common infectious diseases (World Bank 1993). One consequence at the policy level may be the neglect of nutritional improvement as a broad strategy for reducing mortality due to infectious diseases.

MALNUTRITION AND MORTALITY: QUANTIFYING THE EFFECTS

Bearing in mind the "potentiation paradigm" of malnutrition's effects on mortality, the results shown in Figure 2.1 (lower panel) indicate that the absolute level of child mortality can be accurately modelled simply as a function of: (1) the baseline mortality (among those with weight-for-age (WA) > 80%); and (2) the percent of children falling in each of the grades of malnutrition below 80% of median. However, this observation has limited practical utility when stated in those terms, because most countries do not know the mortality level among those with WA > 80% of median. Thus, it would not be possible to estimate the contribution of malnutrition to child mortality in most populations.

An alternative formulation relies upon the fact that the relative risk (RR)[5] of mortality at various grades of WA can be calculated from the data in Figure 2.1. The RRs are 8.4 for severe (WA < 60%), 4.6 for moderate (WA 60–69%) and 2.4 for mild (70–79%) malnutrition. The contribution of malnutrition to child mortality (through its potentiating effects on infectious disease) can then be calculated using the standard epidemiologic statistic of population attributable risk (PAR), which simply combines the RR estimates with estimates of the prevalence of low WA in a given population. The methodology has been fully described and tested elsewhere (Pelletier et al. 1994a). This section simply presents the results emerging from this approach, when applied to 53 countries for which suitable anthropometric data have been published (UNICEF 1993). Figure 2.2 shows the percent of child deaths due to the potentiating effects of malnutrition on disease in each of 53 countries. The total population attributable risk is divided into the portion due to severe malnutrition (WA < 60%) and that due to mild-to-moderate malnutrition (MMM, WA 60–79%). Using the average for all 53 countries, the results indicate that 56% of all child deaths are due to the potentiating effects of malnutrition on disease, of which 83% is due to mild-to-moderate malnutrition. The values for any given country vary in proportion to its prevalence of low weight-for-age. Among the countries shown here, the range for total

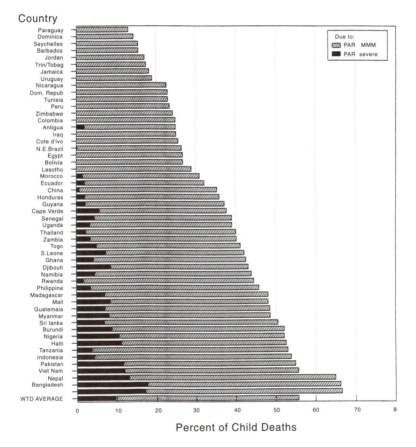

Figure 2.2. Deaths due to the potentiating effects of malnutrition on infectious diseases. (*Source*: Pelletier et al., Bulletin of WHO 1995; 73(4): 443–448.)

population attributable risk is from about 15% in Paraguay to about 85% in India. The percent due to mild-to-moderate malnutrition varies from zero among several countries where severe malnutrition is extremely rare, to a high of 68% in India.

The above estimates are remarkably close to those arising from the Inter-American Investigation of Childhood Mortality over two decades ago (Puffer and Serrano 1973). That study was based on Latin American and selected North American samples and used clinical and verbal autopsy methods to a certain cause of death. As in the present study, it reported that 54% of child deaths (2–4 years) in the Latin American countries had malnutrition as an underlying or associated cause, of which about 15% was severe malnutrition. Among infants (0–11 months), about one-quarter to one-third of all deaths had malnutrition as an underlying or associated cause of death. The estimates for infants are lower than for children, because a large proportion of neonatal deaths are due to congenital and obstetric complications. Thus, the Inter-American Investigation, using a different methodology than the prospective studies shown in Figure 2.1, confirms the quantitative estimates of malnutrition on child mortality and demonstrates that the Latin American results are similar to those from Africa and Asia. In addition, they confirm that conventional methods for classifying cause of death e.g. (World Bank 1993) underestimate the importance of malnutrition by a factor of eight- to ten-fold.

EFFECTS OF MALNUTRITION ON DIFFERENT CAUSES OF DEATH

The consistency in the slope of mortality on weight-for-age shown earlier in Figure 2.1 is striking in light of the differences in ecological circumstances and associated disease exposure, as well as cultural differences across studies. For instance, the Papua New Guinea study took place in the highlands, where acute respiratory infection was noted as a major cause of death and malaria was presumably absent; yet, it has a slope similar to Bangladesh, Tanzania and Malawi, where diarrhea and malaria are combined with acute respiratory infection as major diseases. This empirical observation of relative uniformity in slope across populations suggests that malnutrition may potentiate the effects of many or all of the common infectious diseases.

Somewhat more direct confirmation of this is provided by three of the prospective studies as well as the Inter-American Investigation. The three prospective studies (two in Bangladesh, one in Uganda) collected verbal reports of symptoms at the time of death and, thus, were able to estimate the relative risk (RR) of death due to malnutrition for each symptomatic cause of death separately (Pelletier 1994). All three studies show elevated RRs for diarrhea and measles, the only diseases reported separately in all three studies. In addition, the Uganda study shows elevated RRs for fever and acute respiratory infection. Fever is usually assumed to be due to malaria in clinical practice in Africa settings with endemic malaria, but the Ugandan study did not collect detailed clinical data to confirm this. The two Bangladesh studies grouped fever and acute respiratory infection with other infections, and found elevated RRs for that combined category. Thus, these three studies are consistent with the evidence shown in Figure 2.1, that malnutrition may have a potentiating effect on many or all infectious diseases.

The Inter-American Investigation, based on the 13 Latin American samples, found that malnutrition was an associated cause in 47% of all under-fives deaths (excluding neonatal deaths). It was an associated cause in roughly 60% of deaths due to diarrhea, measles and other infective and parasitic diseases, compared to about 32% in deaths due to respiratory disease or other causes. The latter figure was no higher than that seen in the "other" category which represents a pseudo-control category.

Finally, a recent study from Zaire has challenged the thesis that mild-to-moderate (sub-clinical) malnutrition is associated with elevated child mortality, and has suggested that a major reason for the apparent linkage may be the uniformity with which malaria kills children regardless of nutritional status (Van Den Broeck et al. 1993). It is difficult to interpret this study for two reasons. First, the authors note that it took place in an area that has been the target of an integrated health and development program for the past 20 years. As such, immunization levels are higher and diarrhea is lower than in most parts of Africa, and access to curative care is presumably greater. The authors suggest that this may help explain the absence of an overall effect of mild-to-moderate malnutrition on mortality in their study. If so, it may have limited generalizability to areas that do not share in those characteristics.

A second difficulty relates to the analytical strategy. In contrast to other prospective studies, these authors removed from the mild-to-moderate malnutrition sample any children showing clinical signs of malnutrition. These signs included any muscle wasting (by inspection or palpation), with or without loss of subcutaneous fat, visible skeletal structures or hanging skin. Pitting oedema was also considered a clinical sign. The difficulty in interpretation arises from the fact that children with any of these signs were all considered severely malnourished, but did not come exclusively from the category with $WA < 60\%$. Results published separately

(Van Den Broeck 1994) show that roughly 20% of all children below 80% WA showed these signs and were excluded from the analysis. This makes it extremely difficult to compare this study with the other prospective studies. It appears that the possibility of disease-specific effects of malnutrition is a question that deserves further study, and it may be most amenable to study through case-control analysis of clinical data.

SUMMARY AND POLICY IMPLICATIONS

Analysis of 28 reports from 10 developing countries leads to a number of clear conclusions concerning malnutrition and child mortality:

(1) The inverse association between nutritional status and mortality is a consistent finding across diverse world populations, thereby contradicting the earlier suggestion that the results may be region- or population-specific;

(2) Mortality is elevated even among children with mild-to-moderate malnutrition, contrary to the widely held view that the effects are confined to the severely malnourished;

(3) The association between malnutrition and child mortality does not appear to be due simply to the confounding effects of socioeconomic factors and intercurrent illness;

(4) The long-recognized physiological synergism between malnutrition and infection leads to the prediction that these two factors should have multiplicative effects on mortality at the population level. This prediction is fully consistent with the results from eight epidemiologic studies of malnutrition and mortality. Malnutrition is observed to multiply the number of deaths caused by infectious disease, rather than acting in a simple additive fashion. The effects are strong and consistent across populations;

(5) Applying the results of these eight studies to a larger set of 53 countries for which suitable anthropometric data exist, it is found that malnutrition, through its potentiating effects on infectious diseases, contributes to 56% of all child deaths. This is roughly eight to ten times higher than conventional estimates that ignore the potentiating effects of malnutrition on disease and the effects of mild-to-moderate malnutrition. Of the malnutrition-related deaths, 83% are due to mild-to-moderate malnutrition as opposed to severe malnutrition, which is also much higher than commonly recognized;

(6) The quantitative relationship between malnutrition and mortality is remarkably consistent across eight populations representing diverse ecological, disease and cultural environments. Based on a smaller number of more detailed studies, malnutrition is observed to potentiate deaths

due to several infectious diseases. However, some studies raise doubt concerning its effects on malaria and respiratory infection, leading to the conclusion that further study is required on this question.

These results have a number of implications for health policy and for equity-oriented development policy more generally. The population attributable risk estimates suggest that programs directed at screening and treating only the severely malnourished would have the potential to prevent only about 17% of malnutrition-related deaths (using the average figure for the 53 countries included here), representing only about 10% of all child deaths (i.e., 0.17×0.56). The actual preventable fraction in current health facilities and child survival projects is likely to be even smaller than this, because existing interventions are not 100% effective. Larger impacts could be achieved by pursuing policies and programs that attempt to shift the entire distribution of nutritional status, thereby improving mild-to-moderate malnutrition which accounts for most of the nutrition-related deaths. In addition, because of the multiplicative effects arising from the synergism between malnutrition and morbidity, the largest impacts could be expected in populations with the highest exposure to disease and/or highest prevalence of malnutrition. The results suggest that nutritional improvement of populations is expected to reduce mortality due to several diseases simultaneously (even if not all of them), even if exposure to those diseases remains unchanged. This is as opposed to a disease-focused approach which employs separate interventions to prevent or treat each disease. Clearly, it is desirable to improve nutritional status as well as to reduce disease exposure, but the suggestive cross-disease impacts of nutritional improvement should be taken into account when attempting to design the most cost-effective interventions in the face of resource constraints.

Although this chapter has emphasized the malnutrition–morbidity synergism that increases the severity of disease and likelihood of death, a discussion of policy options to reduce child mortality should also consider the role of curative care. In theory, the effects of the malnutrition–morbidity synergism on mortality could be uncoupled if the affected individuals have access to effective curative care. This is evident in the gender differentials in mortality observed in Bangladesh, where a given degree of malnutrition is observed to have a lesser effect on mortality among Bangladeshi males than females, consistent with the greater access to curative health care among Bangladeshi males (Pelletier n.d.). Such results suggest that the failure to address the synergism, either by reducing exposure to disease or improving nutritional status, places children in a high-risk situation for mortality when access to effective curative health is restricted.

The ability of curative health care to uncouple or weaken the mortality arising from the malnutrition–morbidity synergism has important implications for analyzing the cost-effectiveness and sustainability of alternative approaches to reducing child mortality. Specifically, it suggests that cost-effectiveness calculations could be performed for various combinations of health care improvement, nutritional improvement and reductions in disease exposure, to determine the most cost-effective strategy in the medium term. In the longer-term, however, the sustainability of strategies weighted heavily towards (curative) health care is likely to be lower than those giving more attention to reducing malnutrition and disease exposure, and such strategies would do little to improve social equity.

Finally, it is important to note that the above policy options can be interpreted through the lens of the traditional development paradigm, the new development paradigm, or some combination of the two, although this is not to suggest that the two paradigms are equivalent or substitutable in any sense. The traditional paradigm is based on a service delivery model in which reductions in disease exposure, improvements in nutritional status and improved curative care would all be achieved through selective interventions targeted at high-risk individuals or populations. This is the paradigm that lends itself most readily to the types of cost-effectiveness calculations described above, but incurs high recurrent costs for governments and/or individuals and does not address the underlying causes of these problems.

The "new" development paradigm described in other sections of this volume is based on a grassroots, capacity-building and empowerment model, in which the above "inputs" would be replaced by, or complemented with, community-based action that stresses the mobilization of household, community and external resources to pursue felt-needs of the community. This paradigm is better able to address the context-specific causes and conditioning factors underlying malnutrition, morbidity and mortality, is more likely to lead to sustainable improvements, and is more consistent with the forces of democratization gaining momentum in developing countries. The tight connections between malnutrition and morbidity, and the large quantitative impacts of mild-to-moderate malnutrition on child mortality documented in this chapter, highlight the limitations of the traditional paradigm based on selective, targeted interventions if the desire is to make large, sustainable and equitable impacts on child mortality. The new development paradigm, while requiring a longer time horizon initially, holds greater promise for reaching the goals of large, sustainable and equitable improvements.

NOTES

1. With minor adaptations, this chapter is reprinted with permission from an article that appeared in *Nutrition Reviews* (Pelletier 1994).

2. The Chen et al. study is labelled "Matlab 1d" in this figure, and is based on a re-analysis by Cogill (1982).

3. In this paragraph, terms like "mortality response" and "increase in mortality" are used as a shorthand for attributable risk, which is the difference in mortality rates between the malnourished and the well-nourished.

4. DALY = Disability Adjusted Life Years.

5. Relative Risk is the mortality within a given grade of malnutrition divided by morbidity among the well-nourished, in this case children with weight-for-age > 80%.

REFERENCES

Bairagi, R.
(1985)   "Why Mortality-Discriminating Power of Anthropometric Indicators differs Among Populations." *Journal of Tropical Pediatrics* **31**: 63–64.

Briend, A. and Bari, A.
(1989)   "Critical Assessment of the Use of Growth Monitoring for Identifying High Risk Children in Primary Health Care Programmes." *British Medical Journal* **298**: 1607–1611.

Chen, L. C., Chowdhury, A. K. M. A., and Huffman, S. L.
(1980)   "Anthropometric Assessment of Energy-Protein Malnutrition and Subsequent Risk of Mortality Among Preschool Aged Children." *American Journal of Clinical Nutrition* **33**: 1836–1845.

Cogill, B.
(1982)   "Ranking Anthropometric Indicators Using Mortality in Rural Bangladesh Children." M.Sc. Thesis. Ithaca, NY: Cornell University.

Ewbank, D. C. and Gribble, J. N.
(1993)   *Effects of Health Programs on Child Mortality in Sub-Saharan Africa.* Commission on Behavioral and Social Sciences Education. National Research Council. Washington: National Academy Press.

Heywood, P.
(1982)   "The Functional Significance of Malnutrition: Growth and Prospective Risk of Death in the Highlands of Papua New Guinea." *Journal of Food & Nutrition* **39**(1): 13–19.

Huffman, S. L. and Steel, A.
(1995)   "Do Child Survival Interventions Reduce Malnutrition? The Dark Side of Child Survival." In *Child Growth and Nutrition in Developing*

Countries: Priorities for Action, eds. P. Pinstrup-Andersen, D. Pelletier, and H. Alderman. Ithaca, NY: Cornell University Press.

Kasongo Project Team
(1983)   "Anthropometric Assessment of Young Children's Nutritional Status as an Indicator of Subsequent Risk of Dying." *Journal of Tropical Pediatrics* **29**: 69–75.

Keilmann, A. A. and McCord, C.
(1978)   "Weight-For-Age as an Index of Risk of Death in Children." *Lancet* **1**: 1247–1250.

Lindskog, U., Lindskog, P., Carstensen, J., Larsson, Y., and Gebre-Medhin, M.
(1988)   "Childhood Mortality in Relation to Nutritional Status and Water Supply: A Prospective Study From Rural Malawi." *Acta Paediatrica Scandinavica* **77**: 260–268.

Lipton, M.
(1983)   "Poverty, Undernutrition and Hunger." Staff Working Paper No. 597. Washington: World Bank.

Morley, D.
(1973)   *Pediatric Priorities in the Developing World*. London: Butterworth and Co.

Murray, C. J. L., Govindaraj, R., and Musgrove, P.
(1994)   "National Health Expenditures: A Global Analysis." In *Global Comparative Assessments in the Health Sector: Disease Burden, Expenditures and Intervention Packages*. Geneva: World Health Organization.

Murray, C. J. L. and Lopez, A. D.
(1994)   "Global and Regional Cause-of-Death Patterns in 1990." In *Global Comparative Assessments in the Health Sector: Disease Burden, Expenditures and Intervention Packages*. Geneva: World Health Organization.

Pelletier, D. L.
(1994)   "The Relationship Between Child Anthropometry and Mortality in Developing Countries: Implications for Policy, Programs and Future Research." *Journal of Nutrition Supplement* **124**(10S): 2047–2081.

Pelletier, D. L.
(n.d.)   "The Relationship Between Malnutrition, Morbidity and Child Mortality in Developing Countries." In *Too Young to Die: Genes and Gender* (forthcoming). New York: United Nations, Department of Economic and Social Information and Policy Analysis/ Population Division.

Pelletier, D. L., Frongillo, E. A., and Habicht, J. P.
(1993)   "Epidemiologic Evidence for a Potentiating Effect of Malnutrition on Child Mortality." *American Journal of Public Health* **83**(8): 1130–1133.

Pelletier, D. L., Frongillo E. A., Schroeder D. G., and Habicht J. P.
(1994a) "A Methodology for Estimating the Contribution of Malnutrition to Child Mortality in Developing Countries." *Journal of Nutrition Supplement* **124**(10S): 2106–2122.

Pelletier, D. L., Low, J. W., Johnson, F. C., and Msukwa, L. A. H.
(1994b) "Child Anthropometry and Mortality in Malawi: Testing for Effect Modification by Age and Length of Follow-up and Confounding by Socioeconomic Factors." *Journal of Nutrition Supplement* **124**(10S): 2082–2105.

Puffer, R. C. and Serrano, C. V.
(1973) "Patterns of Mortality in Childhood." Scientific Publication No. 262. Washington: Pan American Health Organization.

Scrimshaw, N. S.
(1968) "Interaction of Nutrition and Infection." Monograph Series 57, Geneva: World Health Organization.

Seckler, D.
(1982) "Small But Healthy: A Basic Hypothesis in the Theory, Measurement and Policy of Malnutrition." In *Newer Concepts in Nutrition and Their Implications for Policy*, ed. P. V. Sukhatme. Pune, India: Maharashtra Association for the Cultivation of Science Research Institute.

Smedman, L., Sterky, G., Mellander, L., and Wall, S.
(1987) "Anthropometry and Subsequent Mortality in Groups of Children Aged 6–59 Months in Guinea-Bissau." *American Journal of Clinical Nutrition* **46**: 369–373.

Sommer, A. and Loewenstein, M. S.
(1975) "Nutritional Status and Mortality: A Prospective Validation of the QUAC Stick." *The American Journal of Clinical Nutrition* **28**: 287–292.

Taylor, C. E. and Ramalingaswami, V.
(1993) "Reducing Mortality in Children Under Five: A Continuing Priority." *Disease Control Priorities in Developing Countries*. ed. D. T. Jamison, W. H. Mosley, A. R. Measham, and J. L. Bobadilla. New York: Oxford Medical Publications.

Trowbridge, F. L. and Sommer, A.
(1981) "Nutritional Anthropometry and Mortality Risk." *American Journal of Clinical Nutrition* **34**: 2591–2592.

United Nations Children's Fund (UNICEF)
(1993) "Child Malnutrition: Progress Toward the World Summit for Children Goal." City Statistics and Monitoring Section.

Van Den Broeck, J., Eeckels, R., and Uylsteke, J.
(1993) "Influence of Nutritional Status on Child Mortality in Rural Zaire." *Lancet* **341**: 1491–1495.

Van Den Broeck, J.
(1994) *Assessment of Child Health and Nutritional Status in a Rural Tropical Area*. Ph.D. Thesis. Leuven, Belgium: Katholieke Universiteit.

Vella, V., Tomkins, A., Borghesi, A., Migliori, G. B., Nidku, J., and Adriko, B. C.
(1993) "Anthropometry and Childhood Mortality in Northwest and Southwest Uganda." *American Journal of Public Health* **83**(11): 1616–1618.

Vella, V., Tomkins, A., Ndiku, J., Marshal, T., and Cortinovis, I.
(1994) "Anthropometry as a Predictor for Mortality Among Ugandan Children, Allowing for Socio-economic Variables." *European Journal of Clinical Nutrition* **48**(3): 189.

Yambi, O.
(1988) *Nutritional Status and the Risk of Death: A Prospective Study of Children Six to Thirty Months Old in Iringa Region, Tanzania*. Ph.D. Thesis. Ithaca, NY: Cornell University.

Walsh, J. A. and Warren, K. S.
(1979) "Selective Primary Health Care: An Interim Strategy for Disease Control in Developing Countries." *New England Journal of Medicine* **301**: 967–974.

World Bank
(1993) *World Development Report: Investing in Health*. Oxford: Oxford University Press.

CHAPTER 3

How Did We Get Here?
A History of
International Nutrition

F. James Levinson and Milla McLachlan

A sustained international effort to address malnutrition in developing countries began after World War II. After roughly 50 years, it now appears both legitimate and appropriate to examine this experience as history. This chapter provides a brief overview of the evolution of major approaches, and suggests that a renewed emphasis on capacity building is a key challenge facing the international nutrition community in the late 1990s.

The trends and challenges faced in nutrition planning and programs mirror, in many respects, broader trends in development approaches over these decades. Early development efforts were greatly influenced by the goals and interests of "donor" nations, and were overwhelmingly supply- and technology-driven. In the latter part of this period, there was a growing recognition of the importance of the human dimensions of development coupled with global political changes. More attention focused on institutional prerequisites for effective social change, reappraisals of the state and civil society in development, and greater emphasis on capacity building to equip actors at all levels to be more effective in their roles (World Bank 1997; and Ch. 4 by Marchione).

EVOLUTION OF INTERNATIONAL NUTRITION PROGRAMS

The inception of large scale international nutrition efforts, as with development efforts in general, traces back to the end of World War II.[1] Each decade has been broadly characterized by a different program and policy emphasis (Figure 3.1).

The leitmotif for early donor-assisted international nutrition efforts in the 1950s and 1960s, and perhaps the continuing leitmotif of such nutrition-related assistance, might be: We give what we have (in surplus), we teach what we know, we look after our own self-interest, and we add to this a pinch of humanitarianism.

Consistent with this philosophy, the primary nutrition activities of the 1950s were home economics extension efforts (often provided by U.S. land grant colleges), milk powder distribution (in surplus worldwide during the 1950s) primarily through schools, the establishment of malnutrition wards in hospitals and later nutrition rehabilitation centers, and the conduct of U.S. government-financed nutrition surveys in developing countries under the auspices of the Interdepartmental Committee on Nutrition for National Defense (ICNND).

During the 1960s, an effort was made through U.N. agencies to consolidate these somewhat scattered and random activities through so-called Applied Nutrition Programs (ANP). These activities, initiated in some 65 countries, were essentially community level programs including small scale food production, food supplementation and nutrition education.

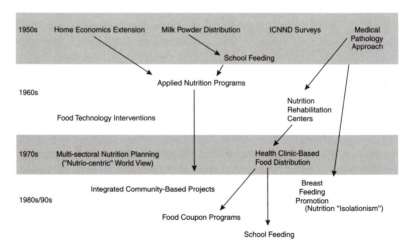

Figure 3.1. Historical progression of nutrition intervention approaches.

Although similar in content to community-based nutrition programs of the 1980s and 90s (except for the omission of growth monitoring), these Applied Nutrition Programs were highly supply-oriented in nature and were, by the early 1970s, generally acknowledged to have been unsuccessful in affecting malnutrition.[2]

At the same time, attention in international nutrition had shifted during the 1960s to what become known as the "protein problem." Based on an emerging western technology producing protein concentrates and isolates and synthetic amino acids primarily for animal feeds and special diets, food companies and research institutes in developing countries sought means of producing low cost protein-rich products from oilseeds, fish, leaves, algae and petroleum.[3] Only after nearly a decade did it become clear that such efforts were based on a largely erroneous understanding of diets in these countries (there are rarely independent protein deficiencies once caloric needs are met), and of the purchasing power limitations of food insecure households.

In the context of the understandings of their time, each of these strategies was logical and elicited committed efforts. In retrospect, they are classic examples of interventions which missed the opportunity to "scale down" through capacity building and, instead, imposed approaches developed in First World contexts. The programmatic implication of this summit decision making was the supply-driven delivery of pre-formulated solutions (and, often, pre-formulated foods actually produced in industrialized countries), solutions often based on a limited understanding of nutrition problems.

A substantial reorientation took place in the 1970s with the introduction of multi-sectoral nutrition planning. While the impetus once again came from industrialized countries—where planning models were in vogue in many development sectors—attention shifted, for the first time, to processes that developing country governments could themselves initiate to come up with combinations of policies and programs designed to meet their specific "basic needs."

Multi-sectoral nutrition planning led to an academic industry of often impractical model building. But it also led to the creation of nutrition planning cells in the governments of 26 developing countries, supported largely by the United States Agency for International Development (USAID) and the United Nations Food and Agriculture Organization (FAO). These cells, usually located in planning commissions, or the office of a president or prime minister, were responsible for identifying and then coordinating shifts in the policies and programs of a range of government ministries (usually including agriculture, food, health, social welfare, industries, and fisheries) for purposes of improved nutritional well-being.

Politicians and officials in charge of line ministries resisted this imposed "nutriocentric" view of development, were largely unwilling to make policy shifts on behalf of consumption or nutrition, and were not at all interested in being coordinated by this or any outside entity. By the late 1970s, most of these cells no longer functioned (Field 1987; Berg 1987a; Levinson 1995).

Viewed in the context of scaling, the multi-sectoral nutrition planning of the 1970s signaled a transition from externally provided prescriptions to an externally provided process of determining at the national (rarely subnational) level policies and programs likely to have a positive impact on malnutrition. This invariably involved some scaling down of capacity from the summit (international donors and western universities) to the national government level—including substantial numbers of national government professionals trained in nutrition planning techniques at M.I.T, Berkeley, and the University of Sussex.

Since the 1980s the effects of the multi-sectoral nutrition planning experience on subsequent developments have been primarily twofold.

First, the inability of nutrition planners and advocates to mobilize other development sectors for nutrition purposes led to a marked retreat from broad-based development thinking, to a posture which, at its worst, might be labeled "nutrition isolationism." The result in many countries has been programs which the nutrition community, for all intents and purposes, has been able to carry out on its own, without the need for any inter-sectoral collaboration. While these programs (primarily micronutrient and breast-feeding activities) are unquestionably important, the presently unbalanced preoccupation with them may have the effect of signaling a reduced commitment to the major needs of calorie deficient populations and, in turn, may risk moving nutrition back to the periphery of the development process.

A second important legacy of the multi-sectoral nutrition planning experience, however, was the carry-over of demand-based, target-directed, systematic thinking into actual project development. Now, for the first time, in large scale projects in Indonesia, south India, and Tanzania, major attention was given to the design of specific activities (e.g., are they targeted to those at greatest risk; are they likely to be cost-effective?); and to project implementation (e.g., are project inputs properly identified and provided; are supervisory systems in place; are projects properly monitored; do management information systems exist which utilize monitoring data for continuous project refinement?) (Zeitlin 1984; Berg 1987b; Vaidyanathan 1989; Soekirman 1995). Frequently, such rational program design and implementation resulted in reduced prevalence of at least severe malnutrition, where the comparable community-based Applied Nutrition Programs of the 1960s had failed.

In terms of scaling, activities of the 1980s, generally operated by subnational, state or district administrations, importantly recognized that central government decision-making was too aggregate a level for either insightful problem analysis or effective program management. Concurrently there was an emerging recognition that programs (based, for example, on activity at centralized health clinics) which did not function at the community level were unlikely to reach the neediest population groups.

The primary scaling issue of the 1990s may be whether the devolution of design/decision making responsibility has gone far enough. UNICEF and a portion of the NGO community, utilizing older concepts of empowerment and entitlement, argue that it is inadequate simply to locate programs at the community level with lip service to community participation. Instead premiums must be placed on community-level empowerment, capacity building and "ownership" of projects. This is all the more essential, it is argued, given resource shortages being faced by national governments and many donors, and the increasing responsibility for resource and labor inputs which is falling to communities themselves (Wisner 1988; Dreze and Sen 1989; Barrett and Csete 1994). At the same time, the importance of a supportive national and international resource and policy environment is stressed (Jonsson 1996).

The argument to the contrary is that, with the exception of those formerly socialist countries with decentralist tendencies and with functioning grassroots political and administrative structures, (e.g. Tanzania, Mozambique, and Vietnam), community decision making is often elitist, individualist, fractious, disinclined towards projects geared to its disadvantaged population groups, and inadequately informed about successful interventions elsewhere. This argument, in turn, is supported by national experiences with social action funds and community-based food security initiatives (Levinson 1993).

Whatever one's conclusions about the proper extent of devolution and the appropriate point to which capacity building initiatives ought to be scaled down from international, regional or national summits, it has become clear over the past decade that the international nutrition community now faces at least two new sets of challenges:

1. Major capacity building efforts at the subnational level are required if nutrition efforts at this level are to be effective and sustainable. This challenge is in the forefront now because programs are less often wholly prescribed or even wholly financed from abroad—for reasons having to

do with program effectiveness, national politics and international budget cuts; because the legacy of nutrition planning requires that programs be responsible to local contexts of need and causality; and because so much program responsibility has devolved to subnational levels.

2. If this is the case, at least a portion of existing nutrition research and training capacity has to be transferred to the critical task of equipping these new cadres of primarily subnational professionals—and those who support them at the national and even international levels—with information on what has worked elsewhere and how specific local needs might best be addressed, and skills to deal with the considerable tasks of program design and decision making.

NOTES

1. Although agricultural and food security systems evolving in most cultures inevitably had some bearing on nutrition, the concept of nutrition as we speak of it today with our explicit concern for child growth, nutrient intake and absorption, deficiency diseases, and related factors affecting these outcomes, is, quite clearly, an imported western phenomenon. The practice is called international nutrition, the public policy and programming aspects of which are called "public nutrition" in other sections of this volume, as proposed by Mason et al. (1996).

2. Perhaps the primary shortcoming of these ANP programs was the virtual absence of targeting. A review by Levinson of early documents pertaining to ANP programs found almost no mention of the need to target resources to those in greatest need. In a listing of 29 recommendations emerging from an international seminar on ANP programs in Africa, for example, (FAO/Africa 1966), and in dozens of recommendations emerging from similar meetings elsewhere in the world, there is no mention of targeting. The implication is that, as late as the early 1970s, the international nutrition community as a whole had not yet become fully aware of the enormous disparities in both economic and nutritional status which exist even in the rural areas of low-income countries.

3. A sense of the contagious enthusiasm surrounding this apparent technological "magic bullet," and related efforts by the U.S. Department of Agriculture to harness the American food industry to address this pressing international need, is found in Scrimshaw and Altschul, 1971 and Milner 1969.

REFERENCES

Barrett, C. and Csete, J.
    (1994) "Conceptualizing Hunger in Contemporary African Policymaking: From Technical to Community-Based Approaches." *Agriculture and Human Values* **2**: 1.

Berg, A.
  (1987a) "Rejoinder: Nutrition Planning is Alive and Well, Thank You." *Food Policy* **12**: 11.

Berg, A.
  (1987b) *Malnutrition: What Can be Done?: Lessons from World Bank Experience.* Baltimore: Johns Hopkins University Press.

Dreze, J. and Sen, A.
  (1989) *Hunger and Public Action.* Oxford and New York: Clarendon Press.

FAO/Africa (Food and Agriculture Organization of the United Nations)
  (1966) "Report of a Joint FAO/WHO Seminar on the Planning and Evaluation of Applied Nutrition Programs in Africa." Rome: FAO.

Field, J. O.
  (1987) "Multisectoral Nutrition Planning: A Post-Mortem." *Food Policy* **12**: 1.

Jonsson, U.
  (1996) "Nutrition and the Convention on the Rights of the Child." *Food Policy* **21**: 1.

Levinson, F. J.
  (1993) "Incorporating Nutrition into Bank-Assisted Social Funds," Human Resources Development and Operations Policy Working Papers 5. Washington: World Bank.

Levinson, F. J.
  (1995) "Multisectoral Nutrition Planning: A Synthesis of Experience." In *Child Growth and Nutrition in Developing Countries*, eds. P. Pinstrup-Anderson, D. Pelletier, and H. Alderman. Ithaca: Cornell University Press.

Mason, J. B., Habicht, J.-P., Greaves, J. P., Jonsson, U., Kevany, J., Martorell, R., and Rogers, B.
  (1996) "Public Nutrition"—Letter to the Editor. *American Journal of Clinical Nutrition* **63**: 399–400.

Milner, M., ed.
  (1969) *Protein-Enriched Cereal Foods for World Needs.* St. Paul, MN: American Association of Cereal Chemists.

Scrimshaw, N. S. and Altschul, A. M.
  (1971) *Amino Acid Fortification of Protein Foods.* Cambridge: MIT Press.

Soekirman
  (1995) "Overcoming Hunger and Malnutrition: The Indonesian Experience." In *The Hunger Report: 1995*, eds. E. Messer and P. Uvin. Amsterdam: Gordon and Breach.

Vaidyanathan, G.
  (1989) "Tamil Nadu Integrated Nutrition Project: An Overview." Case Study prepared for the World Bank, Washington.

Wisner, B.
  (1988)   "GOBI versus PHC? Some Dangers of Selective Primary Health Care."
           Social Science and Medicine **26**: 9.
World Bank
  (1997)   *The World Development Report, The State in a Changing World.*
           Washington, DC: The World Bank.
Zeitlin, M.
  (1984)   "Vol. IV, Household Evaluation, Nutrition Communication and
           Behavioral Change Component, Indonesian Development Program."
           Report to the World Bank, Washington.

CHAPTER 4

The Culture of Nutrition Practice in a New Development Era

Thomas J. Marchione

In the last quarter century, the international development environment surrounding food and nutrition programming has profoundly changed. Transformations which began during the last half of the Cold War (1974–89) became clear in the seven years after it ended. By 1996 a new development era had emerged, characterized by a wider consensus on universal human rights, increased power of civil society, increased role of market economics, and lessened official development assistance. These transformations were accompanied by increased civil conflict and political instability. Combined with other aspects of globalization, the accelerating growth in communications and information technologies, these changes have reshaped the institutional environment affecting food and nutrition problems and the ways the development summit thinks about them and seeks to solve them. This chapter describes how the practice of nutrition intended for grassroots communities must respond within the new development environment: How those at the development summit might scale down assistance to best assist those who are seeking sustainable nutrition security for themselves in the twenty-first century.

49

THE CULTURE OF PUBLIC NUTRITION

Public nutrition in contrast to clinical and laboratory nutrition deals with the problems of social groups and the public policies and programs used to address them (Mason et al. 1996). As a professional culture, it contains the body of knowledge, beliefs, and practices that professionals use for analysis, where they increase their understanding of nutrition problems of human groups, and for programming, where they apply approaches to nutrition problems of human groups. How the profession analyzes problems and designs programs grows with its increasing empirical knowledge and adaptations to changing institutional environmental conditions. The culture can be viewed along six dimensions ranging from the development summit, where nutrition practice is a professional activity, to the grassroots, where nutrition problems and solutions are a matter of life and death (Figure 4.1).

Analysis of Food and Nutrition Problems

The way public problems of nutrition are analyzed can be described using three conceptual dimensions: (1) the nature of problems, ranging from ethical to technical; (2) the causes of problems, ranging from proximate to distal; (3) stocks of knowledge relevant to understanding problems, ranging from the local/indigenous to the universal/scientific.

Nature of Problems: Ethical to Technical

The face of the malnourished child has been entering wired and well-fed homes at ever greater speed and detail since the Ethiopian and Biafran famines of 1974, increasing the tension between technical analysis and ethical concerns. By the 1990s international economic rights relevant to the right to food, freedom from hunger, and the right to nutrition had taken their place along side the technical fields of food, agriculture and nutrition (Eide et al. 1984; Eide, Kracht, and Robertson 1996). A human rights approach to food and nutrition problems rooted in human rights law and political advocacy challenged the ethical detachment of the scientific paradigm (Jonsson 1992, 1996). Oshaug, Eide, and Eide (1994) provided a framework for analyzing state obligations to respect, protect, and fulfill human rights as the key to a normative approach for identifying food and nutrition security-relevant policies.

Causal Nexus: Proximate to Distal

Since 1974, when the World Food Conference defined food security to be a condition of adequate food supply, the extensive linkages between food

Locus

grassroots--- summit

Problem Analysis

Nature:

ethical -- technical

Causal Nexus:

proximate, behavioral----- -- distal, social/systemic

Legitimate Knowledge:

cultural/particular --scientific/universal

Programming Approaches

Planning and Control:

decentralized --- centralized

Sectoral Integration:

horizontal----- ------------------------------------- vertical

Resources:

locally generated------------------------------------ externally provided

Figure 4.1. Scalar dimensions of the professional culture of "public nutrition."

systems, economic systems and nutrition have become much better understood. The concept of food security now encompasses food access or entitlement (Dreze and Sen 1989) by a country's households and the individuals within them. Causal models incorporate distal elements of international food trade to proximate, individual dietary preferences (Maxwell and Smith 1992; Maxwell 1994; Marchione 1976). After two decades of analysis of the causes of malnutrition,[1] UNICEF (1990), among other organizations such as USAID (1993) and international NGOs, have institutionalized conceptual frameworks for problem diagnosis or situation analysis. Poor nutrition always results from immediate biological causes involving the interaction of inadequate consumption of food and infections in the body. Underlying causes are context-specific, arising from household food insecurity or livelihood insecurity, poor care behaviors, and poor health services and health conditions. These in turn result from varying basic causes internal or external to a country, such as availability of resources and who controls them, the political system, economic growth and prevailing cultural ideology, particularly the rights of women (see UNICEF conceptual framework in Ch. 13).

Knowledge: Local to Universal

In the 1970s nutritionists and agriculturists were just being introduced to the diversity of indigenous cultural and sub-cultural (e.g., gender) influences on nutritional knowledge. Few nutritionists recognized the importance of cultural beliefs in shaping behaviors (e.g., Jelliffe 1968). Since then social anthropology and other social sciences have widely influenced nutrition, agriculture, and development. (See Jerome, Kandell, and Pelto 1980 for the beginnings of nutritional anthropology.) Rapid field research techniques for understanding local practices such as breastfeeding and infant feeding and other aspects of food security have proliferated (Ch. 10). Coping strategies unique to localities, such as eating down the food chain and seeking wild foods, are now commonly observed behaviors of households under different situations of food shortage (Frankenberger and Goldstein 1990). In the 1990s, women's nutritional problems and the knowledge women bring to food production, food handling, and child care are analyzed for the sake of the women herself as well as the sake of the child or the family (e.g., Walker 1997).

Programming Approaches

A fuller description of the culture of public nutrition practice involves three programming dimensions: (1) planning and control, ranging from highly centralized "blueprints" to decentralized adaptive processes; (2) sectoral interventions, ranging from vertically targeted to horizontally integrated; and (3) resources, ranging from externally provided to locally generated.

Planning and Control: Centralized to Decentralized

Central planning for food and nutrition was vigorously promoted in the 1970s, when wide-ranging, multisectoral plans were constructed and directed by central governments (see Ch. 3). Such planning responded to a proper understanding of multisectoral causation of nutrition problems, but largely met with limited success in developing countries.[2]

In the early 1980s, starting with the experience of the Iringa project in Tanzania, programmers employed a more flexible and community-controlled approach to design, implementation, and management: this approach has been called "adaptive-programming" (Jonsson 1992). The adaptive process, in contrast to central, or what has been called "blueprint" planning (Maxwell 1994), supports open programs, involving the community in their design and redesign and using decentralized management structures. Iringa's success and program efficacy gave rise to the following lesson:

> Good programs do not just spring up by the implantation of a model observed to be successful elsewhere. They require a visionary cadre of initiators, able to conceptualize, adapt and adopt, mobilize, act and react and manage programs in dynamic situations (Kvishe 1995:377).

The approach, called the "triple A approach" by UNICEF (1990:17) begins with an nutrition *assessment* and a situation *analysis* to determine local causes of malnutrition. Program design and *action* are based on the analyzed causes. Periodic reassessment leads back to re-analysis and redesign and revised action and so forth in an iterative fashion throughout the life of a program.

Sectoral Integration: Vertical to Horizontal

A second dimension of public nutrition programming ranges between vertical sector interventions and horizontal programs, which integrate sectors as necessary. In the 1980s summit institutions, such as UNICEF promoted vertical strategies such as GOBI (growth monitoring, oral rehydration, breastfeeding and immunization). In the 1980–1990s similar targeted vitamin and mineral interventions proliferated.

These stand in contrast to horizontal approaches for addressing general malnutrition and household food insecurity across sectors in one location. For example, a review of UNICEF growth monitoring programs showed disappointing results without the use of better local situation analyses (Pearson 1995). In the case of food security, a "food first" approach is being replaced by a "household livelihood" approach (Maxwell 1994) where the program activity is based on cross-sectoral or holistic analysis at local level (see Ch. 11).

Resources: External to Internal

Among nutrition practitioners deep convictions and strong attitudes surround the use of external versus internal resources for programs.

Well-managed external resources are needed in many of the most poorly nourished areas to build facilities, provide supplies and support, and train staff. Food assistance for example, is often necessary for supplementary and therapeutic feeding of the severely malnourished, and when it is used as an incentive or sold, it can be a fungible resource for a variety of development interventions related to improved nutrition security (USAID 1995). At the same time it often creates dependence by recipients and recipient governments on unreliable external resources, creates preference for foods that are not locally produced, and creates disincentives to local food production. Food supplementation can be costly relative to other interventions (McGuire 1996) and can undermine health and nutrition interventions while serving as an incentive in understaffed health facilities where it is often distributed (Hendrata and Rhode 1988; Marchione 1988). Yet food aid has clearly and unambiguously created benefits for constituencies in donor countries (Ruttan 1996).

THE NEW DEVELOPMENT ENVIRONMENT

The year 1989 marked the end of the Cold War and of the development environment which was shaped by the Bretton Woods institutions and the Marshall Plan implemented after World War II. That year could also mark the introduction of a new development era (Marchione 1996).

The Cold War era was characterized by a political stalemate of the eastern and western blocs that dominated much foreign assistance while stifling both economic and social change in the Third World. Certainly until 1963 and to a large degree until 1989, containment and "security concerns" dominated both economic interests and humanitarian concern in U.S. foreign assistance policy (Ruttan 1996). The direct influence of the Bretton Woods institutions, the World Bank, the International Monetary Fund, and General Agreements on Tariffs and Trade, was limited to the western capitalist bloc (Singer 1995).

This period also encompassed the tail end of the colonial era, but as developing countries became new states, rigid political systems and economic structures rapidly formed. Newly independent states were defined as non-aligned or aligned to the eastern or western blocs and, with toleration—if not encouragement—from the U.S. or the Soviet Union, emerged too often with dictatorial central governments. Governments with low tolerance for grassroots initiatives, suspicious of local economic or political freedom, frequently used central power to co-opt or even oppress grassroots initiatives that did not clearly serve larger political ends. Donor resources were relatively abundant: even the smallest and most remote countries became strategically important and eligible for foreign assistance from one bloc or the other or, for the non-aligned, from both in their race to influence the uncommitted (Ruttan 1996). The new development era is characterized by five specific trends which began in the post-Cold War period. These are likely to reshape the environment and in turn the practice of public nutrition through at least the first decade of the twenty-first century: (1) broadening global support for universal human rights; (2) increasing democratization and rising nongovernmental activity; (3) increasing market-led economic development; (4) declining development resources; and (5) rising political instability.

Broadening Support for Universal Human Rights

Human rights are formal restatements of cultural values that influence social goals and means for achieving elements of human well-being, including good nutrition. Overcoming malnutrition is enabled in an ideological context where basic economic and social needs and civil and political participation are recognized responsibilities of the state and international bodies (Marchione 1984; Jonsson 1996). The right to food, and the more minimalist right to be free from hunger, cover a variety of rights influencing the ability of private groups and individuals to achieve food and nutritional security for themselves. The state's duty is to *respect, protect* and *facilitate* economic and social systems that enable its citizens to maintain their own nutrition security. This encompasses economic rights affecting household food security, the capacity of women to receive and render adequate care to their children, and adequate prevention and control of diseases. Governments, including intergovernmental agencies, would act to *fulfill* nutrition needs only when more proximate systems fail (Oshaug et al. 1994; Kent 1994).

By the end of 1994, the majority of the countries of the world had ratified the 10 international conventions most closely related to the right to food and nutrition. These include rights of children to the highest attainable standard of health, rights of women to be free of discrimination, and economic rights, including food and shelter in peace as well as war (see Messer 1996). For instance, six years after the adoption by the U.N. General Assembly of the Convention on the Rights of the Child in 1989, 191 states (all but the U.S. and Somalia) have ratified it (UNICEF 1997). By 1997 just under 75% of all countries have ratified the Covenant on Economic, Social, and Cultural Rights, which contains the most comprehensive statement of the right to food. Seventy-five percent (including the U.S. in 1992) had also ratified the Covenant on Civil and Political Rights.

Although these conventions were opened for signature in 1966, over 30% of the states that had ratified by 1997 did so in the five years following the end of the Cold War (Marchione 1996).

From 1989 to 1996 no less than seven international conferences have reshaped and articulated the human rights environment.[3] Perhaps most significant was the World Summit for Children which established specific goals and actionable commitments which were reaffirmed at the International Conference on Nutrition (ICN). The ICN reaffirmed that the following seven specific goals will be achieved by the year 2000: (1) reduction by half of severe and moderate malnutrition; (2) reduction of low birth weight to under 10%; (3) institutionalization of growth monitoring and promotion; (4) dissemination of knowledge on how to improve household food security; (5) empowerment of all women to breastfeed for two years and beyond; (6) elimination of iodine-deficiency disorders; (7) elimination of vitamin A deficiency; reduction of iron deficiency anemia (FAO/WHO 1992).

In contrast the goal of the World Food Summit seems distant and diffuse:

> We pledge our political will and our common and national commitment to achieving food security for all and to an ongoing effort to eradicate hunger in all countries with an immediate view to reducing the number of undernourished people to half their present level no later than 2015. (FAO 1996:1)

Implications for Nutrition Practice

Nutrition programmers in this new era must become better informed about the local manifestations of basic economic and social and political and civil rights in the countries and communities where they work. Have international conventions been ratified? How do these international rights articulate with local law and cultural practices? Are women's and minority rights respected in peace and in conflict and population displacement situations? Nutrition programs must increasingly be viewed as ethical processes, where basic rights form the framework for food security goals and program implementation.

Universal rights as they are stated in international instruments and declarations should inspire the specification of nutrition goals and policies not only by governments, but also by NGOs, communities, and private investors. The state should be expected to fulfill needs only in the last resort. Of particular importance are respecting existing food preferences, protecting means of local food procurement, and facilitating new means for universal nutrition security. Equally important is a civil and political rights approach to nutrition programming that enables communities to shape programs that affect their lives. If given full play, this approach should empower the community to eventually realize the interrelated web of basic human rights, including economic rights, such as the right to food. On ethical grounds, the goal of nutritional security for all is not to be compromised, but the route to its achievement must be, particular, iterative, and situationally determined.

Democratization and Rising Non-Governmental Activity

During the Cold War, new states, whether socialist or capitalist, often adopted undemocratic governments. From Guatemala to Mozambique, efforts to address health and nutrition problems in cooperation with communities were life threatening to project personnel (Heggenhougen 1984; Smith-Nonnini 1997).

One of the most positive aspects of the broadening support for human rights after the Cold War is that central governments are under increasing international pressure to practice civil and political rights. In the new development era, democratization is undermining central government dominance over health and nutrition programs in Latin American countries, and to some degree other world regions. Assessments of the proliferation of democratic forms of governance show that the period from the late 1980s to the early 1990s was one of the most expansive periods of democratization since World War II. According to 20 standards of freedom (such as the existence of opposition parties, fair electoral laws, rights of minorities, freedom and independence of the media, existence of trade unions, and the like) the number of countries with free or partly free societies rose dramatically, climbing from 106 (67% of all of the world's states and territories) in January of 1984 to 148 (80% of all the world states and territories) in January of 1993. The proportion of the world's people living under this concept of freedom increased from 59% to 69%. This progress reversed markedly in January 1996 to 62%, and there appeared some ominous indications that free elections may not advance civil liberties (Freedom House 1996; Zakaria 1997). Nevertheless, combined with fiscal constraints, opening markets, and the donor reforms of social services, much of the developing world appears on the road to democratization and political liberalization, if not rapid government decentralization.

NGOs and their freedom to operate locally have been strengthened throughout the 1980s and into the 1990s. Civil society has begun to flourish, opening development activities to NGOs. A world-wide study of NGOs commissioned by the Organization for Economic Cooperation and

Development suggests the magnitude of this increase (Kruse et al. 1997). In Brazil, 4700 autonomous committees were formed in 1993–1994 in response to the National Security Council Declaration of the Campaign Against Hunger, Poverty, and for Life. Following the end of the dictatorship in Chile, church-based NGOs turned in great numbers from political activism to development. NGOs active in Kenya increased from 120 in 1978 to 270–400 in 1988 to 500–550 in 1994. By 1989 40% of Kenyan health services involved NGOs. In 1984 Bangladesh had 104 private development organizations and in 1994 there were 843.

Internationally registered NGOs involved in development and humanitarian activities increased in the early 1990s from 21,000 in 1989/90 to over 31,000 in 1994/95, a massive increase over the less than 1000 in 1972 (Union of International Organizations 1989/90 and 1994/95).

Implications for Nutrition Practice

Democratization challenges nutrition practice to better incorporate community knowledge of nutrition problems in adaptive process approaches to programming. It opens routes to nutrition policy advocacy or politically scaling up activities. On the negative side, nutrition issues become more open to exploitation by unscrupulous politicians, commercial distortion, and unskilled action organizations. NGOs can represent local elites and, though well intentioned, are not always committed to public purposes.

Civil freedoms require nutrition practitioners to better understand and use local culture. Participation and empowerment privileges community members perceptions and indigenous knowledge of nutrition problems. Practitioners should have or use anthropological skills to take advantage of opportunities to learn from communities, respecting and applying the lessons of how communities cope with food insecurity and how they perceive the causes of growth failure and nutritional deficiencies. This will inevitably lead to more variable and flexible programs that stretch the envelope of standard program designs. A major challenge will be to empower communities and local organizations without sacrificing objective evaluation of results.

Active civil societies provide more opportunities to cooperate intersectorally and to advocate to the summit for specific interventions and better policy environments and resources for local programs. The new development environment permits a shift in the balance away from top-down scientific, central programming toward bottom-up advocacy for communities in need.

The new era nutritionist must be self-critical. Hierarchy and dominance do not always derive from central government or from wealthy classes or corporations; they can derive from professionals who will not identify with the plight of people at the grassroots.

Increased Market-Led Economic Growth

The end of the twentieth century has been marked by a global shift toward market liberalization and a decline in government regulation over financial flows. Leading up to and following the end of the Cold War, country after country have structurally adjusted their economies, shrinking government while opening borders to international trade and investment (Uvin 1993). Governments in Asia, such as Malaysia, Korea, Taiwan, Indonesia and Thailand, managed this liberalization in part with the aim to maximize poverty reduction and food security. Countries in Africa have begun to liberalize their economies without apparent solutions to their poverty and food insecurity problems.

The World Bank (1995:4) has described this as a "sea change in developing countries' policies that make them more credit worthy and more attractive to international investors." In 54 low-income countries net private capital flows—at 1984 prices—doubled in the 1980s but have increased more than threefold to nearly $160 billion from 1990 to 1993, while public grants and loans began to decline (World Bank 1995). Regrettably, poorer and more food insecure countries such as those in Sub-Saharan Africa and South Asia have only weakly participated in the surge of private investment.

The comparison of the FAO 1974 World Food Conference and the 1996 World Food Summit starkly contrasts the two development eras. The 1974 conference created a heated debate between northern and southern countries over an "unjust" world economic order. The meeting created the International Fund for Agricultural Development, the U.N. World Food Council, and the Committee of Food Aid Policy and Programs to guide the World Food Program; donors pledged 10 million metric tons of food assistance annually (Ruttan 1996). At the 1996 World Food Summit developed and developing countries alike committed to fair markets and adherence to the trade provision of the General Agreement of Tariffs and Trade (see commitment four in FAO 1996) with little recognition of the asymmetries involved (Raghavan 1997). States with few resources to do so committed themselves to create an enabling economic, political and social conditions for food security although no additional international support for governments was pledged (Hopkins 1997) and no new resources committed. Questions remained if the new trade regime would impact negatively on poorer countries (Singer 1996; FAO 1995), or if food prices would become too high or too volatile as producer subsidies and world food stocks declined, concerns magnified by the economic turmoil of 1998.

Implications for Nutrition Practice

In the new era, nutrition programmers and policy makers have to come to terms with functioning in highly liberalizing economies and reduced government financing and regulation. Food, employment, information, and services essential for nutrition security will be subject to the forces of open markets.

In open economies nutrition problems may be caused or solved in distant markets affecting food prices, food choices, a farmer's agricultural sales, or employment income. Practitioners are required to have a greater understanding of how markets can be used to create sustainable enterprises and income for the poor, and, if necessary, know how to act in the public interest against unfavorable market consequences. For example, codes of conduct, such as those created for the marketing of breast milk substitutes (Marchione and Helsing 1986), may become increasingly necessary to regulate commercial nutrition "education" and protect nutritional status. Similarly, large private enterprises and macro-economic policy planners have greater responsibilities to protect and promote nutrition security.

Practitioners must avoid a "neo-liberal" attitude, that the market will solve the nutrition problem (Maxwell 1994). The role of the practitioner, public and private, should be one of vigilance, cooperation, and advocacy as necessary. The market can be a powerful ally for promoting goods and ideas of nutritional benefit, but an equally powerful foe, requiring practitioners at times to develop strategies to cope with price volatility and to promote countervailing citizen action and information.

Practitioners must also know the economic development implications of poor nutrition, its impact on mortality, mental development, productivity, and morbidity. Yet, conditions such as blindness and mortality due to vitamin A deficiency, or mental retardation induced by iodine deficiency are essentially ethical violations and not merely factors in an economic growth equation.

Declining External Development Resources

In the first half of the 1990s, after two decades of increase at constant prices, official development assistance (ODA) to developing countries began to contract. In 1995 ODA for the governments of the Organization for Economic Cooperation and Development (OECD)[4] was approximately

$60 billion, a 9% drop in real terms from the year before. Contributions as a proportion of GNP as a whole dropped to the lowest level in forty years, ranging from a high of 0.8% from Denmark to a low of under 0.2% from the United States government (World Bank 1997). Private investment is not replacing this assistance. Furthermore, many of the most needy countries are heavily in debt. In 1995, sub-Saharan African governments paid twice as much in debt service than they spent for health services (UNICEF 1997).

After rising to meet the needs in Eastern Europe and states of the former Soviet Union[5] in the post-Cold War period, food aid has precipitously declined from 16.8 million metric tons in 1993 to 7.5 million metric tons in 1996 (WFP 1997) (see Figure 4.2). The U.S. Government, the largest international food aid donor, has decreased its commitment under the Food Aid Convention, and its food aid resources have declined from 7.9 million metric tons in 1993 to a projected 2.7 million metric tons in 1997 (USAID/FFPIS 1997). The bulk of the over 7 million tons in the world's lost food aid from 1993 to 1996 was 4.5 million tons (approximately one

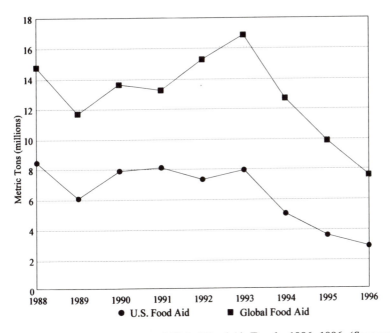

Figure 4.2. U.S. Government and Global Food Air Trends, 1986–1996. (*Sources*: USAID (1997) Food for Peace Information System; World Food Program (1997) INTERFAIS, May report.)

billion U.S. dollars) of government to government "program" food aid. While one might argue that food aid is of dubious direct importance for programs aiming for a sustained reduction in chronic malnutrition, when sold for local currency it has been a useful supplement to recipient government development budgets in the poorest countries. In addition, food aid intended for vulnerable poor in non-emergency situations, such as supplementary nutrition programs for severely malnourished, halved from 1988 to 1996, when it was 1.9 million metric tons (WFP 1997). While much of this decline so far is the result of retargeting away from middle income countries, it is not yet clear how deep the decline will be.

It is unlikely that international NGO resources will substantially attenuate this decline, although they may be able to improve targeting of available resource on the poor. In 1992 after a decade of rapid growth, NGOs managed $8.5 billion in assistance, a small amount compared to the $60 billion of ODA. Of the $8.5 billion, $6 billion was privately mobilized and $2.5 billion was received in the form of ODA from donors. It is likely that the coming decades will see more ODA channeled through NGOs as donors seek alternatives to state-to-state programs, decrease their field staffs, and/or attempt to foster local participation and empowerment. Prospects for substantial increases in private sector funding are far less certain (World Bank 1995).

Implications for Nutrition Practice

In this era of resource scarcity the challenge is how to better target administered nutrition programs while using them to seek sustainable low cost solutions with less reliance on international donor resources.

Practitioners need to be aware that development investments tend to migrate to sectors and populations with high potential for market development and away from the marginal areas where nutrition insecurity and the demand for expensive administered nutrition programs are greatest. Neglect of such areas increases their vulnerability to crises caused by natural disasters or civil disturbances, triggering massive suffering and costly emergency food aid.

The challenge is to use more efficiently the diminishing development resources and to share costs. For example programs may use more efficient area-based strategies that focus on underlying conditions, such as sustained improvements in household income and public health infrastructure, rather than on costly, facility-based nutrition rehabilitation. Understanding local cultural behaviors, such as breastfeeding and complementary feeding practices, can lead to lasting low cost solutions. Similarly solutions involving communities in nutrition surveillance have proved a means to reduce cost and increase effectiveness (UNICEF 1997).

Targeting food aid to the most needy countries and regions and targeting supplementation at the most vulnerable early stages of growth (WHO 1997) are more efficient for long-term nutrition improvement. Monetization of food aid within a country, enabling nutrition service providers to purchase nutrition inputs unavailable from other sources, may be another resource to be tapped. Since the later 1980s, while cash assistance has declined, a growing portion of program needs are raised from the sale of food aid in recipient countries. In fiscal year 1997, nearly 40% of U.S. project food aid provided for development purposes was sold by international NGOs to raise currency for implementing and administering programs (USAID/ FFPIS 1997).

Collaboration between local government, non-governmental organizations, and communities can lead to cost-sharing in cash and kind, more innovation, and more sustainability.

Political Instability

The post-Cold War has seen a proliferation of civil conflicts and state failures, displacing millions of people and putting them at nutrition risk while making nutrition programming both difficult and dangerous (USAID 1997). Nutrition security is undermined for large numbers of dislocated persons created by sectarian conflicts. Worldwide, the numbers of refugees and internally displaced persons reached approximately 40 million in 1994, most of whom were in Africa, where numbers appeared to be increasing exponentially from 1975 to 1995 (ACC/SCN 1994).

Easing ideological tension contributed to the settlement of many conflicts in the early 1990, such as those in El Salvador, Nicaragua, Mozambique, South Africa, and Ethiopia/Eritrea. Yet "complex humanitarian emergencies (CHEs)," (emergencies involving political and civil conflict in combination with resource stress such as drought, flood or crop failure) have proliferated in Africa (The Republic of the Congo, Rwanda, Somalia, Liberia, Sierra Leone), Eastern Europe, and states of the former Soviet Union. Although these conflicts appeared to be abating, after peaking in 1992–1993 (USAID 1997), the lower stakes involved in local and regional conflicts after the Cold War may be leading to higher tolerance of prolonged civil conflicts in the new development era. Donors seeking democratic governance and human rights also may be willing to tolerate more political instability for the sake of political reforms to their liking.

Implications for Nutrition Practice

By definition, the universal right to food transcends conditions of both stable and disrupted societies. Practitioners are obligated to address not only the consequences of natural disasters, but also complex emergencies where food security may be undermined intentionally or unintentionally as a consequence of larger political and military objectives (Messer 1996; Minear and Weiss 1996). This requires a willingness to grapple with the consequences of an ethical stance, such as monitoring food assistance to see that it is used for the hungry rather than the military.[6]

Practice requires application of nutrition skills under dangerous and awkward conditions. In emergency response situations, nutrition practitioners must work in unsecured areas with the arcane problems of food aid selection, logistics and international cooperation in relief camps. They must be able to apply rapid methods of assessment, management, and intervention (WHO 1995). They should be aware of methods for situation analysis using considerations of how the interventions may exacerbate conflict between ethnic or other groups or may hurt local capacities, such as local food production or breastfeeding practices (WHO 1995). Their nutrition interventions should include ways to facilitate return to normal development conditions (Anderson and Woodrow 1993).

CONCLUSIONS

Public nutrition can be viewed as a professional culture with six broad scalar dimensions, ranging from exclusive focus and control within grassroots communities to maximum focus and control within the development summit. Three dimensions relate to problem analysis: nature of problems, causal nexus, and relevant knowledge; and three relate to programming approaches: planning and control over program management, sectoral integration, and the source of program resources.

In the last quarter century the transition of the international development environment has been so profound it has defined a new development era. The features of the new era are closely connected to conditions that led to and followed the end of the Cold War: (1) broadening support for universal human rights; (2) democratization and the rise of non-governmental activity; (3) increasing market-led economic growth; (4) decreasing external development resources; and, associated with the transition to a new era, (5) more political instability and outright civil conflict.

This changed environment is causing the professional culture of nutrition to scale down the summit to better scale up programs from grassroots human and financial resources. The *nature* of problem analysis must move away from strict application of technology toward more considerations of human rights manifestations, such as the right to food and political rights of participation. Analysis of *causes* must incorporate more distal social systemic causes or what are called "basic" causes in the UNICEF conceptual framework. Relevant *knowledge* will increasingly include considerations of local culture in program areas which will shape solutions and the program management context.

The three programming approaches are also being reshaped. *Planning and control* is coming more under the influence of grassroots communities, local governments, and local NGOs. Planning is more process-oriented or adaptive to local realities and less centrally planned by the summit. Programs under local control will be less likely to be confined to targeted interventions *integrated* vertically from summit to grassroots and will be more likely be integrated horizontally across local expressions of development sectors. Finally, *resources* will be more likely to be generated locally than externally provided.

These shifts combined with the wider global reach of communication media and the explosion of digital communication technologies will confront practitioners with a very different world in the year 2000 and beyond. This change is profound enough to claim that the new development era has brought about a new era for the practice of nutrition in society, a shift from the international nutrition of the past to the public nutrition of the future.

NOTES

1. In the early 1990s, UNICEF reviewed many country cases (Brazil, Egypt, Tamil Nadu State in India, Indonesia, Tanzania, Thailand, Zimbabwe, Malaysia, Mexico, Nigeria, and Pakistan) seeking a better understanding of the conditions that lead to nutrition progress (reported in ACC/SCN 1996). See also Ch. 13 for a more discussion.

2. Central planning was reinvigorated by the plans of action proposed under the International Conference of Nutrition in 1992, the results of such are yet to be seen.

3. These started in 1989 with the Convention on the Rights of the Child, followed by the World Summit for Children in 1990, the International Conference on Nutrition in 1992, plus summits on human rights (1993), population (1994), and the FAO World Food Summit (1996).

4. The OECD development assistance contributors include the United States, western European nations plus Australia, New Zealand, and Japan.

5. See a fuller presentation of this in Ch. 1 by Uvin in this volume.

6. See J. Brian Atwood and Leonard Rogers, "Rethinking Humanitarian Aid in the New Era." *International Herald Tribune*, March 12 and 13, 1997, on the dilemmas involved in U.S. Government food relief operations in North Korea and former Zaire in the 1990s.

REFERENCES

ACC/SCN (Administrative Committee on Coordination/Sub-Committee on Nutrition)
(1994) "Report on the Nutrition Situation of Refugee and Displaced Populations." Geneva: World Health Organization.

ACC/SCN
(1996) *How Nutrition Improves.* Written and edited by S. Gillespie, J. Mason and R. Martorell. Geneva: World Health Organization.

Anderson, M. B. and Woodrow, P. J.
(1996) "Reducing Vulnerability to Draught and Famine: Developmental Approaches to Relief." In *The Challenge of Famine: Recent Experience, Lessons Learned*, ed. J. O. Field. West Hartford, CT: Kumarian Press.

Burkhalter, B., Abel, E., and Parlato, P.
(1994) "The Structure and Models Used in Profiles 2.0 with Applications to Bangladesh." Washington, DC: Academy for International Development.

Dreze, J. and Sen, A.
(1989) *Hunger and Public Action.* Oxford: Oxford University Press.

Eide, A., Eide, W. B., Goonatilake, S., Gussow, J., and Omawale, eds.
(1984) *Food as a Human Right.* Tokyo: The United Nations University.

Eide, W. B., Kracht, U., and Robertson, R. E., eds.
(1996) "Nutrition and Human Rights." Special Issue, *Food Policy* **21**(1).

FAO/WHO (Food and Agriculture Organization of the United Nations/World Health Organization)
(1992) *International Conference on Nutrition: Nutrition and Development – A Global Assessment.* Rome: FAO/WHO.

FAO
(1997) *Report on the World Food Summit, 13–17 November, 1996.* Rome: FAO.

Frankenberger, T. and Goldstein, D. M.
(1990) "Food Security, Coping Strategies, and Environmental Degradation." *Arid Lands Newsletter* **30**: 21–27.

Freedom House
(1996) *Freedom in the World: Annual Survey of Political Rights and Civil Liberties 1995–1996.* Washington, DC: Freedom House.

Heggenhougen, H. K.
(1984)   "Will Primary Health Care Be Allowed to Succeed?" *Social Science and Medicine* **19**(3): 217– 224.

Hendrata, L. and Rhode, J. E.
(1988)   "Ten Pitfalls of Growth Monitoring and Promotion." *Indian Journal of Pediatrics*. Supplement 55.

Jelliffe, D. B.
(1968)   *Infant Nutrition in the Subtropics and Tropics*. Geneva: World Health Organization.

Jerome, N. W., Kandel, R. G., and Pelto, G.
(1980)   *Nutritional Anthropology: Contemporary Approaches to Diet and Culture*. New York: Redgrave Publishers.

Jonsson, U.
(1992)   "Nutrition and Ethics." Paper presented at the Meeting on "Nutrition, Ethics, and Human Rights." Norwegian Institute of Human Rights. UNICEF: New York.

Jonsson, U.
(1996)   "Nutrition and the Convention on the Rights of the Child." *Food Policy* **21**(1): 41–55.

Kavishe, F. P.
(1995)   "Investing in Nutrition at the National Level: an African Perspective." *Proceedings of the Nutrition Society* **54**: 367–378.

Kent, G.
(1994)   "The Role of International Organizations in Advancing Nutrition Rights." *Food Policy* **19**(4): 357–366.

Kruse, S. E., Kyllonen, T., Ojanpera, S., Riddell, R. C., and Vielajus, J. L. with assistance from Bebbington, A., Humphreys, D., and Mansfield, D.
(1997)   (DAC Expert Group on AID Evaluation) *Searching for Impact and Methods: NGO Evaluation Synthesis Study*. Volume I Main Report. Helsinki: Ministry of Foreign Affairs of Finland.

Marchione, T. J.
(1977)   "Food and Nutrition in Self-Reliant National Development: The Impact on Child Nutrition of Jamaican Government Policy." *Medical Anthropology* **1**(1): 58–79.

Marchione, T. J.
(1984)   "Approaches to the Hunger Problem: a Critical Overview." In *Food as a Human Right*, eds. A. Eide, W. Barth-Eide, S. Goonatilake, J. Gussow, and Omawale, . Tokyo: United Nations University.

Marchione, T. J.
(1996)   "The Right to Food in the post-Cold War Era." *Food Policy* **21**(1): 83–102.

Marchione, T. J. and Helsing, E., eds.
  (1984)   "Rethinking Infant Nutrition Policies under Changing Socio-Economic
           Conditions." *Acta Paediatrica Scandinavica*. Supplement 314.

Mason, J. B., Habicht, J. P., Greaves, J. P., Jonsson, U., Kevany, J., Martorell, R.,
and Rogers, B.
  (1996)   "Public Nutrition." *American Journal of Clinical Nutrition*, **63**: 399– 405.

Maxwell, S.
  (1994)   "Food Security: A Post-Modern Perspective." Working Paper No. 9.
           Sussex: Institute of Development Studies.

Maxwell, S. and Smith, M.
  (1992)   "Household Food Security: A Conceptual Review." In *Household Food
           Security: Concepts, Indicators, Measurements: A Technical Review*,
           ed. S. Maxwell and T. Frankenberger. New York and Rome: UNICEF
           and the International Fund for Agricultural Development (IFAD).

Messer, E.
  (1996)   "The Human Right to Food (1989–1994)." In *The Hunger Report:
           1995*, eds. E. Messer and P. Uvin. Amsterdam: Gordon and Breach.

McGuire, J. S.
  (1996)   "The Payoff from Improving Nutrition: 1996 Up-Date." Washington,
           DC: World Bank.

Oshaug, A., Eide, W. B., and Eide, A.
  (1994)   "Human Rights: A Normative Basis for Food and Nutrition-Relevant
           Policies." *Food Policy* **19**(6): 491–516.

Pearson, R.
  (1995)   *Thematic Evaluation of UNICEF Support to Growth Monitoring*.
           Evaluation and Working Paper Series, No. 2. New York: UNICEF.

Raghavan, C.
  (1997)   "A New Trade Order in a World of Disorder?" In *World Trade: Toward
           Fair and Free Trade in the Twenty-first Century*, eds. J. M. Greisgraber
           and B. G. Gunter. London and East Haven, CT: Pluto Press with Center
           for Concern.

Ruttan, V. W.
  (1996)   *United States Development Assistance Policy: The Domestic Politics of
           Foreign Economic Aid*. Baltimore and London: The Johns Hopkins
           University Press.

Shaw, J. and Singer, H. W.
  (1996)   "A Future Food Aid Regime: Implications of the Final Act of the GATT
           Uruguay Round" *Food Policy* **21**(4/5): 447–460.

Singer, H. W.
  (1995)   "Rethinking Breton Woods from a Historical Perspective." In *Pro-
           moting Development: Effective Global Institutions for the Twenty-first*

Century, eds. J. M. Griesgraber and B. G. Gunter. London and East Haven CT: Pluto Press with Center for Concern.

Singer, H. W.
(1996) "The Future of Food Trade and Food Aid in a Liberalizing Global Economy." In *The Hunger Report: 1995*, eds. E. Messer and P. Uvin. Amsterdam: Gordon and Breach.

Smith-Nonini, S.
(1997) "Primary Health Care and its Unfulfilled Promise of Community Participation." *Human Organization* **56**(3): 364–374.

UNICEF (United Nations Children's Fund)
(1990) *Strategy for Improved Nutrition of Children and Women in Developing Countries*. New York, UNICEF.

UNICEF
(1997) *State of the World's Children—1998*. New York: Oxford University Press.

Union of International Organizations
(1991) *Yearbook of International Organizations—1989/90*. Brussels: Union of International Organizations.

Union of International Organizations
(1996) *Yearbook of International Organizations—1994/95*. Brussels: Union of International Organizations.

USAID (United States Agency for International Development)
(1993) *Definition of Food Security, Policy Determination 19*. Washington, DC: USAID.

USAID
(1995) *World Food Day Report—1995*. Washington, DC: USAID.

USAID
(1988–1996) Food for Peace Information System, Fiscal Year Budgets. Washington: USAID/BHR/FFP.

USAID
(1997) *1996 Agency Performance Report*. Washington, DC: USAID.

USAID/FFPIS
(1997) (USAID Food for Peace Information System) *Fiscal 1997 Budget Summaries*. Washington, DC: USAID.

Uvin, P.
(1993) "'Do as I say, not as I do': the Limits of Political Conditionality in Sub-Saharan Africa." In *Political Conditionality*, ed. Frank Cass/EADI: London.

WHO (World Health Organization)
(1995) *Field Guide on Rapid Nutrition Assessment in Emergencies*. Alexandria, Egypt: World Health Organization Regional Office for the Eastern Mediterranean.

WHO Food Aid Programs Unit
  (1997) "Protecting and Promoting the Health and Nutrition of Mothers and Children Through Supplementary Feeding." Geneva: WHO.
WFP (World Food Program)
  (1997) "1996 Food Aid Flows: Special Edition of the Food Aid Monitor." INTERFAIS, May. FAO: Rome.
World Bank
  (1995) *World Debt Tables 1994–1995: External Finance for Developing Countries.* Washington, DC: The World Bank.
World Bank
  (1997) *Global Development Finance 1997.* Volume I: Analysis and Summary Tables. Washington, DC: The World Bank.
Walker, S. P.
  (1997) "Nutritional Issues for Women in Developing Countries." *Proceedings of the Nutrition Society* **56**: 345–356.
Zakaria, F.
  (1997) "Democracies That Take Liberties." *The New York Times*, November 2 (editorial opinion) p. 15.

II Scaling Up the Grassroots

CHAPTER 5

Scaling Up, Scaling Down: NGO Paths to Overcoming Hunger[1]

Peter Uvin

Over the last two decades, two profound changes, one institutional and one conceptual, have taken place in the fight against hunger and poverty. At the institutional level, tens of thousands of new community-based organizations have come into being; they now play key roles in the many facets of the fight to eradicate hunger and poverty. At the conceptual level, the definition of food security, and of the ways to achieve it, has undergone profound changes, away from a technical, primarily food production focus, towards an approach that is at the same time much more holistic and more political, involving empowerment and freedom, health and education, agriculture and off-farm employment. These two processes are linked: new actors propose new definitions, pressure old actors, who are in turn influenced by them. Thus, we now have a much greater institutional and conceptual diversity, providing at the same time new opportunities, challenges, and difficulties in the fight against hunger and poverty.

In this respect, the veritable explosion of community-based, participatory, grassroots action in most of the Third World over the last two decades seems to be a most important and encouraging trend. Throughout the world, there are literally millions of grassroots organizations (GROs) and tens of thousands of non-governmental organizations (NGOs) seeking to increase agricultural production, improve basic health care, increase poor people's incomes, design safety nets against exceptional entitlement shortfalls, improve the quality of the environment, change dietary practices, curb fertility rates, and assure access to land, water, and market opportunities. Their creativity and diversity are unparalleled.

Yet, recognizing the importance of these organizations in the fight against hunger does not imply that there is no longer a role for governments, international organizations, private enterprises, research institutions, aid agencies, and the like. All these institutions remain crucial in the fight against hunger: they have financial, legal, and intellectual resources that NGOs and GROs are unlikely ever to possess. Hence, even within a vision that stresses the capacities and creativity of local communities, it remains true that governments and international organizations are crucial actors in the fight against hunger. The issue is not their destruction, or neglect, but rather the creation of links between them and the grassroots. What is required, then, is the creation of interactions between the grassroots and what can be called "the summit," in ways that are beneficial to local communities and poor people. This question of how to "link the grassroots to the summit" is at the cutting edge of current thinking about development strategies.

Linking the grassroots to the summit implies two processes. One is scaling up, a term referring to the process by which grassroots organizations expand their impact and enter into relations with the summit. Less often discussed, but equally necessary, is another process, whereby the summit scales down, adopting modes of functioning that allow for meaningful interaction with the grassroots.

This article proposes a comparative analysis of the process of scaling up of ten grassroots organizations and their programs. It focuses on the issue area of hunger, and draws primarily on the internal files of the Alan Shawn Feinstein Hunger Awards, presented at Brown University from 1988 to 1996.[2] These files provided the information for this study of various types of scaling up, as well as the paths whereby scaling up takes place. In a second part, this article discusses the rationale for scaling down, and presents the extent to which processes of scaling down are currently taking place among international development organizations.

A DEFINITION AND TYPOLOGY OF SCALING UP

We have developed a typology of scaling up, based on our reading of other authors' experiences with the phenomenon. That typology suggests there are different types of scaling up, which often go together but are not identical. Below, we summarily present this typology, looking at scaling up in terms of structures, programs, strategies, and resource bases.

Quantitative Scaling Up

The first type of scaling up occurs when a program or an organization expands its size through increasing its membership base or its constituency and, typically, its geographic working area and its budget. This is the most evident and widely used meaning of the term scaling up, equaling "growth" or "expansion." We call it quantitative scaling up. It happens when participatory organizations draw increasing numbers of people into their realm.

Functional Scaling Up

A second type of scaling up takes place when a community-based program or a grassroots organization expands the number and the type of its activities. Starting in agricultural production, for example, it moves into health, nutrition, credit, training, literacy, etc. This we label functional scaling up. It takes place when participatory organizations add new activities to their operational range.

Political Scaling Up

The third type of scaling up refers to the extent to which participatory organizations move beyond service delivery towards empowerment and change in the structural causes of underdevelopment—its contextual factors and its socio-political-economic environment. This usually includes active political involvement and the creation of relations with the state. This process, similar to a graduation to higher generations in Korten's (1990) parlance, we call political scaling up.

Organizational Scaling Up

Finally, community-based programs or grassroots organizations can increase their organizational strength so as to improve the effectiveness, efficiency, and sustainability of the benefits they provide to their members. This can be done financially, by diversifying their sources of subvention, increasing the degree of self-financing, creating activities that generate income, or assuring the enactment of public legislation that earmarks entitlements within the annual budgets for the program. It can also be done institutionally, by creating external links with other development actors, both public and private (including the enterprise sector), and by improving internal management capacity allowing the organization's staff, members and/or beneficiaries to grow, to learn from mistakes. This we label organizational scaling up.

METHODOLOGY AND PRESENTATION OF THE SAMPLE

For this article, we selected those award recipients that are participatory, community-based Third World organizations, i.e., we excluded all individuals, international agencies, and organizations located in the First World. We used the materials sent to us by the nominators: This usually comprised a selection of annual reports, mission statements, newsletters, and letters of recommendation. For some organizations, we added other readily available sources of information. We dropped two nominees for whom we did not have sufficient information. Together, the total number of organizations retained was ten.

These ten Hunger Award recipients can be taken to represent an interesting selection of organizations that are considered by their peers to have significantly affected hunger. This does not mean that they constitute an exhaustive or in any way a random selection from all that are meritorious, nor even that they really *are* effective in eradicating hunger: Maybe general perception and reality differ, and hard data that could settle the matter are usually unavailable. With these caveats, however, we believe that these organizations constitute interesting material for a closer analysis.

PRESENTATION OF THE ORGANIZATIONS

The ten organizations are (see also Table 5.1):

—Bangladesh Rural Advancement Committee (BRAC)
—Committee for the Fight to End Hunger, Senegal (COLUFIFA)
—Foundation for the Cooperation between Displaced Persons, El Salvador (CORDES)
—Gram Vikas, Orissa, India
—International Institute of Rural Reconstruction Philippines (IIRR)
—National Farmers Association of Zimbabwe (NFAZ)
—Papaye Peasants' Movement, Haiti (MPP)
—Plan Puebla, Mexico
—Sarvodaya Shramadana, Sri Lanka
—Women's Organization of Independecia, Peru (WARMI).

Table 5.1. Basic Characteristics of the Organizations[a]

	Country	Year of Creation	Population Involved	Staff	Budget
BRAC	Bangladesh	1972	550,000 and 11 million in ORT	4,300 (1991)	$21 mill. (1990)
COLUFIFA	Senegal	1984	20,000 (1974)	>10	>$100,000
CORDES	El Salvador	early 1980s			$3 mill.
Gram Vikas	India	1968	60,000 families; 280 villages		
IIRR	Philippines	1960	trained people from over 1,700 organizations in 85 countries	160	$3 mill. (1994)
MPP	Haiti	1973	30,000	>10	$300,000 (1992)
NFAZ	Zimbabwe	1980	200,000 (1990)	25	$500,000 (1990)
Plan Puebla	Mexico	1960s			
Sarvodaya	Sri Lanka	1958	3 million; over 8,800 villages	7,800 staff and tens of thousands of volunteers	
WARMI	Peru	1985	80 soup kitchens (1971)		

[a]These data have to be interpreted with utmost caution. They serve as no more than indicators of an order of magnitude, and not as exact measures of process or output. The "budget" category, for example, typically includes only external funding, and overlooks the contributions of members, volunteers and unpaid labor. Similarly, the "staff" category only includes those with formal jobs in the organization, neglecting volunteers, community activists, and the like. Some cells in the table are empty, either because the data could not be found, or because the category is not very relevant. In the case of IIRR, for example, which works with a few communities in the Philippines and seeks to learn lessons that are then used to train thousands of community organizers from all over the world; it is difficult to come up with a single number for the category "population involved."

Of these ten, three—COLUFIFA, MPP, and NFAZ—are member-based grassroots organizations (GROs), while the other seven are grassroots support organizations (GRSOs), working directly in poor communities, soliciting broad-based popular participation. Sometimes, the distinction is hard to make: The National Farmers Association of Zimbabwe, for example, which we characterized as a membership organization and which has hundreds of thousands of adherents, may well be much more separate from the engagement of its members than Sarvodaya Shramadana, which we classified as a GRSO. The former is a farmers' union characterized by severely deficient dues payments by members and political infighting at the top, while the latter draws on tens of thousands of highly committed volunteers and extremely low-paid staff throughout the country.

The Bangladesh Rural Advancement Committee (BRAC) is probably the single largest community-based non-governmental development program in all of the Third World. It has organized millions of the landless poor in village organizations. It is active in all fields of rural development: agriculture, credit, health, nutrition, education, and artisan production. With UNICEF support, it delivers primary care health services to more than 10 million people.

The Committee for the Fight to End of Hunger (French acronym: COLUFIFA) was created in 1984, after a near-famine hit the normally very fertile Casamance region of Senegal. Its originators are the same people who created and led, more than a decade before, the Association of Young Farmers from Casamance, one of Senegal's first and largest village-based grassroots organizations. COLUFIFA seeks to strengthen communities' resilience against hunger through self-help.

CORDES is a Salvadorean NGO that promotes self-reliance, initially resettling refugees under conditions of war and violence and, since the end of the war, moving into rural development activities in the province of San Vincente, El Salvador.

Gram Vikas in India was created in the late 1960s by a group of leftist students. It set out to improve the fate of the tribal people in the state of Orissa, people who are economically and socially at the very bottom of society. Its first aim was to ensure access to land for the tribal people—a struggle which pit them against the government. Gram Vikas and the communities it works with have also developed a large variety of income generating, public health, and education activities.

The International Institute of Rural Reconstruction grew out of James Yen's massive literacy-cum-rural development movement in pre-revolutionary China. Headquartered in the Philippines and working with local communities in Cavite, but with programs and partners in 12 countries, the organization acts as an action-research and training center for community-based methodologies of rural empowerment.

The "Mouvement Peyizan Papaye" of Haiti is generally considered the largest and most successful peasant self-help group in Haiti. It has worked under adverse political and economic conditions to promote small-scale rural development. It was a major force behind the "Operation Lavalas" that brought to power Rev. Aristide.

The National Farmers Association of Zimbabwe is a countrywide organization representing more than 200,000 small, African communal farmers. It acts as a liaison between these small farmers and government and international organizations. It is also active in rural development programs, and supplies cheap agricultural inputs to its members. In 1991, it merged with another farmers union to form the Zimbabwe Farmers Union.

Plan Puebla is the successful outcome of a motivated team of agricultural technicians working in a participatory manner with small Mexican farmers. As a result, agricultural yields have tripled and innovations expanded from one region through all of Mexico and now even Africa.

Sarvodaya Shramadana is a large and well-known organization, reaching up to 3 million villagers in Sri Lanka. It uses Buddhist values to promote moral, personal and social improvement and to encourage non-violent change in all fields of development: protection of the environment, health, and agriculture.

WARMI consists of hundreds of volunteer women, supported by and linked to CARITAS as well as to progressive politicians, who manage soup kitchens in a poor Lima neighborhood under conditions of rising urban poverty.

QUANTITATIVE SCALING UP

All these organizations have gone through an impressive process of quantitative scaling up. BRAC, which began working in one small region with some hundreds of poor people, currently works with 7,000 village organizations involving 550,000 poor farmers. Its oral rehydration therapy (ORT) program has touched over 13 million people. Sarvodaya Shramadana began in one village and currently involves more than 3 million people, in over 7,000 villages. MPP started as a tiny evangelical klatch of a dozen or so Haitian peasants in one commune, eventually becoming the basis of a 100,000-strong national farmers' movement in dozens of communes. The NAFZ began with some hundreds of peasants; in less than 10 years, it had over 200,000 members, although many did not pay their dues (suggesting that their degree of involvement may be minimal). CORDES now works with what it calls the "third generation" of communities, each one composed of waves of thousands of returning refugees. Gram Vikas began with a few committed students in one district and now works in hundreds of villages in different regions.

Two of the three self-help organizations have grown slowly in size through a process in which increasing numbers of people adhered to the organization and its programs. We call this path of quantitative scaling up "spread." It is typical for GROs to go through a process of slow spread. They usually start very small, with very limited resources; often they are the initiative of one highly motivated person and a few followers. After some time, initial success, or the perception that joining the organization serves their interests, other people are drawn into their realm. The organization spreads out beyond the original group, passing beyond the village borders. As the years go by, the organization can grow to encompass tens of thousands of people.

At least four of the grassroots support organizations—BRAC, CORDES, Plan Puebla, and Sarvodaya Shramadana—also seem to have scaled up quantitatively through spread, although for most of them spread is a mechanism secondary to replication (defined below). This reflects the working style of these organizations, which is not one of simple service delivery or the channelling of money or technical assistance to communities, but rather a deep commitment to self-reliance and participatory learning.

"Replication", whereby a successful program (methodology and mode of organization) is repeated elsewhere, is the path of scaling up that is best exemplified by BRAC. Indeed, BRAC has developed over the years a well-tested sequential methodology for scaling up, composed of experimenting through pilot projects, learning from them, and then replicating them elsewhere on an increasingly large scale (Abed 1986; Lovell 1992).

In a different manner, MPP attempted to encourage replication of its methodology elsewhere in Haiti through the training of "animators" from other regions. "Emerging" grassroots leaders working elsewhere in Haiti for other organizations were invited to spend some time in the region where MPP is active to learn how to work with local communities and stimulate their organization. Both Plan Puebla and the IIRR devote large parts of their resources to replication through training. Organizations such as these have trained generations of rural development practitioners in the use of participatory methodologies, first in Mexico and the Philippines, and later in countries on all continents. In these cases, it is a set of successful methodologies whose replication is sought, and the tool for achieving replication is training by the original developers of the methodology in the original environment. Yet, the actual implementation of what has been learned is done elsewhere by other organizations that employ the persons trained.

Plan Puebla also scaled up through what we call "structural integration." Structural integration occurs when an NGO program is taken over by "existing structures and systems and in particular government structures after it has demonstrated its potential" (Mackie 1992; see too Bebbington and Farrington 1993). Structural integration can come about as a result of demand by the NGO, which persuades a government agency to take over a successful program it launched (e.g., Plan Puebla, where Jimenez Sanchez persuaded the Ministry of Agriculture to take over his program methodology on a large scale), or it can take place on the initiative of the state. Such integration, it is often argued, is an important way to increase impact and assure sustainability of NGO-initiated participatory programs (Allison and Kak 1992; Howes and Sattar 1992; Lovell 1992; Morgan 1990; Tendler 1982). It rarely occurs, however, for it goes against the ideological dynamics of most NGOs and governments. It is also difficult and dangerous, for the mode of functioning of government is often inimical to the flexibility and patience required for successul participatory, community-based action. (See Schorr (1997) for an excellent dicussion of this in the case of the US.)

NFAZ's 1991 merger with the Zimbabwe National Farmers Union, another of the three main farmers unions in Zimbabwe, representing the interests of more than 10,000 small commercial farmers, represents a fifth path to quantitative scaling up, in which different organizations merge with each other creating a single larger one. This path, which can be labeled "aggregation," is very rarely taken: Typical organizational dynamics militate against it. In this case, as Bratton (1994) convincingly demonstrates, a unique combination of government pressure and self-interest by the leaders of the unions explains the process. Generally, the process of aggregation takes place not by mergers, but by the creation of higher-level representative bodies at the regional, national, or international level. Such organizations as the Asian NGO coalition, ANGOC (of which most of our Asian sample NGOs are members) or the Fédération des ONG Sénégalaises, FONGS (of which COLUFIFA is a member) primarily serve as research and advocacy providors for their constituents, although they may also supply other services such as training (Fisher 1992).

FUNCTIONAL SCALING UP

Of our sample organizations, none remained limited to their original activity, and quite a few of them are active in a great many areas of human life.

An organization such as BRAC, for example, now manages dozens of programs in health, education, and economic activity. The three grassroots organizations went through broad processes of diversification, reflecting the needs of their members. They usually started with economic activities (mostly in agriculture), and eventually added to this social service-type of activities. Other organizations followed the opposite path, to arrive at the same end: Sarvodaya Shramadana, for example, began as a social service organization and only later started economic development projects.

In some cases, the functional scaling up that took place was of a "horizontal integration" type, such as adding activities in forestry, environmental protection, education, or artisanal production to agriculture. Sarvodaya Shramadana has become active over the years in preschools, literacy, conservation, drug and alcohol rehabilitation, legal aid, micro-enterprise, relief and rehabilitation in war zones, and water supply. Similarly, Gram Vikas is active in the fields of social forestry, primary health care, adult education, legal aid, small enterprise credit, irrigation, fishery, biogas plants, and disaster relief. This is a process that seems typical of many community-based organizations in that they get drawn into all other aspects of life, eventually becoming "integrated rural development" agencies covering everything from basic human services to income generation.

Other organizations followed paths of vertical integration. WARMI, for example, after a decade of managing soup kitchens, began developing an alternative food purchasing and distribution network; it also entered the health sector. BRAC added factories and outlets to its artisan training program. The most common case of vertical integration consists of the addition of savings and credit mechanisms to the original activities of the organizations. This indicates the great lack of access to credit by the rural poor in the Third World. BRAC, COLUFIFA and MPP, in different ways, all added credit and savings to their original activities. In the case of BRAC, this took the form of the creation of a network of rural banks serving more than 200,000 households, whereas for COLUFIFA and MPP it was limited to accounts in which members deposit their savings and from which they can borrow.

Eight out of the 10 organizations studied primarily focused on economic activities. Indeed, the central aim and the basic type of activity of the BRAC, CORDES, COLUFIFA, Gram Vikas, IIRR, MPP, NFAZ, and Plan Puebla is to improve the economic situations of their members or clients. This reflects the well-known fact that, for the majority of the poor, any investment of their time, energy and money depends foremost on the perceived capacity of that investment to generate additional income. Only later, when a higher and more stable productive base has been assured, are health, nutrition, education and training activities added. One of the two remaining organizations, WARMI, is almost exclusively limited to service delivery, financed through payment for the service by the beneficiaries and voluntary labor of its staff. Sarvodaya Shramadana, finally, usually begins with spiritual renewal and comes only later to income generation.

Looking at hunger and the processes that create entitlements, we observe that only two of the ten organizations focus directly on nutrition: WARMI, with a mandate to feed poor people, and IIRR, for which community health, reproductive health and nutrition is one of its five key programs. The remainder concentrate on activities aimed at increasing income. Investment in cash crops, livestock, artisan production and village industry served the purpose of income improvement and diversification—both important ways to secure increased exchange-based entitlements to food. At least five organizations—CORDES, COLUFIFA, IIRR, MPP and Plan Puebla—have activities specifically to increase food production and decrease the incidence of hunger in the community. COLUFIFA and MPP also invest in improved storage, again with the explicit goal of reducing hunger. Some actions are designed to simultaneously increase income or fight malnutrition. The introduction of vegetable gardening, for example, by COLUFIFA was justified both by improved nutrition and by income generation.

None of the organizations studied started in health but most of them took on health activities. BRAC, COLUFIFA, CORDES, IIRR, MPP, Sarvodaya Shramadana and WARMI all have basic health activities. For most people, recurrent sickness and the impossibility of finding decent health care are among their main frustrations. If people feel they can change that, they are willing to invest their own resources. Note, however, that for most of these organizations family planning or the provision of contraceptives is not a field of action. Only BRAC and IIRR have some activities in that sector as part of their health programs (Lovell 1992). In the light of the importance usually attached by the hunger community to family planning, this is an important observation.

POLITICAL SCALING UP

Here, it is useful to turn back to Korten's (1990) classification of NGOs in generations, distinguishing different strategies for achieving development.

"First generation NGO strategies involve the direct delivery of services to meet an immediate deficiency or shortage experienced by the beneficiary population. The assisting NGO directly relates to the individual or the family and the benefits delivered depend entirely on the funds, staff and administrative capacity of the NGO. Second generation NGO strategies focus the energies of the NGO on developing the capacities of the people to better meet their own needs through self-reliant action. It is the stress on local self-reliance, with the intent that benefits will be sustained by community self-help action beyond the period of NGO assistance, that distinguishes first from second generation strategies. Often the strategy is described as an attempt to "empower" the village people. Third generation NGO strategies look beyond the individual community and seek changes in specific policies and institutions at local, national and global levels. Third generation strategies focus on creating a policy and institutional setting that facilitates, rather than constrains, just, sustainable and inclusive local development action. Fourth generation strategies look beyond focused initiatives aimed at changing specific policies and institutional sub-systems. Their goal is to energize a critical mass of independent, decentralized initiative in support of a social vision."

A small number of the organizations studied—BRAC, CORDES, and WARMI—began as first generation ones. Their aim was to provide direct relief or welfare to poor people. COLUFIFA, Gram Vikas, IIRR, MPP, Plan Puebla and Sarvodaya Shramadana, notwithstanding their many differences on other accounts, were all started as typical second generation organizations. Their goal since their inception was to help people help themselves at the local level, although that local level can cover a large area. Only one organization, the National Farmers' Association of Zimbabwe, started as a third generation one, seeking to represent farmers' interests at the governmental and international level.

Of these ten organizations, six remained at the same generational level; the four others scaled up. One of the three that began as first-generation organizations remained at that level: Peru's WARMI, which essentially remains a soup-kitchen organization. BRAC began as a relief organization, providing relief to refugees from the 1971 liberation war, but its leadership soon discovered the need to go beyond that level and to help strengthen the capacity of poor people to help themselves. It now stands squarely in the second generation.

Among those that began as second generation organizations, IIRR, Plan Puebla, Sarvodaya Shramadana, and COLUFIFA remain firmly at that level. COLUFIFA has recently adopted a strategy of getting its members elected at the local government level but only with the limited objective of being able to work at the grassroots level without being "disturbed" by the state. (Lachenmann 1993)

MPP in Haiti has a turbulent history of political scaling up. In so doing, it went through three phases. In the beginning, it refrained from any political involvement. Fear of repression and the need to establish first a basis of success and confidence explained this situation. In a second phase, the maturity of MPP coincided with the post-Duvalier period and MPP became one of the main rural forces behind Operation Lavalas, which briefly brought Rev. Aristide to power. Following this election, it also was instrumental in the foundation of a national peasants' movement with more than 100,000 members (the "National Peasant Movement of the Congress of Papaye"). After the 1992 coup d'etat, with its leaders in hiding or imprisoned and tortured, and its possessions looted and destroyed, MPP played a less vocal political role, and was subject to severe harassment. Yet, it did remain active, and at great risk prepared reports to the OAS mission on human rights. Hence, MPP has clearly moved to a third generation level, even though the nature of the political scene in Haiti puts extremely tight limits on what is possible.

Gram Vikas was forced to scale up politically from the very beginning. The problems facing the tribal people in Orissa, India often revolve around their lack of access to land and forest produce, as well as to credit, health care and education. All of these issues are strongly conditioned by state policies, meaning that any solution to the problems faced by the tribal people necessarily had to include playing an active role towards the state—and foremost, in the words of its president, Joe Madiath, the unholy trinity of the forest department, the revenue service, and the police. Local elites who benefited from the exploitation of tribal people, such as money-lenders, liquor merchants, and large landowners, were often associated with local government. They too had to be faced, often leading to conflict. Success has been halting and uneven but real. Gram Vikas has even engaged in some collaborative actions with government agencies.

CORDES and the NFAZ show that nice taxonomies never apply to all cases. CORDES started as a first generation organization, providing emergency aid to returning refugees who lacked everything. Yet, at the same time, it was also firmly a third generation organization, having developed a forceful and coherent vision of self-reliance and building up national and international alliances to create the environment conducive to such development. Since the end of the war in El Salvador, it increasingly acts on the second generation level, promoting rural development in the region of San Vincente, working in the fields of irrigation, credit, and marketing. The National Farmers Association of Zimbabwe started as a third generation organization, representing its members' interests at the level of government and foreign donors. Later, taking on rural development activities and the delivery of cheap inputs, it scaled *back* to add second generation types of activities to its scope. Finally, some of the grassroots support organizations have found themelves forced to provide emergency assistance to communities when disaster struck, whether it was Gram Vikas when confronted with flooding, or Sarvodaya Shramadana when faced with the effects of the civil war in Sri Lanka. In those cases, they are temporarily forced to behave like first generation organizations.

What strategies were employed by organizations that moved up to the third generation? Both CORDES and MPP did so mainly through networking, the pooling together of their numbers and resources with like-minded organizations, usually through the creation of federations designed to influence policy making. In 1991, MPP took the initiative in creating a National Peasants Movement with the direct aim of confronting the government. In 1990, CORDES, together with seven other NGOs in the same sector, created an Inter-Institutional Coordination aimed at promoting community development on a large scale. This IIC subsequently went on to organize a conference in San Salvador, attended by representatives of over 100 Salvadoran and foreign NGOs, at which a "New Initiative for Popular Self-Development in El Salvador" was adopted. It is explicitly seen as an attempt to create models that can be expanded nationwide as the political space opens.

Direct entry into politics has been considered (but not executed) by A.T. Ariyaratne of Sri Lanka. None of the other leaders or organizations of our sample entered into the political arena. Gram Vikas may have been the most confrontational of the NGOs in our sample: Often, the tribal people it supports had to occupy state-owned lands illegally. At other times the same organization has sought to support tribal people's capacity to avail themselves of government services and policies. Finally, the NFAZ was created as a lobbying organization and did not really adopt any strategy of scaling up.

In conclusion, only two of the 10 organizations studied are solely first generation. Most organizations are at the second generation level, either from inception onwards, or through scaling up. Few organizations have scaled up politically to become third generation. Only CORDES, Gram Vikas, and MPP did so.

ORGANIZATIONAL SCALING UP

Among the organizations studied, almost all have followed paths of institutional diversification, either changing from one structure to another or adding new structures. Some of the organizations in our sample, COLUFIFA, IIRR, and WARMI, were themselves the result of the institutional diversification of other organizations. In 1993, after the end of the civil war, CORDES changed its name to Foundation for Cooperation and Rural Development of El Salvador (same acronym), reflecting a change in its mission from survival under war conditions to long-term development.

The type of institutional diversification most encountered is the creation of cooperatives. Three of the 10 organizations (CORDES, MPP, and to a lesser extent WARMI) at some point created member cooperatives in the usual areas of purchase of inputs, credit and commercialization. None of them, however, started as cooperatives. The creation of rural banks is also a frequently encountered method of organizational scaling up. In our sample, two organizations, BRAC and COLUFIFA, have ventured into that field. BRAC and Gram Vikas also created autonomous commercial enterprises.

The organizations in our sample have created few institutional links with different actors other than fellow NGOs and donor agencies. Apart from the two cases mentioned above that created commercial enterprises, none of the organizations in our sample seems to have strong links with the private-for-profit sector. Organizations such as BRAC, IIRR and Sarvodaya Shramadana derive steady streams of income from the provision of services and consultancies for donors and occasionally for government agencies (see our discussion of subcontracting below). Plan Puebla set up a training school as part of a Mexican university.

Another important element of organizational scaling up is the search for diversified and secure funding. Most organizations in our sample receive funding from more than one source—in five cases more than 10 sources. BRAC has been able to create a donor consortium, allowing for coordination of its diversified donor support, while Sarvodaya Shramadana has created an endowment fund designed to finance its activities with the interest. IIRR has a donor list of more than 100 organizations and individuals, and a New York office largely devoted to that task, while MPP used the receipts from its Hunger Award to establish a similar office in Boston. Most of this funding is soft money, coming almost exclusively, in order of decreasing frequency, from international private voluntary organizations, multilateral organizations, and the governments of rich countries. Few donors are national philanthropic organizations or rich individuals.

This certainly decreases NGO dependency upon a single donor, although it is quite probable that the small, scattered and uncoordinated nature of external NGO funding rather than a deliberate strategy of donor diversification, is the explanation. Moreover, only few of the organizations—BRAC and IIRR come to mind—managed to secure overall institutional funding, whereby donors do not fund one particular project but the whole program of the organization. As a result, grassroots organizations are forced to adapt their modes of functioning to the divergent requirements of their many donors and to expend human resources in satisfying various administrative requirements.

Successful donor diversification implies two other important points. First, this sample shows that successful grassroots organizations (or, more precisely, grassroots organizations perceived to be successful) can count on large amounts of foreign aid. Donors are, in a way, scrambling over each other so as to be able to finance what they think are the "good" NGOs. It should be clear that donors are not necessarily capable of identifying these good NGOs and often end up financing either NGOs that other donors are already funding (a safe bet), or NGOs with the best public relations. Second, all this implies that none of the organizations in our sample, except WARMI, financed its activities primarily by its own resources, or even by national resources. It seems clear that self-financing is far away for all but a few of the organizations in our sample.

Faced with that problem, our sample of organizations have adopted a variety of strategies. COLUFIFA has a deliberate policy of minimizing its dependence on external aid. According to its founder, Demba Mansaré, it can continue its work without aid, although it would have to shed its more costly activities, such as the construction of health centers. Other organizations such as BRAC or IIRR subcontract for government or international aid organizations, executing training sessions for their staff, evaluation and identification mandates, conferences and workshops, specific consultancies or entire projects. Many analysts caution against subcontracting to the state or to the aid system, arguing that it may tempt or force NGOs to "sell out" their principles for the sake of income—in short, to become co-opted. Yet, in the cases of our sample, extensive subcontracting seems rather to entail a recognition from external actors that the mode of functioning and expertise of these NGOs is valuable. Hence, it seems that for the NGOs this is a way both to expand their impact and to increase their degree of self-financing. Thus, both BRAC and IIRR self-finance more than one quarter of their activities with sub-contracts.

An unresolved issue is that our discussion, reflecting actual practice, has focused exclusively on the sustainability and organizational scaling up of NGOs rather than on the benefits accruing to the poor. Indeed, at the end of the day, what should be sustained is not necessarily the organization providing services, but the progress achieved by its members/clients. A difficult and unanswered question for all organizations concerned, and especially for grassroots support organizations is: To what extent will benefits and progress continue after their departure? To what extent are beneficiaries capable of progressing on their own? There are no clear answers to these questions.

SCALING DOWN

It is generally held that for the interaction between scaled up community-based organizations and the summit to be meaningful the summit should also scale down and adopt structures and modes of operation that allow local communities and their organizations to build their conceptual, operational, and institutional capacities. On the most general level, this implies the need for what Fowler (1988) calls "management for withdrawal," the development of structures and practices that are geared not to perpetuate or enhance the hold of the summit over the grassroots, but rather to enable beneficiary scaling up and autonomy. In other words, what is required is a redefinition of the role of international development organizations and government agencies as one of accommodation, co-adaptation, responsiveness, and flexibility rather than predicting and controlling events (Rich 1994). Only in this way can there be enough space for communities and their organizations to learn, to grow, to initiate, to scale up.

Scaling down thus implies the creation of structures and procedures that allow for information and accountability to local communities in the programs that concern them; the hiring and training of personnel who are respectful and responsive to the needs of poor people; the provision of facilities for self-help such as credit, advice, and legal recognition of grassroots organizations; and the involvement of the people concerned in all phases of the actions. Scaling down is about creating projects and programs that are smaller, more participatory, more flexible and more respectful of local knowledge and local learning. Programs may be slower, may make mistakes, may derail from plans, but at least they are owned by those they claim to support.

Not surprisingly, there is much resistance against scaling down—resistance that cannot be outright discarded or simply wished away. Scaling down is ultimately a political matter, entailing a delegation of power away from the summit towards the grassroots. Nowhere in the world do powerful people, even those committed to development, hand over control of scarce resources voluntarily. Moreover, scaling down implies a profound attitude change, in which the locus for action moves from the experts to the poor, from technologies to communities (Chambers 1997). Such changes are always slow to come about. Finally, strong arguments can be made that certain interventions necessitate financial and technological resources that are almost always beyond the reach of local communities. In all likelihood some things can or should not be scaled down, for their effectiveness would be lost. What exactly those things are, however, or to what extent participation should be reduced, is unclear and subject to heated debate.

Experiences with Scaling Down

To the extent that scaling down has taken place, it has been the result of political processes rather than of intellectual or practical considerations. Three profound political processes can be distinguished that, since the middle of the 1980s, have influenced international organizations to scale down. First is the pressure the NGO community has brought to bear on the summit. Thousands of NGOs (themselves in the process of scaling up) are putting pressure on their governments and on bilateral and multilateral development institutions to adopt a more participative, accountable, respectful, and decentralized mode of functioning. Second, most Third World governments face a profound financial crisis and need to tap new resources for development. This has led to the dominance of a liberal ideological position largely created and fine-tuned by the international financial institutions and the donors but now officially accepted in most Third World countries. This approach to development favors state disengagement, privatization, and community self-help, which are seen as instruments to achieve sustainable, structurally adjusted economic growth. Third is the widespread erosion of the legitimacy of the state and the pressure for political change faced by many governments. The end of the Cold War and the accompanying decline in politically motivated development aid are causal factors in this trend but its main sources are internal to these countries themselves. In many Third World countries, urban and rural populations have been voicing demands for political change, often violently. Powerholders have been forced to provide at least a semblance of change, recognizing organizations of civil society and allowing a greater space for their voices.

Together, these processes have led to the disengagement and decentralization of government structures, increased recognition and funding for NGOs from international donors, and opportunities for participation in the implementation, if not the decision-making, for projects in sectors that were previously under the exclusive control of governments and donors (health, water, and education immediately come to mind). Community-based organizations have found new margins for maneuver, which they have not hesitated to fill, as well as new external financial resources which they have gladly appropriated.

Changes in the Donor Community

International development agencies, whether bilateral or multilateral, have made important changes in their behavior towards Third World NGOs during the last decade. Financial pressure has played a role, but ideological change and direct pressure from NGOs are equally important. Many donors have created disbursement mechanisms to provide rapid financing to small NGO projects. The United Nations Development Program, for example, until recently beholden only to governments, developed a plethora of new initiatives. Since 1990, the Partners in Development Program has offered small grants ($25,000 per country) to NGOs to implement community-based initiatives in more than 60 countries. The Grassroots Initiatives Support Fund, another UNDP initiative, provides small grants to self-help initiatives in Africa; and the Africa 2000 Network (followed by similar initiatives in Asia and Latin America) supplies grants and technical assistance to southern grassroots organizations and grassroots support organizations that are active in ecologically sustainable development. These mechanisms are cheap and small—cynically spoken, crumbs that fall off the table. They do not modify the mode of functioning of the summit, or change the spending patterns of most of their activities—which is what scaling down is really about.

On a more advanced level, international donors now routinely collaborate with local NGOs in project implementation. The United Nations Population Agency (UNFPA), the UN Children's Fund (UNICEF), the Food and Agriculture Organization of the United Nations (FAO), the United Nations High Commissioner for Refugees (UNHCR), and the World Bank all have programs in which NGOs are given sometimes important operational roles. Thus BRAC supplies oral rehydration to millions of people for UNICEF, while Sarvodaya Shramadana is a key partner in World Bank sponsored social dimensions of adjustment projects in Sri Lanka. According to the World Bank, "more than 40% of the total number of Bank projects approved in 1993 involved NGOs" (World Bank 1994). The Bank now has a list of more than 7,000 potential partner NGOs and also publishes a list of "World Bank-financed projects with potential for NGO involvement." The type of involvement sought is almost always "implementation," however, and very rarely "design" (World Bank 1991), suggesting that NGO roles remain limited to sub-contractng rather than partnership. Even bilateral donors such as USAID are attempting to increase their use of and deepen their partnerships with NGOs (USAID 1995). Although such collaborations are on the rise, denoting an increased recognition of the capabilities of NGOs (and supplying increased revenues to the latter) it does not usually amount to scaling down as defined above. Most of the time, the locus for decision-making and control over financing remains squarely with the international donor agencies, while the necessary adaptation is done by the local NGOs, and the collaboration does not extend beyond projects into the realm of national and sectoral programming.

Almost all donor agencies have developed regular consultation mechanisms with the NGO community. In 1984 the World Bank created a mechanism of semi-annual consultation with NGOs. The International Fund for Agricultural Development (IFAD) did so in 1987 and other international agencies such as FAO, UNICEF, and UNHCR now have similar mechanisms. Increasingly these consultations include Third World NGOs, although the mechanisms of selection remain haphazard. Similar meetings take place in the field often on the initiative of a particularly dynamic UN resident representative or NGO leader. Again, these occurrences certainly constitute an advance over the previous policy of mutual neglect, but they do not amount to true scaling down, for they leave inequalities of power and information largely intact.

Other processes, however, do hold the promise of meaningful scaling down. In many ways, it is the World Bank that is most advanced in this respect. First, the World Bank has expressly included in its operational directives consultations with groups, such as NGOs, that will be affected by its projects. This was achieved by pressure from the NGO community, backed by the U.S. government, and against the will of most Third World member states who considered this a violation of their sovereignty. The language of this directive states that consultation shall be done by the borrowing government since, theoretically, the Bank always acts through the government. In practice, however, most NGOs have sought participation in the Bank's deliberations rather than in its actual negotiations with governments. This probably reflects an assessment both of the power of the Bank in these negotiations, and of the fact that it is easier and less dangerous to influence Bank policy than governments' policies. Thus, as part of worldwide networks of political scaling up, Third World NGOs now collaborate with Washington-based NGOs to put pressure on the World Bank (or on the U.S. Congress, which will then pressure the Bank!) to change policy.

As a result, the Bank has been forced to adopt more far-reaching and innovative procedures for working with NGOs. At the end of 1994, it adopted a Participation Action Plan (PAP), which sets out guidelines for the inclusion of NGOs in all stages of project and, for the first time, program lending. These PAPs state that resident missions should meet local NGOs on a monthly basis, that participatory social assessments shall be prioritized, that new, non-economic staff be hired to provide operational support for participatory activities and social assessments, and that headquarters and resident mission staff be trained in participatory tools and techniques. The goal of all these procedures is to mainstream local participation in all of the Bank's activities (World Bank Watchers 1996–7).

Second, following a new policy of disclosure of operational information approved by the executive directors in 1993, the World Bank created a public information system to make available to the public a range of operational documents that were previously restricted to official users. Ordinary citizens now have access to more project information than before, albeit by no means all of it. At the same time, NGOs such as the Washington-based Bank Watchers Project provide inside information on Bank functioning to NGOs everywhere, and seek to increase their knowledge of, and involvement in, the making of country assistance strategies and other policy documents. The Bank is also making its documents available in local university libraries, with a successful case underway in Jamaica, while in another pilot project Bank documents are being translated in local languages in six resident missions (World Bank Watchers 1996–7). Thus, increasingly, local people and their organizations can have access to the information required for meaningful participation.

Third, in 1994, the Bank established an independent inspection panel to hear complaints by private citizens that the World Bank is violating its own procedures, including the ones on participation. During its first two years of existence, five formal requests were received by the inspection panel. Two of these cases have received extensive follow-up: a hydro-electric project in Nepal was abandoned, while at the time of writing the fate of a natural resources management project in Brazil was still pending. Both these projects were advanced in their preparation and it is likely that without the inspection panel procedure these projects would not have been halted (IBRD 1996).

Together, these policy changes have the potential for meaningful scaling down. Through procedures that provide for a multitude of points of interaction with the grassroots, personnel that take such opportunities seriously, widely available information about Bank operations that allows the grassroots to act with knowledge and control mechanisms that allow for accountability, the World Bank has entered a slow process of scaling down. Needless to say, attitudinal and political constraints exist within the Bank and borrowing governments that will counteract these changes. The large majority of Bank staff, for example, remains less than enthralled about venturing beyond the realm of economic and technical considerations in their work. All these processes have only just begun. Their final destination is still unclear and will take years to achieve. Yet, these changes do carry the promise of structural modifications in the Bank's relation with the grassroots.

What is the impact of all this on hunger? Why even discuss scaling down the World Bank in an article about overcoming hunger? In a limited, short-run sense, there is little impact: The World Bank, although by far the most important development agency in the world, does not determine the nutritional situation of the world's hungry people. As such, changing its policy does not immediately affect world hunger. In the longer run, however, the changes we discussed are contributing to a pattern of decision-making that may also affect other development agencies whether bilateral, multilateral or non-governmental. Through them, it will increasingly affect Third World governments. Such a pattern of scaling down is about increased transparency and accountability of those agencies that purport to help the poor and the hungry, increased freedom for maneuver for grass-roots organizations, and respect and external support for their initiatives. Many people believe that no lasting solution to world hunger will come about without these factors. As such, scaling down is a necessary condition for overcoming hunger.

CONCLUSION

In this article, we have distinguished four types of scaling up, and analyzed the paths various community-based organizations have followed to achieve scaling up. Such organizations now routinely implement development programs with million dollar budgets, seek to participate in national and international decision-making processes, propose innovative development models to governments and donor agencies, and generally constitute a major intellectual, social and financial force in the field of development. Not all NGOs have done so equally: Many of them lack both the desire and the capacity to do so. But there is a worldwide trend for grassroots organizations to scale up in the ways described above.

The summit, both governments and international organizations, has its own reasons for allowing this to happen. Some of these reasons are ideological, having to do with a sincere commitment to participation and self-help. Other reasons are opportunistic, the result of budgetary distress and the need to push the cost of services down. Still others are the result of external pressure, from the donor community as well as from the NGOs themselves. Whatever the reasons, opportunities have emerged for the grassroots to link up to the summit as serious, integral actors.

In building links with NGOs, the summit is under pressure to scale down, to adopt more flexible, respectful, and accountable procedures and structures in order to turn interaction into partnership—and, again, there is significant NGO pressure to do so. This does not take place without resistance, but, for the reasons outlined in this chapter, change is taking place, albeit slowly.

If one believes that the solutions to hunger will—and already do—come primarily from the energies, capacities and resources of the poor themselves, together with the institutions they are part of, then the main task of external aid agencies should be to support these capacities and institutions, rather than substituting for them or suffocating them. From such a perspective, the processes of scaling up and scaling down appear to be crucial. Together, they may provide the space for local communities to organize, learn, and innovate; to collaborate, counteract, and propose; and finally, to change their world.

NOTES

1. This article is a revised and updated version of Uvin (1995). Some new organizations have been added and the section on scaling down is entirely new.

2. Brown University has yearly granted three Hunger Awards of $25,000 and two Hunger Awards of $10,000 each. According to the statutes of the awards, the award winners are organizations or people that have made "extraordinary efforts or contributions to the reduction of hunger in the world or its prevention in the future." Yearly, between 30 and 50 nominators—academicians and practitioners from around the globe—present candidates for the awards. Afterwards, Brown University's Board of Trustees, assisted by a special selection committee, chooses the winners.

REFERENCES

Abed, F. A. H.
(1986)   "Scaling Up in Bangladesh Rural Advancement Committee (BRAC)." In *Readings in Community Participation*, ed. M. Bamberger. Washington D.C.: World Bank.

Allison, A. and Kak, L.
(1992)   "NGO/Government Collaboration in Maternal Health and Family Planning Programs." *Transnational Associations* 32(3): 163–66.

Bebbington, A. and Farrington, J.
(1993)   "Governments, NGOs and Agricultural Development: Perspectives on Changing Inter-Organisational Relationships." *The Journal of Developmental Studies* 29(2): 1099–219.

Bratton, M.
(1994)   "Micro-Democracy? The Meger of Farmer Unions in Zimbabwe." *African Studies Review* 37(1): 9–37.

Chambers, R.
(1997)   *Whose Reality Counts? Putting the First Last.* London: Intermediate Technology Publications.

Fisher, J.
(1993)   The Road from Rio: *Sustainable Development and the Nongovernmental Movement in the Third World*. Westport, Connecticut: Praeger.

Fowler, A.
(1988)   "Nongovernmental Organizations in Africa: Achieving Comparative
         Advantage in Relief and Micro-Development." Discussion Paper 249.
         Sussex, England: Sussex Institute of Development Studies.

Howes, M. and Sattar, M. G.
(1992)   "Bigger and Better? Scaling Up Strategies Pursued by BRAC 1972–
         1991." In *Making a Difference: NGOs and Development in a Changing
         World*, eds. M. Edwards and D. Hulme. London: Earthscan.

IBRD/IDA (International Bank for Reconstruction and Development/International
Development Assistance)
(1996)   "The Inspection Panel. Report, Aug. 1, 1994 to July 31, 1996."
         Washington: World Bank.

Korten, D.
(1990)   *Getting to the 21st Century. Voluntary Action and the Global Agenda.*
         West Hartford, CT: Kummarian Press.

Lachenmann, G.
(1993)   "Civil Society and Social Movements in Africa: The Case of the
         Peasant Movement in Senegal." *European Journal of Development
         Research* **5**(2): 68–100.

Lovell, C.
(1992)   *Breaking the Cycle of Poverty: The BRAC Strategy.* West Hartford, CT:
         Kummarian Press.

Mackie, J.
(1992)   "Multiplying Micro-level Inputs to Government Structures." In *Making
         a Difference: NGOs and Development in a Changing World*, eds.
         M. Edwards and D. Hulme London: Earthscan.

Morgan, M.
(1990)   "Stretching the Development Dollar: The Potential for Scaling Up."
         Grassroots Development **14**(1): 2–11.

Rich, B.
(1994)   *Mortgaging the Earth: The World Bank, Environmental Impoverish-
         ment and the Crisis of Development.* Boston: Beacon Press.

Schorr, B. E.
(1997)   *Common Purpose. Strengthening Families and Neighborhoods to
         Rebuild America.* New York: Anchor Books.

Tendler, J.
(1982)   "Turning Private Voluntary Organizations Into Development Agencies:
         Questions for Evaluation." Program Evaluation Discussion Paper
         No. 12. Washington: USAID.

Uvin, P.
(1995)   "Fighting Hunger at the Grassroots: Paths to Scaling Up." *World
         Development* **23**: 6.

USAID (US Agency for International Development)
(1995) "The New Partnership Initiative." Washington: USAID.

World Bank
(1991) *World Bank-Financed Projects with Potential for NGO Involvement.* Washington: World Bank, International Economic Relations Division.

World Bank
(1994) *Working with NGOs.* Washington: World Bank.

World Bank Watchers Project
(1996) *News and Notices.* Washington: Bread for the World.

CHAPTER 6

Scaling Up a Poverty Alleviation and Nutrition Program in Vietnam

Monique Sternin, Jerry Sternin,
and David Marsh

INTRODUCTION

In early 1990, Save the Children/USA, an international non-governmental organization or private voluntary organization based in the United States, received an unprecedented invitation from the Government of Vietnam to create a national community development model, with a special focus on addressing the needs of vulnerable groups placed at special risk by the economic transition to a market economy.

Twenty years earlier the people of Thanh Hoa Province were struggling to survive the ravages of the "American War" which had devastated the province, destroyed all the major industry, and played havoc with the one crop rice culture. The ideological driving force behind efforts to improve food and nutrition until the latter 1980s were collectivists who were as concerned with political dogma as with enhanced productivity. All villages were divided into work brigades with each household responsible for providing labor, while the commune provided rice rations to all its members. Decollectivization was a recognition that the collectives were failing drastically and that the near-famine conditions in the 1980s posed great human as well as political risks. Vietnam's evolution to a market economy began in 1986 and has generally raised living standards. By 1990 it was clear that the shift from the centrally planned economy to a market economy was beginning to have a very positive impact on agricultural productivity. However, under the market economy—which was accompanied by cost recovery policies and an end of state subsidies for certain health, social services and agricultural inputs—there was recognition of a growing gap in wealth distribution. According to the Vietnamese Communist Party, in 1993 rural sub-populations experienced increased vulnerability due to the cessation of the Commune Agricultural Collective Farm's wealth redistribution and the privatization of health care (Berggren and Tuan 1995).

Vietnam has the highest prevalence (52%) of moderately or severely underweight children in the Southeast Asia despite a relatively low underfive mortality rate, 48/1000 (UNICEF 1995). The National Institute of Nutrition (NIN 1995) of Vietnam reported that 45% of children under age five were malnourished despite great success in rice production. In 1990 Vietnam sought strategies to respond to its malnourished children that are both sustainable (unlike feeding programs) and rapid (unlike programs attacking root causes). In response, Save the Children accepted the challenge to develop a Poverty Alleviation and Nutrition Program (PANP) which could measurably and sustainably enhance the quality of life of children and their families.[1]

Despite the high prevalence of malnutrition, Save the Children observed that a narrow majority (55%) of children were actually normally nourished by UNICEF's criterion. Moreover, many, if not most, of these were certain to be from poor families. Save the Children centered its "positive deviant" (PD) approach on these resilient children. Strategically, a positive deviant study asks the question: How do poor families have well nourished children when their neighbors do not? That is, what is their "deviant" behavior (Zeitlin 1990)? The PD approach uses an epidemiological "two by two" table which categorizes a group of individuals according to the presence or absence of two phenomena which are epidemiologically associated and relevant to the community, for example "well nourished child" (yes/no) and "household impoverishment" (yes/no). Positive deviants, a poor family with a well-nourished child, attract attention because they contradict the general pattern. Likewise, a "negative deviant" (Shekar 1992) is a relatively wealthy family with a malnourished child. "Positive" and "negative" refer to a social, rather than numerical, values. Positive deviance is well suited to communities where a problem is common, recognized, important, and remediable through behavior modeled within community norms. The process galvanizes households at risk in poor communities to quickly identify and adopt affordable, lasting solutions to vexing problems from their own impoverished neighbors' experiences.

Thanh Hoa Province

Save the Children introduced the Poverty Alleviation and Nutrition Program (PANP) in the coastal and lowland delta areas of Thanh Hoa Province (population 3 million). One of the country's poorest provinces, Thanh Hoa is approximately 150km south of Hanoi, a four hour drive on the main north-south national highway. Inhabitants were primarily subsistence and cash-crop rice farmers who received small parcels of land after agricultural de-collectivization. Moderate "hungry seasons" (April–June and September–October) preceded each of two rice harvests. Literacy was high among most groups. Women and men worked in the fields. Women were entitled to a monthly "menstruation day" and a three-month post-partum leave, but they generally worked throughout pregnancy. Elderly females and older siblings typically reared young children. Poor rural families expected to educate two children, leaving two to work the land.

Save the Children chose districts with high levels of childhood malnutrition and supportive commune leadership. The extensive social infrastructure included: People's Committee, Women's Union, Health Committee, and Farmers' Committee, among others. The health system included a brigade or hamlet nurse for each hamlet, with a commune health center staffed by a pharmacist, doctor, mid-wife, and/or nurse and a geographically accessible hospital.

National political concern for childhood nutrition facilitated community entry which, in turn, took advantage of existing organizations and systems. The chairman of the People's Committee (mayor equivalent) headed the PANP Commune Steering Committee, other members of which were the chair or vice-chair of the Women's Union, a Health Committee member, and an accountant. Aided by public address systems reaching all hamlet inhabitants, the Commune Steering Committee mobilized community members for PANP.

DEVELOPING THE MODEL: PHASE ONE

During program development early in 1991, it became clear that a phased development strategy beginning with a small, easily monitored, target population would maximize opportunities to build upon lessons learned before going to scale.

Phase One involved establishing a four commune pilot site with a population of 20,000 people in Thanh Hoa. The selected communes became a social laboratory through which a wide range of community development initiatives could be tested. Over a three-year period of continuous testing and evaluation, the Poverty Alleviation and Nutrition Program (PANP) was implemented successfully. The model was based on the belief that in order for development gains to be sustainable, strategies and solutions to community problems had to be identified within the community by the members themselves. Translating this hypothesis into action enabled the PANP to focus on community resources, as well as needs, critical to the model's sustainability and scaling up. The PANP focus on resources includes identification and exploitation of both human and material resources. This process contrasts with the more traditional development approach which focuses on community needs as the principal basis for program development while underemphasizing existing community resources.

One of the principal features of the PANP model was the establishment of a group of Health Volunteers (HV) in each commune. Utilizing the existing commune social infrastructure, Women's Union members and brigade nurses were trained as HVs. This key cadre received health, nutrition, and management training-practice-review incrementally over the two year program implementation cycle as well as a small stipend, initially provided externally, and later paid through the commune endowment fund.

Health Volunteers led a three-pronged nutritional situation analysis. First, each conducted a census of her approximately 80–100 families from which she made rosters of all children under three years of age. Second, she weighed all children less than age three years at the beginning of an every-other-month Growth Monitoring Promotion Program (GMP). Third, she led the positive deviance (PD) inquiry.

Trainers taught Health Volunteers to review the results of the first GMP session, seeking well-nourished children from poor families, according to public wealth rankings based on rice production. After perusing the list, their response was always "co, co" (there are!). Having established that it was possible for some very poor families to have an adequately nourished child, the trainer invited the volunteers and hamlet leaders to construct a list of questions pertinent to their context, including types of foods given, hand-washing practices, snack offering practices, and child care, and to undertake a survey as part of the positive deviance inquiry to learn the secret of these families' success. Visiting four extremely poor families with well nourished children enabled the volunteers not only to interview successful parents, but also to actually observe what went into the cooking pot and the kind of child care which was provided. By consensus, the team identified the likely explanations of the "deviant" behavior resulting in the normal nutritional status despite family poverty. The free, or inexpensive special foods identified through the PD inquiry varied by community and season. They included tiny shrimps and crabs, found in abundance in the rice paddies (but considered inappropriate for young children), sweet potato greens, sesame seeds, peanuts, dried fish, fish sauce, and corn.

Another component of the PD inquiry involved visits to two "well off" families with malnourished children to help the communes understand that good nutrition was not necessarily correlated with economic status. The results of the PD inquiry became the core of the rehabilitation program. The protocol was based on proven, successful dietary practices within the commune, rather than on theoretical concepts of good nutrition.

Four Integrated Programs in the PANP

Four integrated programs within the PANP were developed with a focus on sustainability. Within each program, mechanisms were adopted to ensure financial viability and continuity after the three year PANP implementation cycle was completed.

The Growth Monitoring Promotion Program (GMP): This program weighed all children under three years of age every two months. Trained commune Health Volunteers counseled mothers regarding their children's nutritional status. Mothers whose children were doing well were encouraged to continue the good work. At risk children suffering from second and third degree malnutrition were identified and immediately enrolled in the Nutrition Education/Rehabilitation Program (NERP). Health education, treatment of sick children and bi-annual deworming were also provided at the GMP sites for all children under three years of age.

The Nutrition Education/Rehabilitation Program (NERP): All second or third degree malnourished children under age three identified at the GMP were referred by the Health Volunteers. Each month over a two week period mothers (or caretakers) were invited to bring their children to neighborhood NERP centers established throughout the commune where they actively participated in their children's rehabilitation. Rehabilitation was defined as reaching normal or first degree malnourished status.

The NERP objectives were: (1) to rehabilitate malnourished children and (2) to enable parents to sustain and improve their child's enhanced nutritional status after rehabilitation at home. The first objective, rehabilitating malnourished children, was achieved by providing them with sufficient nutritious food. The real challenge, however, was achieving the second objective which required families to sustain their child's enhanced nutritional status within the existing context of their poverty. Here it was necessary to find the answer in the commune, within the reach of its poorest members. A positive deviance inquiry provided the mechanism.

The actual NERP protocol consisted of a 12 day session in various homes throughout the village. Health Volunteers taught basic nutrition and hygiene messages while supervising the preparation of a nutritious, calorie-dense meal to rehabilitate the assembled second and third degree malnourished children. The meal was comprised of rice, fat, and a source of locally available, inexpensive protein such as eggs or tofu. In addition, each mother/caretaker's daily "price of admission" was a handful of the previously identified "positive deviant" food. The focus of the NERP was to change behavior rather than to transfer knowledge. The behavioral modification which resulted from the mothers' required daily contribution was critical to the success of the program. After the first year, the majority of malnourished children in the commune graduated from the NERP and this aspect was phased out. Approximately 90% of participating children had achieved first degree malnutrition or normal nutritional status. Health Volunteers targeted the remaining 10% of the children and their caretakers through home visits for nutrition counseling and health education.

In addition to the gains realized by NERP participants, nutrition education had been provided for the entire community by demonstrating the dramatic impact good nutrition could have on the health and quality of life of its children. At the time of phase out, almost everyone in the commune had either been personally involved in the program or had had a neighbor, friend, or relative who was in some way involved either as beneficiary or manager, (i.e., HV, steering committee member, hamlet nurse, or leader). Hence, nutrition rose from near oblivion to center stage in the community's consciousness. Individual interviews and focus group discussions revealed that many families in the community which never participated in the NERP noted the changes in the children who were rehabilitated and asked their mothers/caretakers how they achieved such results. A recent independent survey determined that the "positive deviant" foods introduced by mothers during the program implementation were widely used by most mothers of children under three years of age in the commune two years after the NERP portion of the program had ended.

The Nutrition Revolving Loan Program: The objective of this program was to provide immediate access to supplementary food to poor families of malnourished children who had not yet graduated from the program, despite participation in at least two NERPs. Loans in the form of laying hens were made with the condition that five eggs be given to the malnourished child each week. Loans were repaid into the revolving fund which made loans available first to other families with malnourished children and then to other poor families in the commune.

The Healthy Pregnancy/New Mother Program: This program was a critical component of the PANP community health and nutrition strategy. Whereas the NERP and Nutrition Revolving Loan Program enhanced the nutritional status of malnourished children under three years of age, the Healthy Pregnancy/New Mother Program proactively focused on preventive care to address the problem of malnutrition at its source: namely to prevent malnutrition in the fetus, the pregnant woman, as well as the lactating mother. Strategies included targeting and mobilizing men to address women's health issues, providing the program high visibility in the commune through the establishment of a monthly Pregnancy Day and combining quality health care delivery and education for the beneficiaries.

The objectives of this program were to enable all women in the commune: (1) to have healthy pregnancies, (2) to have safe deliveries, (3) to be healthy mothers, and (4) to have healthy babies through the provision of quality reproductive health care, maternal nutrition, hygiene education and counseling.

The program had two main components, the Pregnancy Monitoring Component and the Home Visiting Format. Pregnancy monitoring encouraged all identified pregnant women to have a minimum of three prenatal check-ups during their pregnancy. At a monthly Pregnancy Day at the Commune Health Center, pregnant women received prenatal examinations and pregnancy counseling, anti-tetanus protection, iron supplementation, and weight and blood pressure measurements. Concurrently on that day, Health Volunteers provided hygiene education as well as interactive nutrition education through food demonstrations. Home visiting used HVs to visit the pregnant woman and the new mother at home with their family members, particularly the husband and mother-in-law to provide counseling on the special needs of the pregnant woman, the new mother and baby. Subjects covered were: delivery preparedness, reducing hard workload, maternal diet before and after delivery, breastfeeding management, hygiene, and timely introduction of supplementary feeding.

Strategies for Sustainability

To ensure the sustainability of the above programs initiated during the three year PANP implementation cycle, communities needed the requisite financial and human resources to independently carry on those activities in the post phase-over period. The financial sustainability of the four PANP programs was addressed through development endowments established in each commune. These endowments consisted of grants given to communities for income generating projects, such as milling machines and transport boats. The endowments were managed by the Commune Management Steering Committee composed of commune leaders and established early in the implementation of the PANP. The income from these projects was designated by the Commune Management Steering Committee to fund specific programs within the PANP, such as stipends for Health Volunteers. Through the development endowments, commune leaders were trained in endowment management as well as in the overall management of the PANP.

In addition to financial resources, communities also needed the human resources necessary to manage on-going programs. Human resource development, realized through on-going training of commune leaders, Health Staff and Health Volunteers, was an integral component of the PANP model. The training-practice-review approach of the PANP model provided a series of training workshops for each of the four PANP programs prior to their implementation. To complement these workshops, short evaluation workshops to review results were held after the completion of each program component. This training method, training-practice-review, greatly contributed to the success of the trained commune leaders, Health Staff and Health Volunteers.

Measuring Impact in the Pilot Communes

Baseline census measured for each family member (i.e., those eating together): district, commune, hamlet, household number, couple, and family number; relationship to head of household; date of birth; and sex. Census data were computerized allowing for print-outs of HV rosters of children eligible for each GMP. HVs weighed children on a UNICEF-approved, locally made Seca 25 kg (0.1 kg interval) infant scale, recalibrated between each weighing. At each GMP, HVs plotted weight for age on mothers' "road to health" cards displaying four growth channels: ("normal") ≥ -2 standard deviations (SD) below reference median weight for age; ("moderate malnutrition") < -2 and ≥ -3 SD; ("severe malnutrition") < -3 SD and ≥ -4 SD; and ("very severe malnutrition") < -4 SD.

By early 1993, two years after program inception in the first four pilot communes, the model had already produced significant changes in the nutritional status of the communities. At the beginning of the program, in the first four pilot communes, 36% of all children under three suffered from second or third degree malnutrition. Two years after the inception of the program, this extremely high incidence of physically and intellectually debilitating malnutrition was dramatically reduced to 4% (Table 6.1). Of the more than 1000 children participating in the Nutrition Education/ Rehabilitation Program (NERP) in the first four communes, 93% were rehabilitated. Moreover, they remained so up to two years after their participation in the program (Table 6.2).

Alternative explanations for the improved nutritional status must be considered. A generalized improvement in living standard or nutritional status was unlikely to have occurred, as suggested by similar initial GMP profiles from other PANP cycles begun in other districts. Deworming, as part of the intervention, probably contributed to the effect, but its role was unlikely central since nutritional improvement in some cycles preceded its implementation. Moreover, only children under three years of age were treated rather than all children and/or food preparers. Commune immunization and vitamin A coverage likely improved concomitant with initiation of semi-annual campaigns in November 1993. However, improved national immunization coverage has not correlated with improved child nutrition. Finally, one should at least consider factitious data, perhaps manipulated to achieve targets. However, independent evaluations by the National Institute of Nutrition confirmed improvements in child nutritional status in other PANP cycles (NIN survey as quoted in Berggren and Tuan, 1995). Moreover, targets were either not used or not communicated to field staff. Finally, computer-assisted monitoring of HVs showed that they randomly, rather than systematically, misclassified nutritional status in the

Table 6.1. Nutritional Status Among Children Under Age Three Years in Four Pilot Communes: Quang Xuong District (1991–1993)

Program Phase**	Nutritional Status* (%)				
	Normal	Moderate Malnutrition	Severe Malnutrition	Very Severe Malnutrition	Total
Baseline (n = 1765)	32	32	30	6	100
Phase-over (n = 1626)	69	27	4	0	100
Post Phase-over (n = 1876)	66	32	2	0	100

* normal ≥ -2 standard deviations (SD) below reference median weight for age; moderate malnutrition < -2 and ≥ -3 SD; severe malnutrition < -3 SD and ≥ -4 SD; and very severe malnutrition < -4 SD.
** Baseline (February 1991), Phase-over (December 1993), Post Phase-over (August, 1993).

Table 6.2. Nutritional Status Among NERP Attenders in Four Pilot Communes: Quang Xuong District (1991–1993)

Program Phase	Nutritional Status* (%)				
	Normal	Moderate Malnutrition	Severe Malnutrition	Very Severe Malnutrition	Total
Entry Status** (n = 1624)	0	0	89	11	100
Phase-over (n = 1251***)	63	33	4	0	100

* normal ⩾ −2 standard deviations (SD) below reference median weight for age; moderate malnutrition < −2 and ⩾ −3 SD; severe malnutrition < −3 SD and ⩾ −4 SD; and very severe malnutrition < −4 SD.
** Entry Status (March 1991–March 1993), Phase-over (December 1993): 6–24 months after participtation in NERP (Nutritional Education and Rehabilitation Program).
*** 11 deaths and 362 children not reweighed (well-nourished children were less likely to be reweighed).

approximately 10% of assessments in which they erred; this also argues against data manipulation.

From the beginning of the program in early 1991, Save the Children shared impact data with a wide range of Vietnamese and foreign development experts with an interest in nutrition. As data began to show significant reductions in malnutrition, curiosity was peaked and the pilot villages were visited by many Vietnamese officials and international development personnel, including UNICEF, UNDP, the World Bank, the Vietnamese National Institute of Nutrition, the Committee for Protection and Care of Children and health staff from districts and provinces throughout Vietnam. While appreciating the extraordinary nutritional gains realized by the program communes, most visitors were skeptical about the replicability of the model. "Save the Children has had control over all the program inputs," they argued. "When anything went awry in the villages, you were able to change course immediately. How do you replicate that degree of surveillance in thousands of communes throughout the country?"

GOING TO SCALE WITH QUALITY INTACT: PHASE TWO

In March 1993, Save the Children was authorized to expand the program to an additional ten communes with a population of 60,000 people in Thanh Hoa province. Six staff members from the Vietnamese National Institute of Nutrition (NIN) were seconded to Save the Children to assume responsibility for scaling up the program while maintaining its positive outcomes. The primary objective for the expansion of the PANP to fourteen communes was to demonstrate that the dramatic results achieved in phase one could be achieved on a larger scale utilizing national staff. Going to scale while maintaining the quality of the original model presented a set of critical challenges. Among these was the transfer of responsibility for program implementation, training, and evaluation at the field level from expatriate staff to Vietnamese staff. Extended visits to the original four villages provided the new NIN staff with direct encounters with the model in addition to the conceptual framework presented through numerous workshops. NIN staff were asked to evaluate the ongoing project, a process which afforded them broad access and contact with village leaders, program beneficiaries and villagers at large.

Utilizing National Institute of Nutrition staff as program trainers provided, not unexpectedly, both advantages and challenges. As trained professionals, their knowledge of nutrition improved the technical component of the NERP protocol. As Vietnamese, their understanding of the socio-political context of the village led to structural innovations in program management, beyond the reach of the expatriate staff responsible for the original model. The other side of the "expertise" coin, however, has been a skepticism about the value of villagers' knowledge, experience and wisdom: the "doctor knows best" syndrome. Inherent in the success of the original model was the reliance on villagers to identify solutions to their own problems. It was the conscious absence of a preconceived plan of action which led, for instance, to the development of the NERP, based on untapped, but readily available food resources found in the villages. Modification of the NERP diet and introduction of poultry loans were also the direct results of villagers' ownership of problems and responsibility for finding their solutions. Without a genuine belief in the villagers' wisdom, the model simply could not have succeeded. Hence, the success of program expansion was contingent to a large measure on the ability to inculcate that conviction in the trainers. The conversion of National Institute of Nutrition staff from technical experts to process-sensitive trainers was a significant challenge.

The NIN staff, as described above, made valuable contributions both in the content and form of the program during the first phase of program expansion. What emerged from the experience, however, was a clearer understanding of the requisite skills for program trainers. These tended to be heavily weighted towards process rather than technical expertise. The efficacy of the technical content of the NERP, GMP, and Healthy

Pregnancy/New Mother Program had been demonstrated and documented. Still required to scale up were the skills to transfer that knowledge and to add to it, by effectively tapping the experience and knowledge of villagers in new communes.

Expansion of the Program

Since the primary challenge of the expansion phase was the transfer of program implementation and management to NIN staff, a three-step geographic expansion maximized opportunities to build upon lessons learned and problems perceived. The first expansion began in March 1993 in three new villages, followed by another three in July, and a final expansion to four villages in a new district, Tinh Gia, in November 1993. In all, ten new villages, with a population of 63,774, were selected by the districts and Save the Children staff based on the results of a nutritional baseline carried out by the Vietnamese National Institute of Nutrition.

After providing the new health volunteers with training in GMP, the NIN staff and Health Volunteers undertook the positive deviance inquiry to determine the appropriate content for each village for its Nutrition Education/Rehabilitation Program protocol. Unlike the old villages where locally available shrimp, crabs and greens were the principal foods provided to their children by the poor "positive deviant" families, the new villages, lacking these foods, depended on other free or inexpensive foods such as peanuts, sesame or dried fish.

A newly installed computer Management Information System provided a check on the accuracy of the health volunteers' manual GMP report. The program compared each child's date of birth and weight and corresponding nutritional status with the manual calculation reported by the Health Volunteers. Hence, errors could be detected and analyzed and then used as a basis for retraining Health Volunteers in the GMP protocol. Lessons learned from the first GMP in the first three new villages (March 1993) demonstrated that the training of the Health Volunteers was inadequate.

Consequently, NIN staff held additional workshops to upgrade growth card plotting skills of the Health Volunteers, and of equal importance, increased the time allowed for GMP training in the subsequent two groups of new villages. Similarly, the training schedule for other program components for the second and third set of new villages was based on experience in the first expansion villages. Time allotted for training was increased where necessary, and training materials were improved based on the experience gained in the first expansion villages. These intense training demands for time and personnel and the surveillance were necessary only during the program development stage. Improvements over time in training techniques and materials enabled Health Volunteers, for example, to greatly improve accuracy of GMP plotting. Hence, the manual system at the village level now proves sufficient.

The expertise gained over the first two and a half years by villagers in the original program communes provided an excellent resource for the people in the villages added to the new expanded program. Health volunteers, People's Committee and Women's Union leaders and members took an active part in training new villagers in program objectives, implementation and protocol. The utilization of "old villagers" as consultants not only contributed to a smoother program implementation in the expanded villages, but reinforced the knowledge and sense of empowerment of the contributing consultants and their villages.

The creation by the NIN staff and villagers of an NERP Management Committee in the expanded program villages proved to be an important innovation and an effective vehicle for increased program participation and ownership at the highest levels. In the original pilot villages, the NERP was managed by an individual such as the Women's Union chairperson or the head of the clinic. The managing committee in the expansion villages was comprised of the head of the People's Committee, the Party chairman, the head of the Women's Union, and one commune health center staff. The committee members viewed their role as "ensuring the overall management, implementation and monitoring of the program." Committee members attended NERP sessions and checked on hygiene, menus, and eligibility of attending children. Their assistance not only contributed to the overall conduct of the NERP and other programs, but also greatly enhanced the commune's official commitment to children's health and nutrition.

New District, New Opportunities

The expansion of the program to a new district, Tinh Gia, in November of 1993 provided an opportunity to utilize the commune NERP Management Committee concept at the district level for the first time. Meetings held at the Tinh Gia People's Committee focused on expectations, roles and responsibilities. Unlike the program in the original villages, where district level Women's Union, People's Committee and Health Cadre had a somewhat peripheral role, those entities were asked to assume a principal management role for program implementation and monitoring. The assumption of a management role for the district has proven critical not only for sustainability of the program, but for scaling up as well.

As managers of the program, the district assumed responsibility for the overall implementation and quality of the program. Women's Union leaders visited NERPs and Pregnancy Day programs. People's Committee members checked on the commune's financial management of loan programs and development endowments. District health and family planning cadres participated in training village health staff for pregnancy monitoring. Growth Monitoring and NERP results were passed by the commune to the district rather than to Save the Children as in the original communes. Hence, after program phase-over at the commune level, the district remained responsible for resolving problems. The District Management Steering Committee developed a comprehensive understanding of the specific programs and their impact. This enabled them to replicate individual components on their own in other communes throughout the district. With only minimal external financial assistance, specific components of the program, (i.e. GMP, NERP, Healthy Pregnancy/New Mother Program) could be implemented in non-program villages by district level cadres who participated in training and management of these protocols. One district, Quang Xuong, implemented the Pregnancy Day in all 43 villages throughout the district. This strategy facilitated a redefinition and enhancement of roles: "district leaders as program catalysts" rather than the more passive role of "district leaders as program partners."

The ability to build on content and process lessons learned in the original program villages combined with structural innovations (such as the management steering committee), enabled the NIN staff to get off to a more rapid start in the expanded program villages. Program impact was similar to that seen in the initial development stage (Table 6.3). Indeed, it was faster. Because the NERPs had been refined, village mothers/caretakers rehabilitated their children in an average of 2.8 sessions, rather than the 3.3 required in the original communes. As a result, the NERP program was phased out in the second group of 10 communes in an average of 10 months rather than the 23 months required in the first four communes.

A detailed cohort analysis (Sternin et al. 1997) was performed of the impact of PANP in Group C, the last four of these added communes. Children's weight for age improved, on average, by 0.36 Z-score (from -2.14 to -1.78 Z-scores). Moreover, the nutritional status of severely and very severely malnourished children improved by fully 1.44 Z-scores (from -3.58 to -2.14 Z-scores). Very severe malnutrition vanished (Table 6.4), while severe malnutrition decreased from a prevalence of 19–4%, and the normal group increased by a third (from a prevalence of 42–56%). Indeed, Vietnamese colleagues dramatically succeeded in using local solutions to alleviate childhood malnutrition over the 24 month program.[2]

Table 6.3. Nutritional Status Among Children Under Age Three Years in 10 Expanded Communes: Quang Xuong and Tinh Gia Districts (1993–1995)

Program Phase	Severe and Very Severe Malnutrition* (%)			
	Group A**	Group B**	Group C**	Total
Baseline	24	29	29	27
One Year	11	7	3	7
Two Years	1	2	2	2

* normal ≥ −2 standard deviations (SD) below reference median weight for age; moderate malnutrition < −2 and ≥ −3 SD; severe malnutrition < −3 SD and ≥ −4 SD; and very severe malnutrition < −4 SD.
** Group A (April 1993–February 1995), Group B (July 1993–July 1995), Group C (November 1993–September 1995).

Table 6.4. Follow-Up Nutritional Status* of Children Under Age Three Years at Baseline in Four Expanded Communes: Quang Xuong and Tinh Gia Districts (1993–1995)

Baseline Status Age 0–35 Months (n, [%])	Endline Status** (month 24: Age 24–59 months) [%]				
	Normal	Moderate Malnutrition	Severe Malnutrition	Very Severe Malnutrition	Died
	(n = 1060)	(n = 738)	(n = 76)	(n = 0)	(n = 9)
Normal (791, [42])	74	24	1	0	1
Moderate Malnutrition (668, [35])	50	44	4	0	1
Severe Malnutrition (362, [19])	36	57	6	0	1
Very Severe Malnutrition (72, [4])	24	61	14	0	1
Total (1893, [100])	56	39	4	0	1

* normal ≥ −2 standard deviations (SD) below reference median weight for age; moderate malnutrition < −2 and ≥ −3 SD; severe malnutrition < −3 SD and ≥ −4 SD; and very severe malnutrition < −4 SD.
** 60 children were lost to follow-up: we assumed that their nutritional outcomes were identical to their baseline-specific counterparts.

Living University and Further Geographic Expansion

By the spring of 1994, it was clear that program expansion and implementation managed solely by Vietnamese staff in no way compromised the quality or impact of the PANP. Many international and Vietnamese organizations which had earlier visited the program now expressed interest in replicating it in their respective geographic areas.

Major development organizations involved in nutrition, health and poverty alleviation in Vietnam, including UNICEF, and a host of international non-governmental organizations demonstrated keen interest in accessing the model for replication. Increased attention highlighted the need to create a mechanism through which the model could be made available to the maximum number of communities throughout Vietnam. "The Living University," which opened in July 1994, responded to that need by using the 14 program communes as an open classroom where the PANP model was experienced as well as studied.

Participants attending the Living University in Thanh Hoa gained experience in each of the four integrated programs which made up the PANP, visiting existing communes where the model was in full operation. The curriculum integrated direct field experience with theory-based workshops to provide an in-depth foundation for implementation of the PANP. This direct practical experience enabled participants to gain a full understanding of the implementation and management of the PANP prior to initiating the program in their own communities.

By December 1995, the Living University graduated seven classes consisting of representatives from 11 international NGOs, as well as Vietnamese commune and district level Women's Union, health services and people's committee cadres. The PANP was introduced by these graduates in 20 communes in nine provinces throughout Vietnam. Four of the organizations were already using their newly initiated model communes as their own mini-Living University providing a vehicle for program expansion to other communes within their program areas. Thus, the Living University provided an excellent vehicle through which Save the Children's mandate to create a national Poverty Alleviation and Nutrition Program could be realized.

A major shift occurred after March 1995 when Vietnamese district officials became the primary clients of the Living University. Previously representatives from international non-governmental organizations such as CARE or Plan International would attend the Living University course and then directly train health volunteers in a few of their program communes before implementing the PANP. After March 1995, District People's

Committee, Women's Union and Health Department officials attended two-day pre-training management workshops before selecting district trainers to attend the Living University's two-week training of trainers (TOT). Upon completion of the course, the district trainers trained Health Volunteers in two additional communes and in collaboration with the People's Committee, Women's Union and Health Department personnel, supervised the overall program. The sense of program ownership by the district greatly enhanced the long-term sustainability of the program. District leaders felt greater responsibility for program success than when implementation was under the supervision of an international non-governmental organization.

After several months of training Health Volunteers in two new communes, the district trainers were "up to speed" in training techniques and fully conversant with the first few PANP components. They were then ready to expand the model to additional communes in the district. Hence, each district developed its own mini-Living University, greatly facilitating program expansion. This means of qualitatively scaling up the program proved highly effective. By early 1998, the Poverty Alleviation and Nutrition Program, including its Nutrition Education/Rehabilitation Program (NERP) component, had reached more than 200 communes. In seven years, the population being affected grew from 20,000 to 1.2 million.

Other Processes and Strategies for Scaling Up

Learning from the Students

The Living University not only provided an excellent mechanism for geographic scaling up, but also served as a basis for ongoing modification and improvement of the model. Because Living University graduates returned to areas throughout the country to implement the model, innovations and modifications occurred based on local conditions, interpretations and, sometimes, chance. The staff visited "graduate" programs to provide consultancies but also to learn from the satellite programs. Innovative practices or successful modifications were then incorporated into the curriculum and shared with subsequent participants.

Cooperation, Co-options, and Partnering

Save the Children has borrowed staff from other Vietnamese organizations concerned with nutrition on one or two year contracts. Arrangements with the National Institute of Nutrition and the Community Health Research Unit of Hanoi Medical College, have for example, enabled Save the

Children to add additional personnel to the Living University staff, while providing invaluable practical training and experience for those individuals which later can be utilized when they return to their respective institutes. First hand experience with a community-based nutrition program like the NERP can help broaden the perspective of local institutes whose world view is often much more academic than reality-based.

Save the Children's relationship with the Community Health Research Unit includes funding of PANP implementation in two communes by the unit. The program communes not only enable unit staff to gain direct experience in managing a community based nutrition program, but also provide a training ground for medical school students in preventative health care and nutrition.

Functionally Scaling Up

Save the Children made a strategic decision to minimize the number of interventions required to measurably and sustainably impact nutritional status. Although it is clear that water and sanitation projects, increased agricultural productivity, and income generation would certainly further enhance nutritional impact, the cost of these additional components would militate against broad program replication. Poor communes with high levels of malnutrition in Vietnam simply do not have the financial resources to access these inputs, nor is it likely that the central government will be able to provide them in the foreseeable future. With a current one time cost of less than two U.S. dollars per beneficiary for the PANP, funding needs could easily be met by bilateral and multi-lateral funders and international non-governmental organizations. Hence, Save the Children has placed replicability above optimum impact in prioritizing ultimate program objectives.

Political Scaling Up: From Service Delivery to Advocacy

During the creation of the model in the first four communes, Save the Children's role was limited to that of service delivery agent. In the second stage, with the expansion to an additional 10 communes under the management of NIN staff, that role broadened to include trainer and partner. With the creation of the Living University, Save the Children has further expanded its role to include advocacy. Advocacy in the context of the Save the Children program means utilizing the program, now operational in more than 200 communes, to demonstrate that nutrition can be addressed at the grass-roots level today. The Vietnamese have a saying, "*tram nghe khong bang mot thay, tram thay khong bang mot so"* ("One hundred hearings is not worth one seeing, and one hundred seeings is not worth one doing"). Lying somewhere between "Seeing is believing" and "One picture is worth a thousand words," the expression is indicative of Vietnamese pragmatism and unwillingness to accept things on faith.

Therefore, one of the objectives of the Save the Children program has been to provide a demonstrably successful low cost, high impact nutritional model which can be used to advocate the viability of addressing malnutrition without addressing all causal factors. The conventional wisdom in Vietnam and elsewhere is that the causes of malnutrition are so closely related that the problem can not be solved before all the contributing factors are addressed. This perspective has often led to resignation and a "do-little" attitude regarding the inevitability of high degrees of malnutrition in the context of Vietnam's poverty. Hence, Save the Children, by involving a variety of key leadership partners and community organizations in a high visibility model project, has attempted to demonstrate that malnutrition can be impacted before all causal factors are addressed.

In this regard, Save the Children has played a role in joining others in Vietnam over a five year period to place malnutrition on the political screen. As more and more data have become available confirming the impact of the NERP, Save the Children has increased its advocacy for the need and viability of acting now to address malnutrition. Through the efforts of the Vietnamese National Institute of Nutrition, the Vietnamese Committee for the Protection and Care of Children, UNICEF and others, enhanced nutrition is now a stated goal of the government where there is considerable will to enact a National Plan of Action for Nutrition.

Our final thoughts, then, rest on the likely conclusion that PANP works. How widely applicable is the PANP experience? Is Vietnam a "positive deviant" from which other peoples can learn? Literacy since "the American War" is nearly universal. Communism's heritage of central planning through targets, although often misguided, has instilled a quantitative culture. National policy endorses population control and child nutritional improvement. Classless, casteless Vietnamese people may be easy to mobilize because of their discipline, obedience, and reverence for education and training. The ubiquitous public address systems certainly facilitate information education and communication. Another advantage was community-level service organizations that were formed to serve state purposes, were readily available. Finally, the positive deviant food is, in many communes, "free" for the gathering. Other settings could capitalize on these or different strengths.

Wiser through discovering apparent solutions for an intractable problem, we would not be surprised to learn that other common, recognizable, important problems, can be dramatically ameliorated through local, nontechnical solutions. While not a panacea, neither is positive deviance a "niche-tool" to be rarely used. Resting squarely on equity, positive deviance not only targets those in need, but requires guidance from them. Positive deviance strategies deserve wide usage.

NOTES

1. The nutritional status of children as measured in national surveys during the time this program was implemented improved only by a few percentage points (NIN 1995). The 40% reduction in real prices of rice in the early 1990's was a benefit to net buyers of rice, nearly half of households in Vietnam, but the vast majority of the recipients of this program were net rice sellers whose incomes would have been adversely affected by the price rise. Furthermore, only nine percent of rural persons in Vietnam did not produce rice in the early 1990s; the three percent of these households that are in the lowest income groups would have benefited most from the lower price (IFPRI 1996).

2. Pelletier et al. (1995) reported that risks of child mortality due to infectious disease were remarkably dependent on severity of nutritional status and were similar across numerous developing country settings. The relative risk for death compared to children with normal nutritional status increased geometrically for worsening nutritional category: 2.5 for mild, 4.6 for moderate, and 8.4 for severe (closely approximating our categories B, C, and D). If we apply these risks to our children (including 1 for category A), using an indirect standardization approach, PANP averted 30.3% (standardized RR compared to normally nourished population: 2.499 at baseline versus 1.741 after year two) of childhood deaths due to infection. A birth rate of 29/1000 (UNICEF 1995) in this population of approximately 25,000 yields 725 live births annually. At least half of an under five mortality rate of 55/1000 (UNICEF 1995) could be due to infection, claiming 40 children over two years. Thus, PANP could avert up to 12 (40×0.303) of the projected child deaths over the period of the project, assuming most deaths occurred before age three.

REFERENCES

Berggren, G. G. and Tuan, T.
   (1995)   "Evaluation of the Save the Children (SC) Poverty Alleviation/ Nutrition Program (PANP) Thanh Hoa Province, Vietnam."

IFPRI (International Food Policy Research Institute)
(1996)   "Rice Market Monitoring and Policy Options Study." Prepared for the
          Asian Development Bank, Washington, D.C.: International Food Policy
          Research Institute.

NIN (National Institute of Nutrition).
(1995)   Personal Communication, National Institute of Nutrition, Vietnam.

Pelletier, D., Frongillo, E. A., Schoeder, D. G., and Habicht, J.-P.
(1995)   "The Effects of Malnutrition on Child Mortality in Developing
          Countries." *Bulletin of the World Health Organization* **73**(4): 443–448.

Sternin, M., Sternin, J., and March, D. L.
(1997)   "Rapid, Sustained Childhood Malnutrition Alleviation Through a
          'Positive Deviance' Approach in Rural Vietnam: Preliminary Find-
          ings." In *Hearth Nutrition Model: Applications in Haiti, Vietnam, and
          Bangladesh*, O. Wollinka, E. Keeley, B. R. Burkhalter, and N. Bashir.
          Arlington, VA: Basic Support for Institutionalizing Child Survival-
          (BASICS) Project for USAID and World Relief Corporation.

Shekar, M., Habicht, J.-P., and Latham, M.
(1992)   "Positive–Negative Deviant Analyses to Improve Programme Targeting
          and Services: Example from Tamil Nadu Integrated Nutrition Project."
          International Journal of Epidemiology **21**(4): 707–713.

UNICEF
(1995)   State of the World's Children. Oxford: Oxford University Press.

Zeitlin, M., Ghassemi H., and Mansour, M.
(1990)   *Positive Deviance in Child Nutrition*. New York: UN University Press.

CHAPTER 7

Evaluation of the Hearth Program in Haiti: Mothers Help Scale Up a Nutrition Program

Gretchen G. Berggren, Warren L. Berggren,
Erve Bottex, Barton R. Burkhalter and
Robert S. Northrup

Hearth programs[1] seek to improve the health and nutritional status of preschool children by working closely with mothers with knowledge of child care and locally available foods. This chapter describes and evaluates the Hearth program developed at the Hopital Albert Schweitzer (HAS) in Deschapelles, Haiti. The HAS Hearth program initiates the rehabilitation of malnourished children during two weeks of intensive feeding, and in so doing also educates and motivates the mothers to continue the appropriate feeding. It also motivates the network of Hearth volunteer mothers to engage in other community health activities with HAS.

BACKGROUND

Despite an emerging democratic government facilitated by the end of the Cold War, Haiti's Hearth program takes place against a grim picture of deterioration in the agriculture and economic sectors. Haiti faces intense population pressure with annual population growth of about 2% and population density of about 250 persons per square kilometer, highest in the Caribbean. Agriculture accounts for 32% of the entire GNP and is a major source of employment for the 20% of the population living in rural areas.

The economic disruption that occurred after the military coup in 1991 exacerbated an already disastrous economic situation in Haiti. During the subsequent military regime and trade embargo, apart from human rights and security concerns, the events caused (1) a breakdown in social services, (2) a sharp reduction in mobility of goods, services and people, (3) price increases, and (4) reduced household income.

Haiti's inadequate food and nutrition conditions add another layer of suffering. The 1987 Household Expenditure and Consumption Survey found that 70% of Haitians received insufficient calories and 50% insufficient protein. The 1994 Demographic and Health Survey found that one-third of Haitian preschool children were moderately or severely underweight-for-age. According to FAO data the average Haitian consumed a meager 2000 calories per day in the 1960s and only 1700 in the 1990s, whereas the average adult needs 2300 calories per day.

Cassava, yams, and bananas are important food crops in terms of production, but cereal-bean mixtures have long been the staple of the Haitian diet (Riordan et al. 1997). Food aid is only a partial answer. Since the early 1980s Haiti has received about 100,000 metric tons of food aid per year, with about two-thirds distributed directly to beneficiaries, mainly school children instead of higher risk preschoolers. The Hearth program, in contrast, uses locally available foods and local human resources to sustainably improve the nutritional status of the more vulnerable preschoolers.

Anthropologists observed in the late 1980s that rural families survived by cutting back on meals and meal portions, and by allotting portions equally, sometimes without regard to age. Coping mechanisms of Haitian mothers were stretched to the breaking point, with most rural Haitian families down to one meal per day, including young children (Alvarez and Murray 1990). Apparently Haitian adults did not always realize that this created an impending disaster for the child who is not able to consume a daily energy requirement in one sitting.

A study of CARE/Haiti's food and nutrition programs concludes with nine findings about feeding and nutrition in rural Haiti: (1) children weaned completely from the breast get only one or two meals per day; (2) the quantity of food at a single meal is often very small, and not enriched with oil (not "calorie-dense"); (3) preschool children are often left at home alone or in the care of older siblings who are also hungry and competitive for food; (4) variety is lacking in food used by poor families at any given season; (5) household food insecurity is partly due to inadequate grain storage, insects and rodents devastate stored foods; (6) seasonal variation affects food availability ("hungry season" just before harvest); (7) children displaced from their biologic families; (8) heightened problems occur in single-parent households; (9) high rates of diseases that precipitate malnutrition: diarrhea, measles, respiratory infections, intestinal parasites and malaria. Despite all these problems, mothers with extra knowledge about the causes of malnutrition seemed better able to stave it off (Berggren et al. 1993). This list suggests that while Haiti awaits solution of its basic development problems, poor families must protect their children from malnutrition through better care: supporting breastfeeding, keeping babies clean, feeding at adequate frequency, and seeking prompt treatment when illness strikes.

Hopital Albert Schweitzer (HAS), a private non-profit hospital providing health care to the approximately 240,000 people living in the rural Artibonite Valley in central Haiti functions as a part of the district health care system. During these hard times HAS continued a Community Health Unit to provide preventive care that reaches into the surrounding communities. Working with the existing network of Community Development and Health Agents (*Agents Communautaires*), the Unit strengthened several fledgling programs that were providing preventive care such as immunizations, deworming, vitamin A capsule distribution, growth monitoring and nutrition counseling. The Unit also designed and implemented the Hearth program.

ANTECEDENT MODELS

The Hearth model is rooted in several decades of experience and learning from rehabilitating malnourished preschool children. Earliest was hospital-based nutritional rehabilitation. While often successful, hospital rehabilitation was costly, able to handle only a small fraction of the malnourished children, and generally unsuccessful in prevention of recurrences. Hospital rehabilitation "medicalized" malnutrition and its care, leading to the inappropriate belief that it is a medical rather than a social or behavioral problem which can and should be handled in the home.

In response to these failings, Mothercraft Centers were implemented in Haiti and elsewhere in the 1960s and 70s (Beaudry-Darsime and

Latham 1973; Berggren et al. 1984; King et al. 1968, 1974, 1978). The Mothercraft Centers, located in rural villages, employed women nutrition educators (*monitrices*) to care for and demonstrate how to feed moderately and severely malnourished children daily for three months. Caretakers of the malnourished children were incorporated into the rehabilitation process so they would learn how to prevent malnutrition in future children. Inexpensive local foods and a specially devised weaning food (ground corn or rice and beans) demonstrated that food alone, usually without medicine, would rehabilitate the child. Mothers observe that children would lose their edema, smile, gain back their appetite and become more active, and learned to walk again. The montrices taught hygiene and family planning, used demonstration vegetable gardens, and made home visits. If the Center was able to eliminate severe childhood malnutrition in the community, the successful Mothercraft Center was closed and the monitrice was moved to the next community.

Numerous studies of Mothercraft Centers (King et al. 1968, 1978; Berggren 1971) reported improvements in family diets, nutritional status of participating children, mother's food selection and preparation practices, and survival of the younger siblings of participants. Berggren et al. (1985) found that weights and heights of participating children improved significantly compared to country-wide advances. Beaudry-Darisme and Latham (1973) found that centers in Haiti and Guatemala clearly improved nutritional status of participants in the short-term, but the results were less clear-cut in the long-term, showing farming and fishing families doing better. However, as Berggren et al. (1984) note, Mothercraft Centers had serious limitations: (1) they were expensive—about $6,000 per center per year in Haiti in 1980; (2) they were slow to reach the entire population of needy children; (3) they relied too often on animal protein rather than on local grains and legumes; (4) they became permanent fixtures in many communities with associated problems of absenteeism and dependence.

To address these concerns, Berggren and colleagues (1984), developed the less expensive "Nutrition Demonstration Foyer" (NDF). Nested within a growth monitoring, counseling and periodic deworming project, the NDF drastically shortened the exposure from three months to two weeks. Malnourished children gathered daily in a volunteer outdoor kitchen ("foyer") loaned by a local family to eat nutritious snacks and a supplementary meal prepared with local, calorie dense foods. Mothers often assisted the monitrice in preparing and feeding the meals. The basic hypothesis was that two weeks was enough time for mothers to be convinced of the efficacy of the practices: manifested by the return of child's appetite and positive social interaction and weight gain. The NDF built on lessons from the Mothercraft Centers: mothers learn by doing, nutritious menus can be developed from inexpensive local foods, and ill children should be referred to nearby primary health care centers. The monitrices worked in three week cycles: two weeks to implement an NDF and one week to set up an NDF in the next community. With 20–25 children per NDF, each monitrice directly reached about 340–425 children per year.

A follow-up study (Berggren et al. 1984) found lower death rates in NDF children than in similarly malnourished children who had merely undergone growth monitoring and counseling (GMC). Although deaths were few, the follow-up study reported significantly lower death rates of younger siblings of NDF children (Berggren et al. 1981).

Modified versions of the NDF introduced into several countries by Save the Children/USA report positive findings. Dubuisson et al. (1995) found the prevalence of moderate and severe underweight children dropped from 77% to 47% in a foyer program children after two years compared to a constant 63% in controls, although this finding may be compromised because potential confounders are not analyzed. In Bangladesh, Kaye et al. (1995) reported significant reduction in the mortality rates in younger siblings of foyer children relative to controls, although this result may be confounded by regression to the mean. In Vietnam, Save the Children developed an extended version of the NDF that virtually eliminated moderate and severe malnutrition. (See Sternin et al. in Ch. 6.)

THE HEARTH PROGRAM AT HAS

In 1993 Berggren and colleagues introduced the Hearth program at HAS, building on the success of the earlier NDF programs but relying on greater input from the communities themselves (Wollinka et al. 1997: Introduction). Volunteer mothers from the communities were trained by monitrices to implement the program in their own communities. Menus were developed in each community jointly by the monitrices and animatrices from practices of local mothers with well-nourished children, using principles of positive deviance (Zeitlin et al. 1990) and transferred to local mothers using principles of adult education (Wollinka et al. 1997: Ch. 2). The Community Health Unit at HAS built a staff of 14 monitrices who systematically implemented the program throughout the district.

The evolution of child nutrition concepts in Haiti from hospital rehabilitation to Mothercraft Centers, NDF, and finally Hearth was accompanied by a dramatic drop in the cost per participant (Figure 7.1). The cost reduction was made possible by the increasing involvement of community resources

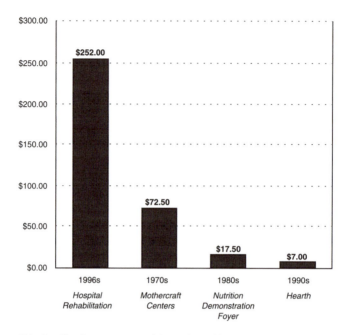

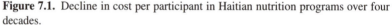

Figure 7.1. Decline in cost per participant in Haitian nutrition programs over four decades.
Note: Costs for hospital rehabilitation and Mothercraft Centers obtained from Beaudry-Darisme and Latham (1973), for NDF from Warren Berggren (personal communication), and for Hearth from this chapter. All costs in U.S. dollars at the time of the program.

in the program. These two developments—cost decrease and increased community involvement—have enabled the program to scale up to the district level.

HAS initiated Hearth to reduce the number of children requiring hospital care for malnutrition. But the program evolved beyond this limited objective. By establishing a large network of community volunteers living throughout its service area, HAS has been able to implement numerous outreach programs aimed at reducing malnutrition and promoting the health and welfare of all residents.

The HAS Hearth program uses three types of health workers: community development and health agents (*Agents Communautaires*), nutrition educators (*monitrices*) and volunteer mothers (*animatrices*). The approximately 60 Agents Communautaires employed by HAS are selected by the several communities they serve (about 700 families per agent). They have a broad range of duties, many directly relevant to the Hearth program, such as vital event recording and organizing community gatherings called Rally Posts where mothers bring their children for immunizations, growth monitoring and counseling and other preventive health services. The 14 monitrices are women with an eighth grade or higher education employed by HAS's Public Health Unit, who are recruited, hired and trained for several months by HAS. They work in pairs to train and then supervise the animatrices during the implementation of the foyers and subsequent follow-up activities. The animatrices are the front line volunteer workers in direct contact with the mothers of malnourished children. Typically there are 10 to 20 per community. Thus, the 200,000 people in the HAS service area, living in roughly 150 communities and neighborhoods averaging about 1300 persons each, are served by 60 full-time paid Agents Communautaires, 14 full-time paid monitrices, and a total of about 1900 volunteer animatrices.

Once the monitrices are trained, the Agents Communautaires recruit animatrices from communities scheduled to receive Hearth. Each animatrice selects tend to be congenial, willing and vivacious. Most households in the community hear about the Hearth program at this point.

Next the animatrices are trained by the monitrices (Figure 7.2). As their first assignment, the animatrices select 15 families with whom they want to work and complete a "picture" of those families. The animatrices visit their 15 families and obtain house numbers, children, and birth dates. During the visit, the animatrice explains about Hearth to each mother, and invites her to a weighing of all the preschool children taking place later in the week.

Following training in the use of growth cards, each animatrice selects a normal weight child among their 15 households by looking at growth cards of children who have participated in the regular weighing program, and identifies the foods most frequently fed to these children from interviews with their mothers, but does not attempt to estimate quantities consumed. This process attracts attention in the neighborhood, and begins to confirm the idea that good nutrition is possible in this environment, using the foods available to every household, even those who are poor. The animatrices then collectively determine the menu to be served to the malnourished children in their community, based on the foods served by the "positive deviant" mothers. The animatrices may or may not be such positive deviant mothers—indeed, numerous animatrices had malnourished children of their own who joined the foyer because they were underweight.

Experience shows that the menus derived from the "survey" of positive deviants turns out to be nearly identical from place to place, as does their cost in the local markets. The consistency has produced pressure to shorten

DAY 1: The 10 to 20 animatrices-in-trainning from one community or sub-community meet with the two monitrices responsible for organizing the health program in that community to receive motivating information about the program and their role as animatrice. They learn how to interpret a growth curve on a standard growth card, and to identify malnourished children on the basis of that curve or a single weight. Finally they learn to carry out a simple 24-hour recall dietary history that focuses on the types of food rather than the quantity of food consumed. They are assigned to seek out a child with normal or mild malnutrition on the basis of his/her growth card (a positive deviant), and then to carry out the simple 24-hour recall dietary survey on that child, for reporting the next day.

DAY 2: Each animatrice reports the foods consumed by the positive deviant child she studied. The monitrice tabulates these reports, noting the frequency of each foodstuff, and then reports these frequencies to the animatrices in the form of a menu of the most frequently used foods in the positive deviant diets. Quantities are adjusted by the monitrices at this point to provide a nutritionally balanced menu. (At HAS, the resulting positive deviant menu has been the same in all communities – rice or corn, bean sauce and a vegetable.) Together the animatrices and monitrice estimate the cost of each item in the marketplace.

DAY 3: Each animatrice is given enough money to purchase two of the positive deviant meals at the local market. Meanwhile one of the monitrices purchases the same items at the same time in the same market, to breed an atmosphere of competition for getting the lowest price. The monitrice weighs the purchased items to estimate their nutritional value in calories and proteins, confirming that a nutritionally complete diet can in fact be purchased for the money provided.

DAY 4: Called the Rehearsal Day, small teams of animatrices rise early to prepare the specified diet so they can feed it to neighborhood children by 8–9 o'clock in the morning. This shows the animatrice that the food is satisfying to the children, is sufficient for children up to 5 years of age, and also that the process of preparation early in the morning is feasible. That afternoon the animatrice trainees visit their 15 selected homes to get all children between one and five years old to attend the weighing scheduled for the following day.

DAY 5: When the children and their parents (usually mothers) have assembled, all the preschoolers are weighed by the monitrice together with the animatrices. The program is explained, including reasons for giving children a balanced meal of affordable local foods used by mothers of well-nourished children. Parents of children with moderate or severe malnutrition are then invited to participate in the foyers. Most accept or are persuaded, and frequently some mildly malnourished children are also accepted into the program.

Figure 7.2. One week training course for animatrices.

the course and merely prescribe the effective menu without rediscovering the menu each time. The program leaders have strongly resisted this pressure, both because of their conviction that the "discovery approach" to adult education is valid, and *because the derivation of the menu from the positive deviant survey and the local market exercise is critical to convince mothers to participate in the foyer.*

At the weighing, the mothers are informed more fully about the purposes and activities of the program and deworming medicine is administered to all children in attendance. Preschool children over one year who are moderately or severely underweight-for-age (WAM < 75%) are invited to participate. Although the program established the policy of only inviting moderately or severely underweight children over one year of age, in fact the foyers included many mildly underweight children and a few less than a year old. (The sample of 192 program children used in the evaluation included 52—27%—who were mildly underweight.) Sometimes malnourished children not from one of the 15 selected families attend the group weighing, either at the urging of the Agent Communautaire or monitrice, or because they heard the news on the community grapevine. These children are encouraged to attend the foyers. In this way, the program ends up reaching most of the malnourished children in the community.

After the weighing, mothers of underweight children receive a full description of the program from the monitrice, including the process used to determine the positive deviant menu that will be served to the children at the foyers. The similarity of the positive deviant mothers to those in attendance is emphasized: they live in the same neighborhood, usually in similar economic conditions, and buy in the same marketplace at the same prices as the other mothers. Thus the mothers believe that they can provide the same menu to their own children. HAS staff noted that some mothers are insulted by the invitation to participate because it carries the insinuation that they have not provided adequate care and food to their own child, and as a result some mothers do not readily agree to participate. In these cases the animatrices negotiate with the reluctant mothers, using enticements such as, "participation will enable us to find out if your child has a disease," and "if your child does not grow adequately s/he will be referred to the hospital for care." Refusals to participate are described as rare.

The following Monday the animatrice prepares the first of 12 meals at her own hearth. The feeding occurs between 8 and 9 A.M., a time chosen because it does not compete with any other mealtime and which allows enough time to cook the beans into a sauce, the most important source of protein. Some children come to the foyer themselves, while others are brought by their mothers or older siblings. Most importantly, the animatrices never harangue the mothers at the foyers. Rather they focus almost entirely at getting a nutritionally rich diet into the participating children.

Participants eat the foyer meal for 12 days (daily except Sunday). The menu is changed from day to day with regard to type of grain (rice, corn) and type of vegetable (various types of leaves, okra, tomatoes), but pureed beans seems to be a constant component, ensuring adequate protein intake.

The severely malnourished children, who often arrive listless and disinterested in food, are often transformed by the enhanced nutritional intake, becoming active, playing, losing their cranky whining, and developing such an intense appetite that they consume astonishing amounts of food at a single foyer session. This behavior change alone is a very powerful motivator for the mothers of these children and the animatrice, providing visible evidence that the recommended menu really works.

Following the two weeks of foyer feedings, full responsibility for feeding reverts to the mother, who is encouraged to continue the foyer menu. The HAS program also encourages increased feeding frequency.

Repeat weighings are scheduled by the monitrices at four and eight weeks following the foyers. The weighings are accompanied by counseling to encourage mothers to continue the foyer diet. Children who have not gained at least 200 grams during the eight weeks are considered failures, and are referred to the hospital. A small sample indicates that approximately 30% of the participants in the HAS program are referred. Of these, about 30% had tuberculosis; the remaining 70% face a mix of other medical and social problems.

HAS operates a Women's Microenterprise Program to assist families of Hearth participants who continue growth failure for one year. During the first half of 1996, 65 women were offered the opportunity to participate in this program, and 53 accepted. Following training, the women were given paying jobs associated with school feeding, with the payments structured so that after about five months the women amass enough capital (approximately US$50) to start a small enterprise.

The HAS program costs about $7.00 (U.S.) per program participant, including about $3.00 for food ($0.25 per meal), and $4.00 for all costs associated with salaries, transportation, and supervision. (Additional details about the program can be found in Wollinka et al. 1997: Chs. 1 and 3.)

EVALUATION OF THE HEARTH PROGRAM AT HAS

This evaluation assesses the impact of the Hearth program on the weight-for-age malnutrition in program participants over a period of one year. It does not address the immediate (2–8 weeks) rehabilitation of the moderately and severely malnourished program participants during the program, changes in practices and attitudes of mothers, reduction of the prevalence of malnutrition in the general population, nor the creation of a sustaining network of effective volunteers. These limitations mean that the evaluation can not be used to judge the broader value of the program. Nevertheless,

the evaluation indicates that the program is headed in the right direction.
(See Wollinka et al. 1997: Ch. 3.)

Methodology

The evaluation compares the one year weight gain of 192 children who
participated in the Hearth program to the gain of 185 similar children who
participated in growth monitoring but not Hearth. The program sample
was selected systematically (every seventh name) from all children participating in Hearth during its first six months (October 1993–March 1994, a
period referred to as the intervention period). The program sample children were weighed when they enrolled in the program and again one year
later.

The comparison sample includes preschool children from communities
which had not participated in the Hearth program, and who were underweight during the intervention period as evidenced on their road-to-health
cards. To obtain the comparison sample, a team attended Rally Posts in all
communities that had not yet participated in the Hearth program where
they identified all children who qualified for the comparison group,
recorded pre-weights from road-to-health cards, completed and recorded
post-weighings, and gave various other health services. Whenever possible
the younger siblings of the children in the comparison group were
weighed and the mothers were questioned about younger sibling mortality.

Program data were collected in two distinct phases, one for foyers
implemented during October–December, 1993, and the second for foyers
implemented January–March, 1994. Information was not obtained about
the results of the four and 8-week weighings, about whether or not a program participant was referred to the hospital as a result of the 8-week
weighing, about the diagnosis, treatment or outcome of referred children,
or whether or not the program children had a road-to-health card.

Weight and age data were transformed into weight-for-age as a percent
of the international reference median (WAM) and into weight-for-age
Z-score (WAZ) using the anthropometric calculation package in EPI-INFO
(Table 7.1).

Results

Multi-variate analysis was used to compare one-year WAZ gains in the
program and comparison groups. The multi-variate model predicts WAZ at
the end of the program (WAZ2) as a function of initial WAZ (WAZ1),
age of child, phase (earlier or later foyer), treatment group (program or

Table 7.1. Program and Comparison Samples[a]

Characteristics	Program	Comparison
Sample Size	192	185
Percent participating		
in Hearth program	100%	0%
Percent participating	33%	100%
in growth monitoring (GMP)	(approx)	
Average age in months	34.5	29.0
Initial nutritional status: weight-		
for-age (W/A) Z-score (WAZ1)		
Average initial weight-for-age		
Z-score	−2.75	−2.68
Number (%) between 0 and		
−1.99 (normal and mild)	11 (6%)	11 (6%)
Number (%) −2.00 and below		
(moderate and severe)	181 (94%)	176 (94%)
Initial nutritional status: % of		
W/A reference median (WAM1)		
Number (%) 75% or above median		
(normal and mild)	52 (27%)	44 (24%)
Number (%) below 75% of median		
(moderate and severe)	140 (73%)	143 (76%)

[a]The discrepancy between the figures for WAZ1 and WAM1 is due to the fact that the categories of mild, moderate and severe underweight are defined differently in the two systems. In the WAZ system, mild, moderate, severe and very severe malnutrition are defined as −1 to −2, −2 to −3, −3 to −4, and below −4 respectively. In WAM, mild, moderate and severe malnutrition are defined as 90–75%, 60–75%, below 60% of the reference median respectively.

comparison), and an interactive variable combining treatment group and initial WAZ. Initial WAZ, treatment group and their interactive term all made significant contributions to final WAZ but age and phase did not (Table 7.2).

This analysis shows that the program has a strong, positive, and highly significant effect on nutritional status, but only for children with relatively higher nutritional status (i.e., mild-to-moderately underweight) at the beginning of the program. The program's effect on children with lower initial nutritional status (i.e., severe-to-very severely underweight) is not statistically significant. This counterintuitive result may be due in all or in part to selection bias from exclusion of children who died from the sample as discussed below.

To determine whether this counter-intuitive result is a statistical artifact caused by imposing a linear model on the data, the program and comparison groups were divided into four equal categories by WAZ1 quartiles, and a WAZ gain regression analysis was performed for each quartile. The model predicts WAZ gain as a function of treatment group, age and phase. Children in the top WAZ1 quartile (which includes all of the mildly and many of the moderately underweight children) do decidedly better if they are in the program than in the comparison group; program and comparison children in the middle two WAZ1 quartiles have about the same WAZ gain; and children in the bottom WAZ1 quartile (which includes all the very severely underweight children) do better in the comparison group, although this difference is not statistically significant. Thus this analysis confirms the multi-variate analysis.

The multi-variate model (Table 7.2) was used to estimate the size of the effect of the program. The results of this simulation, reported in Table 7.3, show that program children with WAZ1 equal to -2.0 average about 0.3 higher WAZ gain (in other words, three-tenths of a standard deviation higher in the program children, which works out to be about one pound of additional weight in a 36 month old) than the comparison children with the same WAZ1. Program and comparison children with WAZ1 of -3.0 average about the same WAZ gain, and program children with WAZ1 of -4.0 average 0.36 less WAZ gain than the comparison children, although as noted above the difference between the program and comparison groups at WAZ1 $= -4.0$ and -3.0 is not statistically significant.

Potential Threats to the Validity of the Observed Results

Growth Monitoring Program (GMP) effect. One-third of the children in the program sample and all of the children in the comparison group were

Table 7.2. Analysis[a] of Final Weight-for-Age (Z-score) of Children participating in the Hearth Program and in a Comparision Group

Term	F Value	Significance
Treatment	9.8	$p = 0.002$
Phase	3.6	$p = 0.058$
Initial (WAZI)	47.6	$p = 0.0001$
Age	0.8	$p = 0.368$
Treatment $\times$ WAZI	8.9	$p = 0.003$

[a]The dependent variable (WAZ2) is the final weight-for-age Z-score. TREATMENT signifies program or comparision group children. PHASE refers to different periods of the program. INITIAL (WAZ1) is the weight-for-age Z-score of children when the program began. This analysis used an ordinary least squares regression model calculated using SAS, GLS procedure.

Table 7.3. Predicted Impact of the Hearth Program on the Gain in Nutritional Status for Participant Children of Different Initial Weight-for-Age Z-Scores[a]

Initial WAZ (WAZ1)	WAZ Gain		Gain in WAZ due to program
	Program	Comparison	
-2.0	0.11	-0.19	0.30
-3.0	0.21	0.24	-0.03
-4.0	0.31	0.67	-0.36

[a] This table shows the results when the model from Table 7.2 is used to predict WAZ2 for three assumed values of WAZ1. WAZ gain equals predicted WAZ2 minus assumed WAZ1. Phase and age do not influence the results. In a seperate analysis by WAZ1 quartiles (see text), the difference between the program and comparison was statistically significant in the highest quartile of WAZ1 but not in the lower three quartiles, thus suggesting that in this table the WAZ gain reported when WAZ1 equals -2.0 may be more reliable than the loss in WAZ gain when WAZ1 equals -4.0.

active in the GMP. Therefore, any GMP impact on growth will manifest in both groups but to a greater extent in the comparison group. The *absolute* gain in nutritional status observed in the program group will overstate the true program effect because part will be due to the GMP, but the *net* gain in nutritional status observed in the program group (program gain minus comparison gain) will understate the true program effect because the GMP will have a larger effect on the comparison than the program group.

Historical effects and regression-toward-the-mean. Although historical effects and regression-toward-the-mean are confounded with each other and potentially with the GMP effect, the comparison group controls for their combined effect.

Age, phase, and initial nutritional status. These three factors were addressed in the multi-variate analysis. Age was not related to WAZ gain in the multi-variate analysis, and not related to initial WAZ in a separate analysis. This is surprising because others have reported contrary findings (Schroeder et al. 1995). The phase variable addresses the possibility of program learning as a result of fine-tuning by the Hearth program staff during the implementation period. If such learning occurred, then a phase effect should have been apparent in the program group but not in the comparison group. In fact, phase had no significant effect, nor did the addition of the interactive term (PHASExPROGRAM) to the multi-variate model.

Community effect. The program might have caused a community effect. For example, the program might have improved the nutritional status of non-participants. However, the data set did not permit such an analysis. Other behavioral change programs that have looked for such a community effect have often found it (Hornik 1990; Hornik et al. 1992). If the Hearth Program did have a community effect, then the present analysis would underestimate the true effect of the program.

Selection bias. Several types of selection bias may have influenced the results. First, participants in GMP are self-selected. Mothers who self-select into GMP may be better mothers on average than the more inclusive group of mothers in Hearth. If so, this selection bias may have caused an underestimation of the true effect of the program. (This selection bias is subsumed in the GMP effect.) Second, the program sample was selected by picking every seventh child on the roster of participants, a method which systematically excludes siblings (including twins). It is uncertain whether this tends to over or underestimate the program effect. Third, some of the children nominated for the program sample by the "every seventh name" method were not actually found in the field for various reasons including death and moved. Other names were substituted for the children not found (the next participant listed on the roster). It is uncertain whether the children not found were systematically different from the found children, and whether this potential bias would tend to over or underestimate program effect. Fourth, some underweight children may not have enrolled in the program, and if so, may have differed from the enrolled children, thus creating the potential for bias. It is not clear how this would influence the results. Fifth, mothers of mildly underweight children self-selected into the Hearth Program and may differ from the mildly underweight in the comparison group. This potential bias may have caused the observed results to slightly overestimate the actual effect of the program. Sixth, the sample excludes all children dying between the initial and final weighing in the comparison and possibly some in the program group. Because death is more likely to strike more severely underweight children, this bias may have caused the observed results to underestimate the actual effect of the program, especially for moderate-to-severe undernourished children.

DISCUSSION AND CONCLUSION

The Hearth program developed at the Hopital Albert Schweitzer in Haiti by Dr. Warren Berggren and his colleagues builds on earlier programs (Mothercraft Centers, Nutrition Demonstration Foyers) in Haiti and elsewhere. Hearth aims to reduce the cost of the antecedent programs while maintaining or increasing the effectiveness so that it can be expanded to a sustainable district-level program. The present effort to document and evaluate the program produced several surprising results and raised a number of interesting issues.

The main difference between Hearth at HAS and the antecedent programs is the increase in community participation designed into the Hearth program, especially participation by community mothers. In one sense of the term, Hearth scaled down so that it could afford to scale up. The program scaled down in several ways: from few large permanent mothercraft centers serving several communities to many small hearths of local mothers each serving a few families; from paid staff to volunteer mothers; from foyers with many children to foyers with only a few children; from three months of demonstration feeding to 12 days; and from several demonstration meals a day to one per day. This not only reduced the cost but also made the whole affair more accessible and apparent to the local families. Analysis and problem-solving moved closer to the community: the positive-deviant approach incorporated local practice/wisdom to convince mothers that they could do the same thing; and the teaching/learning strategy shifted from demonstrations by knowledgeable persons to self-discovery by the mothers themselves in a partially structured environment. By working with and relying on the communities and individuals in these ways, the HAS staff was able to focus on scaling-up issues: implement the program throughout the entire district and functionally scale up, that is identify new problems, and introduce new activities in the fledgling network, such as micro-enterprises.

The evaluation compared the one-year gain in nutritional status in a sample of 192 program participants to a comparison group of 185 non-participants. Although the initial purpose of the Hearth program was to rehabilitate moderately and severely malnourished children, a multivariate analysis showed that the program prevented nutritional deterioration in mild-to-moderately underweight children relative to the comparison group, but not in moderate-to-very severely underweight children. What can explain this surprising result?

The first part of this result, preventing deterioration in mild-to-moderately underweight children, might reflect learning by the mothers of these children combined with a lower burden of serious infectious disease. Many volunteer mothers (animatrices) maintain informal contact with mothers in their group after the foyers, and it is not implausible that such contact is greater and more effective with mothers of the mild-to-moderately underweight children who may be more responsive and competent than mothers of more severely malnourished children. Further, the extra effort required to enroll mildly underweight children in the foyers is a selection bias that may contribute to this result.

The second part of the result, namely, the lack of impact on more severely underweight children and even the probability that very severely underweight program children do worse than the comparison children, might be explained at least in part by selection bias that excluded dead children from the sample. Possibly most important, the results suggest that a growth monitoring program (GMP) is more effective with very severely underweight children over the course of a year and the Hearth program is more effective with mild-to-moderately underweight children. The severely underweight may require the more persistent attention and appropriate referrals of a well-run GMP program. If so, then the combination of GMP and Hearth should produce the best of both worlds.

The HAS version of the Hearth program differs significantly from antecedent programs. Its objective of "jump-starting" a network of volunteer mothers (animatrices) who can then deliver community oriented primary care is important and goes well beyond the nutritional rehabilitation goals of earlier efforts.

Many outreach programs develop networks of volunteer community health workers where each volunteer worker is supposed to serve all the residents of a defined area where the worker also lives. Not so with the HAS Hearth program, where volunteers are selected because they have personality and interest, not because they live in a particular section of the community. In fact, several volunteers may live near each other, and they serve whichever families they wish. The HAS Hearth model thus taps into the dynamics of the community. We suspect that the HAS approach is better suited to the high mobility of families which is characteristic of Haiti.

Much has been made of positive deviance as a method to identify local foods and practices that are both effective and feasible. However, in the HAS hearth program, positive deviance is primarily used to promote effective foods and behaviors to the mothers, rather than to discover the best menu in each community. In fact, all of the communities "discovered" the same positive deviant menu from the 24-hour recall of positive deviant mothers. This menu was well-known to the nutrition educators (monitrices) from the start. The use of the positive deviance approach to convince mothers of the value and economic feasibility of the Hearth Program menu has made a very important contribution to the success of the HAS program.

The HAS Hearth program uses a different teaching strategy than other nutritional rehabilitation programs. It stresses self-directed discovery. Mothers are helped to discover for themselves by observing the public implementation of the program and its dramatic rehabilitation of their children, instead of being told what to do. This contrasts with the learning-by-demonstration approach used by the Mothercraft Centers, and with the learning-by-doing approach used in the Hearth program in Vietnam described elsewhere in this volume.

Additional work is needed to understand the full impact of the Hearth program. The analysis here does not address the effect of the program on other mothers and children in the communities where it is implemented ("community effect"), nor the extent to which the effects of the program are sustained through time. Representative samples drawn from the entire population in the program and comparison communities are probably required to assess the community effect. A prospective study could resolve most of the selection bias.

Improvements to the program could be found by analyzing the relative contribution of different program components, including the contribution of individual monitrices and animatrices, the contribution of the 12-day foyer component, and the hospital referral component for children who do not gain weight after eight weeks. Another issue that requires long-term evaluation is whether the structure of monitrices and volunteer mothers sustains and delivers other effective health services. Finally it is important to understand how best to integrate the GMP and the Hearth programs.

NOTES

1. The HAS Hearth program was developed with the resources and support of Hopital Albert Schweitzer and its staff. The evaluation was supported by the BASICS Project/Partnership for Child Health, and World Relief Corporation, in addition to HAS. Special recognition is owed to the staff of HAS, to Muriel Elmer of World Relief Corporation who was instrumental in conceiving and organizing the evaluation, to Laura Caulfield, Faisal Faruque, and Dory Storms of The Johns Hopkins University for valuable technical advice, to Jay Ross of the Academy for Educational Development who was instrumental in conceiving, performing and interpreting the multi-variate analysis, and to Jeff Grant who conducted most of the data collection for the evaluation. Although these friends and colleagues have been vital to the conduct and success of the work reflected here, any misinterpretations, errors or other problems with this report are the sole responsibility of the authors.

REFERENCES

Alvarez, M. and Murray, G.
  (1990) *Socialization for Scarcity in Rural Haiti*. Port-au-Prince, Haiti: U.S. Agency for International Development.
Beaudry-Darisme, M. and Latham, M. C.
  (1973) "Nutrition Rehabilitation Centers—An Evaluation of Their Performance." *Environmental Child Health* **19**(3): 299–332.

Berggren, W. L.
(1971) "Evaluation of the Effectiveness of Education and Rehabilitation Centers." In *Proceedings of the Western Hemisphere Nutrition Congress III*, ed. P. L. White. Chicago: Department of Food and Nutrition, Division of Scientific Activities, American Medical Association.

Berggren, G., Alvarez, M., and Gay, M.
(1993) *Causes of Malnutrition in Rural Haiti: Evaluation Report on the RICHES Project of CARE/Haiti*. Port-au-Prince, Haiti: CARE.

Berggren, G. G., Hebert, J. R., and Waternaux, C. M.
(1985) "Comparison of Haitian Children in a Nutrition Intervention Programme with Children in the Haitian National Nutrition Survey." *Bulletin of the World Health Organization*, 63(6): 1141–1150.

Berggren, G., Alvarez, M., Genece, E., Amadee-Gedeon, P. M., and Henry, M.
(1984) *The Nutrition Demonstration Foyer: A Model for Combatting Malnutrition in Haiti*. HOVIPREP Monograph Series, No. 2, International Food & Nutrition Program. Cambridge, MA: Massachusetts Institute of Technology.

Berggren, W. L., Berggren, G. G., and Ewbank, D.
(1981) "Reduction of Mortality in Rural Haiti Through a Primary Health Care Program." *New England Journal of Medicine* 304: 1324–1330.

Dubuisson, St. E., Ludzen, S., Zayan, A., and Swedberg, E.
(1995) Impact of Sustainable Behavior Change on the Nutritional Status of Children. In *Community Impact of PVO Child Survival Efforts: 1985–1994*. Proceedings, A Worldwide Conference sponsored by USAID, Bangalore, India, October 2–7, 1994, eds. D. Storms, C. Carter, P. Altman. Baltimore, MD: Johns Hopkins University Department of International Health.

Hornik, R.
(1990) "Alternative Models of Behavior Change." Working Paper No. 131, Center for International Health and Development Communication. Philadelphia: Annenberg School for Communication, University of Pennsylvania.

Hornik, R., McDivitt, J., Yoder, P. S., Zimicki, S., Contreras-Budge, E., McDowell, J., and Rasmuson, M.
(1992) "Communication for Child Survival: Evaluation of Projects in Ten Countries." (Draft working paper). Philadelphia: Center for International Health and Development Communication. Annenberg School for Communication, University of Pennsylvania.

Kaye, K., Kahn, N. H., and Hossain, A.
(1995) "Effect of a Nutrition Education Program on the Weight of Younger Siblings of Malnourished Children in Bangladesh." In *Community Impact of PVO Child Survival Efforts: 1985–1994*, eds. D. Storms, C. Carter, P. Altman. Proceedings, A Worldwide Conference sponsored

by USAID, Bangalore, India, Oct 2–7, 1994. Baltimore, MD: Johns Hopkins University Department of International Health.

King, K. W., Fougere, W., Webb, R. E., Berggren, G., Berggren, W. L., and Hilare, A.
(1978)   "Preventive and Therapeutic Benefits in Relation to Cost: Performance over 10 Years of Mothercraft Centers in Haiti." *American Journal of Clinical Nutrition* **31**: 679–690.

King, K.W., Fougere, W., Hilaire, A., Webb, R. E., Berggren, G., and Berggren, W.
(1974)   "Costs in Relation to Benefits for Mothercraft Centers in Haiti, 1964–1974." Paper presented at Western Hemisphere Nutrition Congress IV, Bal Harbour, FL.

King, K. W., Begin, I. D., Fougere, W., Dominique, G., Grinker, R., and Foucald, J.
(1968)   "Two-year Evaluation of a Nutritional Rehabilitation (Mothercraft) Center." *Achivos Venezolanos de Nutricion* **18**: 245–261.

Riordan, J. T., van Haeftan, R., Augustine, A., Blemur, M., Guengant, J.-P., and Locher, U.
(1997)   *USAID Strategy to Improve Food Security in Haiti.* Port-au-Prince, Haiti: USAID.

Schroeder, D. K., Martorell, R., Rivera, J. A., Ruel, M., and Habicht, J.-P.
(1995)   "Age Difference in the Impact of Nutritional Supplementation on Growth." *Journal of Nutrition* (supplement) **125**: 1051S–1059S.

Wollinka, O., Keeley, E., Burkhalter, B. R., and Bashir, N.
eds. *Hearth Nutrition Model: Applications in Haiti, Vietnam, and Bangladesh.* Arlington, VA: Basic Support for Institutionalizing Child Survival (BASICS) Project for USAID and World Relief Corporation.

Zeitlin, M., Ghassemi, H., and Mansour, M.
(1990)   *Positive Deviance in Child Nutrition—With Emphasis on Psychosocial and Behavioral Aspects and Implications for Development.* Tokyo: United Nations University.

CHAPTER 8

Equity and Sustainability of the Health System: A Community Agenda in the Central Region of Togo

K. A. Pangu, K. Aflagah, M. Kaba,
El Hadji Tairou, and N. Tchedre

Improved nutrition of children and women in developing countries is associated with improved primary health care, poverty reduction, and expanded community involvement (UNICEF 1990). After the mid-1980s, many Third World governments faced severe budgetary crises. In Sub-Saharan Africa, governments began implementing both structural adjustment programs and health reforms in efforts to expand coverage and improve quality and equity of health care. The shared components of structural adjustment and health reforms often included severe cutbacks in real government spending along with organizational decentralization, community involvement, and re-allocation of resources to new priorities.

Togo is one of the Sub-Saharan countries where centrally managed health systems had been rapidly deteriorating. As in other countries, this increased the importance of community participation in decision-making in sectors that were previously under the exclusive control of government officials or health professionals (World Health Organization 1996). With the decentralization and democratization process under way, scaling down management responsibility and scaling up community participation was considered a key element to restoring accountability and confidence in public health services.

This chapter describes how, from 1989 through 1991, the Primary Health Care Project (PHCP) in the Central Region of Togo confronted these trends and programming opportunities. Although it was not a part of the "Bamako Initiative" developed in 1987, the activities implemented in Togo were inspired by the principal goal of the Initiative: to improve access by households to a minimum package of services, including immunization, prenatal and postnatal care, nutrition, family planning, correct case management of common diseases in children and other local priority problems (UNICEF 1992).[1] The PHCP used the Bamako Initiative's basic strategies of decentralized planning, essential drugs policy, and participation of households in the financing and management of basic services.

PROJECT BACKGROUND

Togo is a small country in Western Africa bordered on the west by Ghana, on the north by Burkina Faso, on the east by Benin, and on the south by the Atlantic Ocean. Its total population is estimated at 3.5 million. For three decades, the country has made significant progress in improving the health status of its population. The under-five mortality fell from 264 to 135 between 1960 and 1993 and infant mortality from 154 to 84 (UNICEF 1995a). However, despite these improvements, when the PHCP started in 1989, the general social and economic environment was weak and unstable, partially due to the democratization process the country was going through. Other health status indicators were also low. Some 20% of newborns were underweight, 22% of children between six and 11 had a goiter and the maternal mortality rate was high: more than 640 per 100,000 live births (WHO–UNICEF 1996).

The Central Region town of Sokode, where the project is based, is situated on the main north-south road that runs through the country linking it to Burkina Faso, Mali and Niger to the north and to the capital city of Lome some 350 kilometers to the south. Estimated at 350,000 people, the region's population lives primarily from agriculture and small trade. A very limited proportion of the people are involved in public administration and other non-farm employment. The region has no manufacturing industry. In 1990, the average net income of a farmer was estimated at CFA 5,000/month (US $1 = CFA 250) (PHCP 1991). The Central Region was considered as a transition region between the relatively wealthy south of the country, where the capital and the port are located, and the poor arid north region.

The region is divided into three health districts. Every district is headed by a district medical officer associated with a referral hospital. There is also a regional hospital with specialists in Sokode. Some 55 health centers/dispensaries (HC) are spread throughout the region, which represents a ratio of one health unit per 6,000 inhabitants. The government's contribution to the functioning of health services is important. In addition to paying the staff's salaries, it provides each health center with an annual budget of CFA 700,000 for the purchase of drugs.

However, when the project started, health centers experienced frequent drug shortages. Togopharma, the para-governmental organization which imported and distributed drugs to health units, mainly supplied brand name products. With their annual budgets, health centers could not afford to buy drugs and supplies which would enable them to cover the needs of the population for a whole year. Since the use of drugs was not well rationalized, a six-month supply barely lasted a couple of months. After that period, patients who consulted the health units were given prescriptions to buy drugs either from depots or private pharmacies. Also, as the system was centralized, funds generated at health centers were used by the health staff without any system of accountability to the community and the health authorities.

THE PROJECT

The Primary Health Care Project (PHCP) was funded by the German Agency for Technical Cooperation (GTZ). The support to Togo's Central Region's health care system included the technical assistance of a public health expert. The total of US $330,000 annually included the salary of the expert. The expert was to assist the three district doctors in the planning and management of primary health care, including training of staff. The project provided technical equipment to health centers, and supplied the first lot of drugs to communities. It also helped organize the first regional store for essential drugs.

The project adopted and modified the three strategies used by the Bamako Initiative (BI) in other African countries: (1) decentralized planning to the district level; (2) implementation of an essential drugs policy;

and (3) improvement of governance through the participation of households in the financing and management of basic services. These scaling down strategies are designed, on the one hand, to improve the quality of services by establishing a more balanced dialogue between health professionals and communities, and, on the other hand, to increase accessibility of health care by reducing the costs of services and by introducing outreach activities for preventive care (McPacke et al. 1992). A health unit is considered as revitalized or full functioning when: (1) staff are trained in communication skills and use of generic drugs; (2) the facilities and equipment have been improved; (3) it is supplied with essential drugs on a regular basis; (4) the population of the catchment area is known; (5) it is managed by the community; (6) it is supervised by the District Health Management Teams (DHMT). In Togo the teams were composed of the district medical officer, the responsible administrator, the chief nurse and the heads of specific health programs.

SCALING UP THE ROLE OF THE COMMUNITY

To scale up local capacity to manage sustainable and equitable health care systems, four actions were taken: (1) define the catchment areas and the potential role of the communities in each catchment area; (2) establish the communities' ownership over the health units; (3) strengthen existing social structures of the communities needed for management; (4) improve the management capacity of the communities.

Defining the Catchment Areas and Consulting the Community

In order to begin the process of revitalization, a "census," a specially designed needs assessment, was organized in the areas covered by the health units. Each area comprised several villages using the same health facility. Some areas had two or three health units, but there were no problems identifying the health area to which the village belonged. (The population using a health unit (in the catchment area) is called the "community" in this chapter.)

The census was conducted by health center teams with the help of designated community members and took approximately one month to be completed. The census collected basic information on the households through interviews with household members and the village chiefs. The information collected on a household included, the name, age, sex, chronic diseases (e.g., tuberculosis, and leprosy), for each member of the household, the status of immunization for children under-five, and for women, the number of pregnancies and the number of children alive. The census form provided a space for registering any health problem reported by the household's member and what was done for the problem.

The census was conducted progressively in all (55) catchment areas in the region as the first step in the process of health unit revitalization. It established a baseline for the activities to be carried by the health unit. One of the aims was to listen to people's opinions, discuss with them the expected changes in the functioning of the health units, and their new role. It offered a good opportunity for the staff to discuss the role and responsibilities of the community in the fields of finance, drugs, and staff management. They also discussed the role of the community in achieving health goals, and the importance of outreach activities. It appeared to be a very useful exercise for the staff as they discovered, among other things, that some people hardly used the health centers at all.

All the households registered during the census were classified by village and by distance from the health center. The purpose of the classification by village was to give a clearer picture of how the different villages were using the preventive and curative services provided by the health center. By knowing members of households with chronic diseases or serious health problems the team of the health center was able to better target their home visits or to refer patients to the social services. A map of each catchment area showing the population of each village was posted at the health unit. The regional social and rural development services agencies provided additional information on the social, cultural and economic background of the villages.

Reinforcing Community Ownership of the Health Unit

After consulting the population, it was felt that having the people pay an initial financial contribution for the improvement of the health unit would contribute to reinforcing each community's ownership over its health unit, in the same way that a dowry seals the bonds of matrimony between husband and wife. The money was collected by health committee members of each village under the supervision of the village chiefs. According to the size of the population covered by the health center, the initial fee was set by the District Health Management Team at CFA 100,000. This was equivalent to approximately CFA 20 per capita.

Each community determined how the money was going to be collected. In some villages the money was collected locally, in others the money came from people from the village living in the capital or even abroad as part of their contribution to the development of their villages. The financial aspect did not slow down the program at all. The people were, in effect, paying to have the right to decide how the health center was going to function and, later on, to become owners of the health center.

Fifty percent of the money was deposited into a bank account opened for the health unit in a local credit union as a reserve enabling the community to pay for the poor for example. The other fifty percent was deposited in a regional bank account as a solidarity fund and was managed by the regional management team. The money was used to pay for the operating costs of the regional drug store where the various health units could buy generic drugs at a reasonable price. The first lot of drugs was provided by the PHCP free of charge. For its part, the government, through its program of cooperation with the German Agency for Technical Cooperation, refurbished the health centers' buildings and the regional drug store and equipped them.

During a public ceremony chaired by regional health officials, political and traditional authorities, the health center was handed over to the community for co-management. The participation of officials at this ceremony was important. It contributed, among other things, to convincing the community that the change in management was real, desired, and supported by everybody.

Strengthening Existing Social Structures of the Community

It was important to rely on existing organizations in the community to implement the program and avoid the temptation of establishing new parallel structures or communication channels. People in the Central Region did not wait for the project to be launched to start getting together, discussing, and finding solutions to their problems. It is a tradition for members of a community to assemble and talk things over: men and women, young and old, merchants or peasants, all gather together or around their chief on a regular basis to settle their affairs. Understanding how those meetings were organized and how things worked made it possible to integrate the Primary Health Care Project into the daily routine of the community.

The chief of a village is traditionally vested with the authority of spreading information among the villagers. He is the one who calls for meetings and conducts them. His role was recognized and valued from the very beginning of the project. Because the implications of the proposed actions were discussed with the people and accepted by them, it was not difficult to reach a consensus and obtain the necessary human and material resources from the community. This strategy allowed the activities related to primary health care to fit into the organization and development of the community, making them less vulnerable to external influences.

Building Community Capacity to Manage the Health Unit

Ensuring transparency and accountability at the health unit was considered as an important step in restoring the confidence of the community after years of deterioration and low usage. The DHMT and the regional health authorities in coordination with the local authorities decided that the community should take an active part in the revitalization process from the beginning. Each community would have a say in the management of important components of their health unit, such as drugs, finances, and staff management, which traditionally was considered a privilege of professionals. Selection of health committee's members as secretary, bookkeeper and president was done through a consensual process between the villages covered by each health unit. The chiefs of villages oversaw the functioning of the health units, including overall management of staff, in close coordination with the DHMT, whose members were responsible for the day to day operation of the health units.

During a two-week session some community members were trained by the DHMT in simple accounting and bookkeeping, drug management, record keeping, simple health information collection (death, birth, selected diseases) and in basic communication skills. During the monthly participatory planning session, the data collected were reviewed and discussed by the health staff, the health committee members and the DHMT, and decisions were taken to improve the functioning of the health unit. One important area of discussion was the identification and achievement of the health objectives (e.g., immunization, percent of the needy population covered, improvement of nutrition) by the different villages. The chiefs of the villages were asked to mobilize the population and give support to the health unit team visiting the villages. The additional cost of this activity was covered by the money collected through cost sharing (i.e., fees for consultation and drugs).

The District Health Management Team assisted this process by regular supervision. Before the start of the Primary Health Care Project, supervision was irregular and limited to administrative aspects. The methodology and importance of supervision were discussed with the three district medical officers. Training sessions in supervision were organized for the DHMT, and supervision tools were developed. It was agreed that the supervisors would broaden the scope to include the quality of care, progress in achieving health objectives and community involvement. The three DHMTs held a monthly meeting and shared the results, progress, or problems they noted during supervision. Monthly health statistics reports prepared by health centers were reviewed at those meetings, and health center staff received quarterly feedback on their activities. At the beginning of the revitalization process, frequent visits were necessary. Afterward, on average, revitalized health centers received one supervising visit per month.

RESULTS

Utilization of Health Centers

In 1991, eight centers out of 55 were revitalized but only five had been functioning for at least one year. Those five are considered in the following analysis.

Figure 8.1 compares the before and after utilization rates for curative services in the five revitalized health centers in 1990 and 1991. The utilization rates are percentages of the total catchment populations that were new attenders (excluding patients coming from outside the catchment area) over the period of a year. There is a significant increase in the use of health centers, which after revitalization ranged from 32% to 95%. In three health centers, the utilization rates have more than doubled. The increases occurred despite the fact that patients now had to pay some fees for service. The variation in use from health center to health center can partially be explained by the fact that health centers are not equally accessible. Some have very scattered population. An important improvement was also introduced in preventive services. Before the revitalization, vaccination

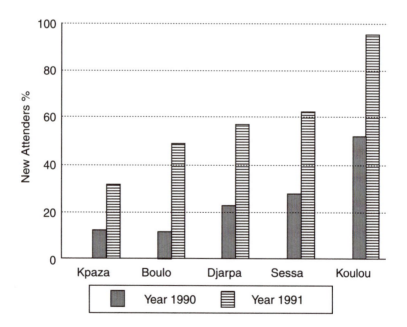

Figure 8.1. Use of health centers before and after revitalization.

campaigns had been conducted by district mobile teams on a very irregular basis. Now that health centers had resources, and were made responsible for a defined area, preventive activities were performed in a much more regular and efficient way by the health center team through outreach activities. Preventive services, including nutrition surveillance, were extended to people living in remote villages, on a more regular basis and at a lower cost than through mobile teams from the district.

Another point to underline is the gender issue, which strengthened the communities sense of ownership. An early analysis of health center data by gender and age groups showed that the centers were mostly used by women and children. They were also the first to benefit from immunization and prenatal care programs. Men complained that the health units were not fully responding to their needs. From data available at hospital and private mission health centers, hypertension was one of the common health problems in men. With the resources the health units had, it was possible to add basic essential drugs for hypertension. With the agreement of the DHMT, sphyngometers were provided to the health units, and nurses were trained in the management of hypertension at first level health units. With the introduction of this new activity, the community realized that, given some additional resources, it was possible to expand, within certain limits, the services the health units were offering.

Utilization Patterns

With the establishment of a regional drug store and a community-based management system, the use of the health units became more regular and sustained. In the past, people had gotten into the habit of rushing to the health centers as soon as drugs were delivered; the health centers were then deserted until the next drug delivery. They used the health centers in a typically sporadic fashion, with peaks corresponding to arrivals of drugs.

Figure 8.2 shows the use of health center services after revitalization. The figure gives quarterly rates for one year after implementation of the program. For several health centers, the utilization rates are more than twice the initial levels. But the most remarkable observation is the fact that, thanks to the regional store of essential drugs, drugs were always available and the utilization rates remained stable all year long.

To define the performance levels of the revitalized health centers in the region, they were regularly compared to Pagala, a reference health center run by expatriate missionary nuns. The Pagala Center was judged suitable and desirable both to the community and to health authorities. Figure 8.3 shows the utilization rates of the five health centers for the year 1991,

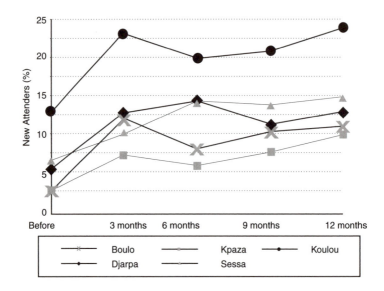

Figure 8.2. Use of health centers before and during first year of revitalization.

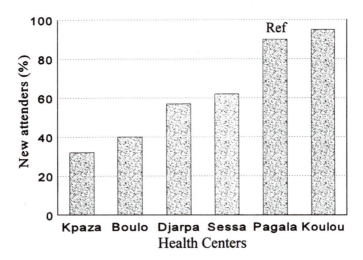

Figure 8.3. Health center utilization rates in 1991.

compared to the reference center. Although all health centers have increased their utilization rates, only one had better performance than the reference. Several reasons could explain the higher performance of the Pagala Health Center. Pagala is a small city, the population is more dense, the nuns were more qualified in health service delivery than the local nurses. The important fact is that all health centers made progress toward reaching the reference rate. This reference was considered as a challenging but realistic and reasonable goal to pursue. Having a clear goal to pursue made health centers more eager to emulate and to compete.

Payment for Health Services

Pricing and payment of health care often give rise to discussions and controversies. Who should determine prices? Should they be applied uniformly throughout the country? When should they be changed? In a study reviewing the cost recovery of public services in English- and Portuguese-speaking African countries, it was found that out of 20 countries, 15 had a national system of charging for services in place.

Among these, nine had local systems of charging patients in addition to the national systems (Nolan and Turbat 1995). For this study, prices were set by health committees after discussions with the district team. To have a level of reference the health committees could refer to the price charged by the Pagala health center. The Pagala Health Center performed well and its prices were considered reasonable with respect to financial accessibility.

The two most important issues considered by communities when fixing the prices were accessibility of services to the whole population and health center solvency. A flat rate per sickness episode was adopted. This type of payment promotes solidarity between patients because patients suffering from serious diseases pay the same amount as those with minor ones.

As shown in Figure 8.4, prices charged by health centers were not uniform. The charge per sickness episode, including consultation and drugs, varied between CFA 200 and CFA 500. Communities determined themselves how much they could pay and set prices. Three health centers had prices exceeding the reference price. It was observed that as communities start getting financial resources, their needs for improvement also increased. There was a great temptation to increase the income by increasing the fees. It was the duty of the supervisory team to raise this issue during the monthly supervision, ensure that the community take into account all aspects when setting prices, and discuss alternative solutions for raising funds.

In several African communities, paying for services is culturally well accepted (Van der Geest 1992). What is new in this project is the retention

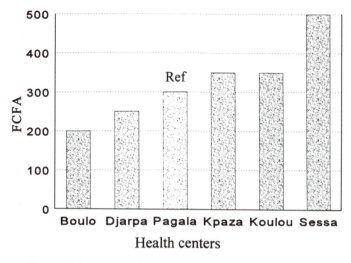

Health centers

Figure 8.4. Cost per sickness episode at health centers in 1991.

and the use of all resources (from central government and locally generated) at health center levels, as well as local co-management of the financial and human resources. Previously, patients had to pay a modest lump
sum for consultation, i.e., CFA 100 for an adult, and CFA 50 for a child.
The money collected was sent to the central government. However, since
nurses did not have enough drugs to distribute, they issued a large number
of prescriptions. Patients then had to buy their drugs from official depots
or private pharmacies.

The Problem of Patients Who Cannot Pay for Services

As stated earlier, the government granted subsidies in drugs to health centers and provided free of charge drugs for those suffering from tuberculosis and leprosy. A national social service was also giving some support,
generally food for malnourished children and pregnant women. Although
very significant, these actions were not sufficient to cover the needs of all
those who couldn't afford to pay. Consequently, for everyone to have
access to health services, the community took the initiative of instituting
an exemption system for those who cannot afford to pay the cost of care.
The DHMT decided to support this initiative. Under the recommendation
of health staff and the management committee's chairperson, some people
were exempted from paying for care and drugs. They received a certificate,
signed by the chairperson or the chief of the village, entitling them to free

care. Once again, the exemption rate of Pagala Health Center was taken as reference.

As observed for the fee levels, the exemption rates varied noticeably between health centers. In 1991, only one health center had an exemption rate exceeding the reference rate of 12% observed at Pagala. The nuns did not have formal exemption criteria, but since they have been working in the area for many years and were fully aware of the social environment, they were able to determine who needed free care, much like the community.

This 12% reference rate was considered as a maximum not to be exceeded by other health centers, because beyond this, their viability could be compromised. For example, some health centers decided to include all students in their exemption programs. This decision resulted in an over-utilization of the centers by the students, with significant decrease of income. To solve the problem, schools were encouraged to buy kits of first-aid drugs from health centers and teachers were trained to treat their pupils on the spot. They were exempted at the health center only if their school referred them. It is interesting to note that, when the decision to exempt students was taken, nobody in the community contested it. Only later on, when the students began to overuse the centers, did the community react and take corrective action, learning by doing.

At Boulo and Djarpa, a different situation was encountered: exemption rates were very low, only 2%. This suggests that the exemption criteria established by these communities were much too rigid. The problem was raised with health center staff and representatives of the communities during supervision visits. In communities where everyone considers oneself poor, it was indeed difficult to set objective criteria of poverty. A recent study of different African countries showed that in order to develop solidarity mechanisms, it is more effective to rely on the community's perception of poverty and exclusion, rather than on external predefined criteria (de la Rocque 1995).

Use of Locally Raised Funds

The fact that revenues are retained and managed locally allows communities to have control over the financial situation of their health centers. This approach ensures transparency and accountability. Communities' organizational abilities were stimulated by translating decisions into immediate action within the scope of their own financial resources, giving them the opportunity to see the results of their involvement.

Local level decision-making, however, is a process that needs to be practiced and supported, especially in the African context, where the highly centralized top-down approach through political parties has been the rule. Some communities were skeptical at first. They did not believe that they had full responsibility for the functioning of the unit. But progressively, after witnessing the results of their actions, they developed confidence in the new system and in their capacity to carry out actions. The decisions taken by the communities in the five health centers over one year covered a variety of issues, including transport for referred patients, extension of services to remote villages, services during the night, security of the health center, additions to the list of drugs, maintenance of the village pump, etc. For some issues the health committees made decisions to use money collected by the health center. Some decisions were left pending, and others were referred to district authorities. The learning exercise consisted also in defining the problems for which they needed help from external sources.

Figure 8.5 shows how revenues generated were used at the Koulou, Sessa, and Kpaza Health Centers. The way the funds were used depended on how long the center had been functioning. At the beginning, because of the initial contribution of drugs from the project, the health centers did not have to buy drugs. The most important item on the budget was usually the salary paid to support staff. Later on, health centers started spending on other items, usually in the following order of importance: reordering of drugs (40–70% of all revenues), salaries of support staff (5–13%), and

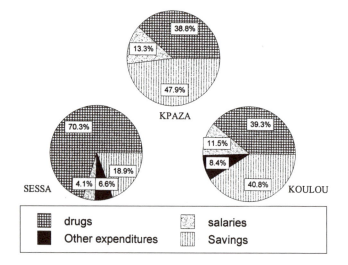

Figure 8.5. Use of funds by health centers in 1991.

miscellaneous operating costs (6–8%). The funds remaining, if any, were saved for the future.

Health centers had different incomes, depending on their frequency of use. Monthly revenues of the health centers varied between CFA 100,000 and 350,000. Because drugs and salaries have to be paid regularly on a monthly basis, the health center management committees have very little discretionary power over such recurrent costs. However, they have greater control over other operating costs (classified "other expenditures" in Figure 8.5). It is up to the committees to decide on the allocation, amount and priority of such expenditures.

Figure 8.6 shows the details of other expenditures made by the communities in 1991. The most important expenditure, representing nearly 60% of the total costs, is care for patients who are unable to pay, which demonstrates how much solidarity is valued in communities. Transportation for referred patients represents 15% of expenses, which consist of difficult deliveries or other emergencies requiring immediate evacuation. Training of staff in the form of allowances for enhancement or refresher courses at the district level, accounts for 12% of expenditures. Miscellaneous expenses (reception, purchase of books, procurement of food for patients, maintenance of village water pumps, etc.), also total 12%. Finally, maintenance of buildings and facilities accounts for 3% of the budget.

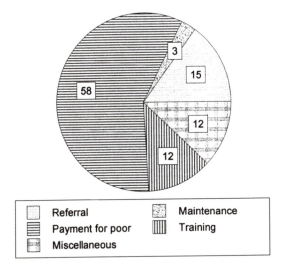

Figure 8.6. Funds allocation by communities.

Impact of Reorganization on Sustainability

Sustainability is highly dependent on the values the community gives to the program and their capacity and willingness to influence its functioning. As stated by Van Balen (1990), activities requiring efforts that jeopardize the realization of values the community considers to be more important will not be sustained. A community will strive to sustain health services only if those services respond to its needs and are within the scope of its capabilities and expertise. Two examples can be used to make this point. During the democratization process in Togo, the country went through a period of political unrest. Health centers that were best able to cope were those which had adopted co-management and cost-sharing (UNICEF 1995b). Similarly, in the area of Kasongo (in former Zaire), where support from the outside or from the district level had long ceased, health centers which relied on the principles of community participation and decentralized management were able to maintain an acceptable level of functioning in spite of economic and social deterioration (Pangu 1988).

The definition of sustainability should also include a distinction between the responsibility of governments and donors and the responsibility of communities. In the present study, capital costs, such as the purchase of expensive equipment that communities cannot normally afford, are considered a government responsibility, whether or not donors contribute. Salaries of professionals are also paid by the government. Within the limits of their capabilities, communities pay for critical components essential for improving the functioning of their health centers.

Equity and sustainability are closely related. This study shows that communities are equity conscious, and that this concern is addressed when they have the necessary power and means. Before introducing more complex systems to achieve equity, it is therefore essential to have a thorough understanding of the existing social solidarity mechanisms in communities. A good knowledge of the internal dynamics of the community will guarantee that initiatives undertaken are successful and sustainable.

CONCLUSIONS

The urgency of moving forward with health reforms is viewed as a vital consideration, and several countries in Sub-Saharan Africa have embarked on reforms. Health sector reforms are occurring in a context of democratization and reduction of resources, with communities asking for more involvement in decisions directly affecting their lives. Decentralization, an increased role for local governments, and equitable and efficient allocation are the main elements of the reforms. This study has drawn attention to the fact that success depends greatly on the capacity and the willingness of communities to add critical resources to those provided by government and external donors. Empowering the community is a process of building the community's capacity to manage their own services, improve their capacity to innovate, generate resources and improve their organizational capacity. As defined by Lecomte, scaling up is a matter of autonomy, self-reliance, and independence (see Uvin 1995, and in this volume).

Several conditions were necessary to gain the confidence of the community in such new types of management: people were well-informed of their role and function; co-management was effective and all stakeholders recognized and accepted the community's new role; existing community structures were respected and used to coordinate the activities; essential components of perceived and technical quality were in place before the introduction of any fees (i.e., a new system of drug provision). Two aspects not discussed in this chapter should also be considered: training of health staff in technical matters and in basic communication skills, and regular supervision of activities at all district levels.

Under these conditions, the study shows a significant increase in utilization rates after revitalization, despite the introduction of a fee for services. Preventive activities were extended to remote village, thanks to additional resources generated by the health units, leading to more equity in the functioning of the district health system. The system was designed to cover the whole region in 10 years. It has been adopted by other regions, and it has been considered as a model to be applied countrywide.

NOTES

1. The Bamako Initiative was launched in 1987, during the regional meeting of African Ministers sponsored by WHO and UNICEF, in Bamako, Mali. It aims at the revitalization of public health systems by decentralizing the decision-making from national to district level, reorganizing health care delivery, instituting community financing and co-management of basic health services and providing a minimum package of essential health services at the level of the basic unit. The principles of the Initiative had been adopted by more than 40 countries throughout the world.

REFERENCES

de la Rocque, M.
(1995) *Problem of Equity and Access to Health for all: Study on the Identi-fication and Support to the Poor. Synthesis Report.* UNICEF–CIDR.

McPacke, B., Hanson, K., and Mills, A.
(1992)   *Experience to Date of Implementing the Bamako Initiative: A Review and Five Case Studies.* London: London School of Hygiene and Tropical Medicine.

Nolan, B. and Turbat, V.
(1995)   *Cost Recovery in Public Health Services in Sub-Saharan Africa.* Washington: The World Bank.

Pangu, K. A.
(1988)   *Kasongo: Mission Report.* URESP–IMT. (Unpublished document)

PHCP (Primary Health Care Project), Central Region
(1991)   *Socio-Economic Survey of the Population.* Unpublished document of the GTZ (German Agency for Technical Development) project.

UNICEF (United Nations Children's Fund)
(1990)   *Strategy for Improved Nutrition of Children and Women in Developing Countries.* New York: UNICEF.

UNICEF
(1992)   *The Bamako Initiative Progress Report.* E/ICEF/1992/L.6. New York: UNICEF.

UNICEF
(1995a)   *The State of the World's Children.* 1995. New York: UNICEF.

UNICEF
(1995b)   *Workplan for 1996.* UNICEF Regional Office for West and Central Africa.

Uvin, P.
(1995)   "Fighting Hunger at the Grassroots: Paths to Scaling Up." *World Development* **23**: 6.

Van der Geest, S.
(1992)   "Is Paying for Health Care Culturally Acceptable in Sub-Sahara Africa? Money and Tradition." *Social Science and Medicine* **34**: 6.

Van Balen, H.
(1990)   "An Adequate Interface with the Community: The Contribution of the Basic Health Services." In *Implementing Primary Health Care*, eds. P. Streefland and J. Chabot. Amsterdam: Royal Tropical Institute.

World Health Organization (WHO)
(1996)   "Achieving Evidence-Based Health Sector Reforms in Sub-Saharan Africa." WHO/SHS/HSR96.

WHO–UNICEF
(1996)   *Revised 1990 Estimates of Maternal Mortality, a New Approach by WHO and UNICEF,* WHO/FRH/MSN/96.11.

CHAPTER 9

Increasing Micronutrient Intakes in Rural Bangladesh: An NGO's Search for Program Sustainability

Ted Greiner and M.A. Mannan

Innovative and practical communication combined with increased production of local foods can be both an efficient and sustainable solution to widespread micronutrient deficiency, even in the poorest countries. Given the right knowledge through exposure to modern and traditional media in a way that empowers people at the grassroots level, they themselves can overcome deficiencies which diminish the quality and shorten the length of their lives.

This chapter documents how one non-governmental organization, Worldview International Foundation (WIF), established blindness prevention programs run by local staff to address vitamin A deficiency among the poorest citizens of Bangladesh. It focuses on the innovative communication activities developed and the lessons learned on how these programs were transformed, scaled up, struggled to identify sustainable approaches, and coped with changes in the availability of donor funding over the life of their activities.

NUTRITION PROBLEMS IN BANGLADESH

Ever since winning independence from Pakistan in 1971, Bangladesh has been among the poorest countries in the world. The proportion of the population below the poverty line decreased from an estimated 73% in the early 1970s to 47% in the early 1990's, but this still placed it, along with Nepal, as one of the two poorest countries in the South Asian region (Vyas 1997). Not surprisingly, in the 1990s Bangladesh had some of the most serious nutrition problems in the world. Rates of low birth weight were on the order of 50% and rates of young child malnutrition were even higher. In the 15 years following 1980, foodgrain production has risen, however, and there is evidence of gradual improvement in rates of young child protein energy malnutrition (PEM) during that period (UNICEF 1996).

In 1982, a national survey found that vitamin A deficiency was a public health problem throughout the country (3% of preschool-age children were night blind, abbreviated as XN). Some 30,000 children were estimated to go blind annually from this unnecessary deficiency disease, about half of them dying soon thereafter (Helen Keller International and Institute of Public Health Nutrition 1985; Cohen, Rahman et al. 1985). The average dietary intake was 38% of recommended levels while only 10% of families consumed recommended levels or above. Another smaller national study in 1989 found some signs of improvement, with a rate of XN of 1.8% (Bangladesh Rural Advancement Committee 1989). Khan and Nazin (1974) found iron deficiency to be widespread, but new studies of the problem are needed. Iron consumption is less than 10 mg/day per capita, far below the requirement (ACC/SCN 1993). Some 60% of the population is at risk of iodine deficiency (UNICEF 1996) although iodized salt is becoming increasingly available throughout most of the country.

Universal Vitamin A Capsule Distribution

Throughout the 1970s and 1980s, both government and donors in Bangladesh relied almost exclusively on the "universal" vitamin A capsule (VAC) distribution program to address the vitamin A problem. Since 1973, large-dose (200,000 IU) VAC have been distributed by primary health care workers to all villages twice a year to all children six months to six years of age. Run by the Institute for Public Health Nutrition with technical support from Helen Keller International (HKI), this was funded by UNICEF although major funding came from the Swedish International Development Cooperation Agency (Sida) in 1981–1993.

In one area of the country, 100% VAC coverage was reported for two rounds in a row, reducing night blindness to nearly 1%, giving a 73% efficacy rate (Darnton-Hill, Sibanda et al. 1988). However, in most places coverage rates were so low that effectiveness was far below this level. National surveys found coverage in the previous six months to vary between 46–35% (Bangladesh Rural Advancement Committee 1989; Helen Keller International and Institute of Public Health Nutrition 1985). Thus in most areas coverage rates rarely if ever achieved the 60–65% level required to make a substantial impact on the problem (Karim, Hassan et al. 1988).[1]

WORLDVIEW INTERNATIONAL FOUNDATION INVOLVEMENT IN NUTRITION

At about the time that the first national vitamin A survey was done in 1982, the Bangladesh office of Worldview International Foundation (WIF), an international non-governmental organization with its headquarters in Sri Lanka, was looking for a serious, practical problem to which it could apply its communication skills. Registered as a non-governmental organization (NGO) under the aegis of the Ministry of Education, it had obtained funding from many donor agencies in several countries in Africa and Asia aiming to provide developing countries with self-reliant capacity in the methods and skills of mass communication. As a grassroots support organization (GRSO) in the terminology used by Uvin (1995), WIF strove to empower developing countries in the communication field where dependency on industrialized countries (and thus their views of world issues and events) has been high.

WIF decided that an innovative and practical communication approach could provide a sustainable solution to the problem of vitamin A deficiency and designed the Nutritional Blindness Prevention Programme (NBPP). WIF saw the problem of vitamin A deficiency as something that the poor could overcome themselves if they possessed the right knowledge, and felt that a mix of mass media and interpersonal, modern and traditional media could provide that information in an empowering way.

Run entirely by local staff, NBPP and an outgrowth of it called the Comprehensive Nutrition and Blindness Prevention Programme (CNBPP) have been in operation ever since. This chapter documents the evolution of this program, including its functional scaling up in 1993 into CNBPP. It focuses on the innovative activities developed and the lessons that can be learned from the way the program scaled up, struggled to identify sustainable approaches, and coped with changes in the availability of donor funding over the years.

THE PROGRAM: NUTRITION AND BLINDNESS PREVENTION

Approach

The NBPP used both modern and traditional media, interpersonal as well as mass media channels, to educate and motivate two target groups, the rural poor and the general population, "to take preventive measures which are available to them in order to reduce the number of nutritional blindness cases among children."[2] Groups of traditional folk singers were hired to give free performances in the villages, weaving messages about nutrition into their songs, chants, and playful debates. NBPP also utilized women volunteers (WVs) who became temporary paid staff, albeit with very low salaries, chosen for their interest in serving the community. The idea was to serve an entire district (usually with population of 1–2 million) for a period of about three years, and then to leave. Effective communication was thought to be capable of creating permanent change. In Korten's terminology, the NBPP was thus a second generation strategy, "developing the capacities of the people to better meet their own needs through self-reliant action" (Korten 1990).

Coverage

The WIF nutritional programs have so far covered a total population of over nine million in six districts, staying for 3–7 years in each. WIF originally obtained large grants for 7–8 years each from three donors. But in later years the WIF program received only small grants from three other donors. (See Table 9.1.)

WIF worked only in districts that had been identified as high-risk areas for vitamin A deficiency and xerophthalmia by the national survey (Cohen, Rahman et al. 1985). By 1990, WIF had developed plans for undertaking similar projects in other areas of the country, but the government requested it to complete coverage of the northern high-risk zone first. The three major donors, in one of several donor meetings held in the early 1990s, also expressed their concern that WIF would not be able to focus adequately on the three existing districts if it spread itself too thin by seeking additional donors. Ironically, this proved to be the end of an era of expanding development aid and all three of these donors had ceased funding WIF

Table 9.1. WIF Nutrition Program Donors

District	Donor	Dates
Rangpur	SMF (Norway)	1984–1989
Dinajpur (8 subdistricts)	NOVIB (Holland)	1987–1993
Lalmonirhat	SMF/NOVIB	1990–1993
Gaibandah	Sida (Sweden)	1989–1993
Thakurgaon	Sida	1993–1996
Panchagarh	Sida	1993–1996
Dinajpur (2 subdistricts)	ODA (UK)	1994–
Four districts (school gardening only)	UNICEF	1995–
Thakurgaon (4 subdistricts)	PATH (Canada)	1997–1998

within the next few years. Finding new donors for large-scale projects has proven to be nearly impossible.

Pressures for Change

The Nutritional Blindness Prevention Programme continually evolved. Staff often took initiative based on lessons learned from their own field experience, as well as observation of successful approaches developed by other NGOs. Twice new project directors were appointed and made substantial changes in program direction. Responses were made to evaluation findings and recommendations.

WIF's program was remarkable in being able to attract donors with a wide range of interests. This put great demands on management and staff flexibility. Among the first three large-scale donors, Pastor Strömme Memorial Foundation (SMF) was mainly interested in effective, empowering communication. NOVIB, a Dutch NGO, wanted to support participatory community action programs. The third major donor, Sida, was pleased to support a diet-based nutrition program, since it had for years supported the universal vitamin A capsule distribution approach. Among the three smaller-scale donors, the ODA-funded Bangladesh Ministry of Agriculture/ Department of Agricultural Extension (DAE) was interested in an agricultural project that could successfully improve diets. UNICEF wanted to support only school gardening. Partners in Advanced Technology for Health (PATH), a U.S./Canadian NGO, was interested in broad micronutrient programs, with innovative supplementation and fortification approaches, not just the diet-based aspect.

Difficulties arose when donor interests shifted. For example, NOVIB put pressure on WIF to make substantial changes in the project in response to its own consultants' project assessments. The consultants, supported by agency staff, preferred to channel support to third generation grassroots organizations (GROs). Some of NOVIB's requests were implemented and probably increased program effectiveness and sustainability such as procedures enabling women volunteers to function independently after WIF pulled out from an area.

Some of these changes fit the various categories of qualitative and quantitative scaling up mentioned by Uvin (1995) and the remainder of this chapter will discuss them accordingly.

QUANTITATIVE SCALING UP

NBPP began with a large-scale pilot study which ran for three years. Several different communication approaches were tested in three unions of the Pirgonj subdistrict or Thana (population 241,000) of Rangpur District in northern Bangladesh. The pilot study enabled project staff to learn management and other lessons that allowed replication on a larger scale to take place with a short start up time. The pilot study lasted for over two years, allowing it to cover the three stages required for scaling up to be successful, according to Greene and Kevany (1994):

> "... a process stage to test whether the proposed intervention will be effective under field conditions; a feasibility stage to determine the likelihood of achieving accepted output/outcome levels, an efficiency stage to establish optimum costs and effectiveness relationships" (p. 228).

As illustrated in Figure 9.1, scaling up to a level covering about four million people occurred quickly. It was possible to maintain implementation at about this level, shifting to new districts, for about seven years before cutting back to only about 2.3 million in 1994 and about one half million in 1997 (not counting the four-district secondary school gardening project).

The first quantitative scaling up occurred in 1987 when the final evaluation of the pilot project, contracted out to the HKI (Cohen and Mitra 1986), recommended expansion. Strömme Memorial Foundation provided funds to cover the entire district of Rangpur (1989 population about 3 million). Later that year, NOVIB funded further expansion to 8 of the 13 subdistricts in Dinajpur (about 1 million). In 1990, the districts of Lalmonirhat (1 million) and Gaibandah (2 million) were added. As Rangpur was phased out, staff were shifted to Gaibandah. When the three-year Gaibandah

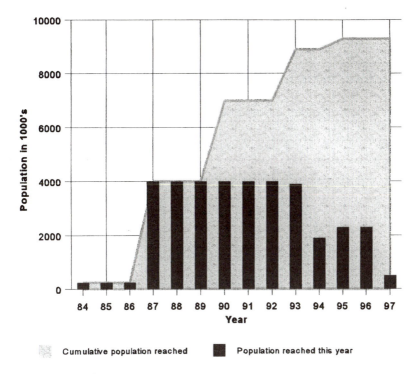

Figure 9.1. Population reached by NBPP & CNBPP.

project was completed, many staff were shifted to the districts of Thakurgaon (about 1 million) and Panchagarh (about 0.9 million). In 1995, two of the uncovered subdistricts in Dinajpur (population 0.4 million) were added for a two year period. In 1990–1992 the project was running at full scale in three districts simultaneously and staffing was at its highest level, employing 13 staff at central level, 86 staff in the districts, and 534 staff on a contract basis, mainly the women volunteers.

FUNCTIONAL SCALING UP

NBPP started as an attempt to find a good communication model to improve intakes of vitamin A. The following section describes its gradual evolution into a comprehensive micronutrient program empowering the poorest groups in one of the most neglected areas of Bangladesh to improve family health by growing, selling, and consuming better foods, and purchasing iodized salt, iron tablets and deworming medication.

Efforts to Increase Demand for Vitamin A-Rich Foods

During its early years, most project effort went into increasing demand for affordable vitamin A-rich foods.[3] During the pilot project a mass media component reached the entire district (indeed, some mass media messages reached the entire country). However, its evaluation (Cohen and Mitra 1986) found the use of schools and of folk media to be most cost-effective of the communication approaches tested. The comprehensive approach was most effective, but also most expensive.

The evaluation also recommended a new approach, the use of women motivators. Initially, these WVs worked part-time using flip charts and other media to convey messages, usually to groups of mothers. They followed up all identified cases of night blindness,[4] encouraging the parents to take these children to a health worker and to increase the amount of green leaves and other carotene-rich foods given to the children.

This first scaled-up version of the project included several other components. Using a generator, a film called "Amulyadhon" (Invaluable Treasure) about the problem of vitamin A deficiency made in the classic melodrama/comedy style was shown in the villages in the evenings. Radio spots and jingles were broadcast on national and district radio and awareness-raising messages were shown at movie theatres throughout the district. Billboards with important messages were placed at strategic locations around the district. Posters and calenders with project messages were also distributed. Homestead gardening was encouraged but not directly assisted. Forty schools were chosen in each subdistrict and given support to start school gardens, and to assist enterprising students who were inspired to start such gardens at home.

As the project expanded to other districts with other donors' support, feature articles and paid advertisements were placed in local newspapers and paid television spots were added for a limited period to reach decision-makers and educated elites to ensure they understood the problem and supported the goals of the program.

Efforts to Increase the Supply of Vitamin A-Rich Foods

In 1991 a new program director made major changes in the program. WVs began to concentrate more on helping families do homestead gardening, partly by establishing "green banks" (playing on the similar-sounding name of the famous "Grameen Bank") for seed and seedling production in model gardens at their own homes. Though intended to be given free to families with night-blind children, seeds and seedlings were to be sold to other women in their "territories" consisting of half a union, an area composed of several villages.

The mass-media approaches gradually assumed a less important role. This created controversy among some of the senior program staff who felt more at home with media than other approaches and felt that the second project director was betraying WIF's original mandate.

Homestead gardening assumed major importance. Other major changes included upgrading the WVs to full time and asking them to form women's groups which, in the name of program sustainability, were encouraged to save and borrow money to undertake income-generating projects. The poorest and landless groups were targetted for special attention. Free seed was distributed to all households for three carotene-rich vine crops that could be grown on rooftops or in nearby trees. Women's groups were organized in such a way as to combine landowners and the landless. WVs were to negotiate arrangements by which the landless did most of the work but at least got a fair share of the produce.[5]

Another change made in 1993 was to tighten targeting to the 60% of the population with less than one acre of land. This not only increased cost-effectiveness, it actually made the project easier to implement. The poorer target groups are much more interested in the small income increases offered by homestead gardening, seem to be more open to project messages, and positive toward simple new technologies for improving their health.

The "health worker approach" was included in the early stages in each Sida-funded district. Training seminars were given to the largely male cadre of health assistants to increase their knowledge of nutritional issues. By encouraging them to do home visiting with the WVs, communication with village women on all health issues was improved. Sida's intention was also to increase their awareness and that of the Ministry of Health in general on how nutrition issues could better be solved by encouraging increased production as well as consumption of nutritious foods. However, in each district WIF gradually phased out the "health worker" approach, feeling that for their goals at district level it was ineffective.

The Role of Evaluation and Research

Many changes in WIF's programs were based on the results of external evaluations. In two districts baseline surveys of reasonable quality were lacking. In one of these, a post-project survey (Hassan, Bhuyan et al. 1994) was done. In the other, a quasi-experimental design was used to measure the effects of the third year of a three-year project, comparing the project district to an equally large nearby portion of two other districts

(Greiner and Mitra 1995). Two other projects conducted on district-wide scales were evaluated using before and after surveys but without non-project comparison areas (Ali, Sukanta et al. 1993; Hussain, Kvåle et al. 1993).

The Rangpur and Dinajpur evaluations gave clear indications that household production of carotene-rich foods increased substantially and rates of night blindness decreased. One evaluation recommended increased attention to production by the poorer groups to give them the wherewithal to increase consumption (Pollard and van der Pasch 1990).

The Gaibandah evaluation (Greiner and Mitra 1995) showed that, compared to a control area, NBPP increased homestead production and particularly consumption of important foods in only one year, albeit the third year of the project. Changes in one key outcome indicator, consumption of green leafy vegetables by preschool age children, are shown in Table 9.2.

Without a comparison area, the full magnitude of the increase in consumption would not have been apparent. This is because green leafy vegetable consumption decreased in the comparison area, probably due to a collapse in the price of rice at the time. (More expensive and higher status foods than leafy vegetables are then bought to accompany the staple, rice.) In the project area, the educational messages overcame this factor and even increased consumption further.

One project review in 1992 found that night blindness usually did not disappear until green leaves were consumed in large amounts daily for months. This suggested that some other problem was also involved, probably low consumption of fat in the diet. Therefore, the message was added at that time to cook the green leaves in oil.

A study was designed to see if increased consumption of fat would indeed shorten the time required for the regression of the night blindness (Wallén 1994). Night blind children were given deworming medication and divided into two groups, one of which received 16 grams of soybean

Table 9.2 Change in the percentage of children 1–6 years of age who consumed green leafy vegetables the day before the interview

	Project Area		Non-project Area	
	%	N	%	N
March 1992	40	2559	34	2529
March 1993	52	2522	26	2518

oil daily. There was a small improvement in cure times for the group that got fat in their diets, six compared to seven weeks, but both groups got better much more quickly than had ever been experienced previously. While there were several possible explanations for this, a likely one was that the deworming had been beneficial, perhaps leading to higher levels of absorption of carotene from the diet.

Project Expansion Beyond Vitamin A Deficiency

As night blindness rates declined, WIF became interested in nutrition problems that were more severe and yet feasible for them to have an impact on: iodine and iron, the other two common micronutrient deficiencies,[6] and helminth infection and incorrect infant feeding practices.

In 1993 under a third program manager, CNBPP was functionally scaling up to include these nutrition components. The role of income generation among the women's groups was played down to increase attention on health issues. The new components are described below:

1. *Preventing iodine deficiency disorders (IDD).* In Thakurgaon and Panchagarh districts, a baseline study revealed that many villagers did not understand the importance of consuming iodized salt and very few used it. CNBPP decided not only to convey messages about this, but also to sell the salt itself, since on local markets at that time it cost twice as much as non-iodized salt. At first, high quality salt was provided. However, little was bought until WIF purchased the cheapest variety of iodized salt. Once people understood its value, they were willing to pay the extra 30–40% above the cost of locally available non-iodized salt. Women's groups say that nearly everyone uses it now. They said during group discussions in 1996 that they saw so much benefit from using it that they would continue to do so once the project left and they had to pay retail prices of up to 100% higher than for non-iodized salt.

2. *Alleviating iron deficiency/nutritional anemia.* If consumed with or close to meals, the vitamin C content of fruit would increase the iron absorption from the entire meal. As in most countries, when fruit is available it is usually only consumed between meals. But mothers said there was no taboo or objection to consuming fruit directly with or after meals, so messages were added through the various media accordingly.

For women of reproductive age, dietary improvement is not enough to offset blood loss from menstruation and pregnancy. Yet women in these districts obtained very few prophylactic iron-folate tablets from the health care sector. WIF began to supply them. By purchasing in bulk, WIF could sell iron-folate tablets via the WVs at slightly over half what these tablets cost over the counter in local pharmacies. However, pills were offered only to women presenting with pale mucous membranes. Also, the use of the same large doses recommended by health workers (3×60 mg iron per day) led to side effects.

The focus was shifted to all pregnant and lactating[7] mothers, along with the message to take just two tablets per week. This eliminated side effects, increased compliance and, since tablets were sold in 50 or 100 at a time, increased the chances that women would take them for the long periods required to improve their iron status. (Studies also suggest that taking iron once or twice a week is nearly as effective in preventing iron deficiency as taking it daily.) Women now said that they appreciated the lack of side effects and getting a benefit even if they did not remember to always take the pills on exactly the right day. Those who had taken the pills for some months said they could feel the benefit and many said they would continue to buy it at commercial rates when the project ended.

3. *Deworming*. WIF negotiated with a local drug company to produce large single-dose tablets of mabendazole (500 mg), a broad spectrum anthelminthic drug which is safe and effective against the common intestinal parasites in Bangladesh (Ascaris, hookworm and Trichuris). Sold at WIF's cost, it was much cheaper than the three-dose version available locally over the counter. Women are pleased with its low cost and the fact that it does not require them to remember to take it for three days in a row. WIF requires that families purchase one tablet for each family member (excepting any women who could possibly be pregnant and children less than two years of age) and recommends that it be taken every six months.

4. *Promoting exclusive breastfeeding*. Various fluids are given occasionally from birth onwards in Bangladesh, and thus exclusive breastfeeding for any length of time is rare. WIF now has changed its messages to the following:

—Breastfeeding should be initiated as soon after birth as the infant is rested; mother and baby should not be separated at this time; washing of the baby is best done later.
—No other feeds, not even water, should be given before five months of age; honey is actually dangerous for infants.
—Complementary foods should be provided from 5–6 months, starting with small quantities and gradually increasing the amount, but not disturbing the breastfeeding pattern. WIF is unusual in presenting information on complementation in this way. Often "weaning foods programs" pressure mothers to give so much additional food so often from such an

early age that breast milk production is probably reduced, perhaps doing more harm than good (Greiner 1996).
—Breastfeed as long as the mother and child want to, the longer the better. (In Bangladesh breastfeeding sustained even beyond 2–3 years is the major factor protecting against vitamin A deficiency (Cohen, Measham et al. 1983; Mahalanabis 1991).)

ORGANIZATIONAL SCALING UP: ACHIEVING TECHNICAL AND FINANCIAL SUSTAINABILITY

Obtaining Access to Technical Expertise

In its early years, WIF involved both government and other NGO staff in an Advisory Message Council. This group decided on which messages would be promoted by the program, vetted some of the mass media productions, chose the agency that should evaluate the pilot test, and examined and approved the evaluation methods to be used. At the beginning of the project, when training needs were high, WIF hired its own experts in agronomy, health and training. Additional technical expertise was obtained through outside experts brought in for short times by the donor agencies. They also helped spread awareness of the project in international fora. While no doubt cost-effective, this approach never put WIF in the same league as leading NGOs such as Helen Keller International (HKI) (which always had an expatriate director for its Bangladesh office) and the Bangladesh Rural Advancement Committee (BRAC), which had a research department staffed with PhDs, some of international repute. This lack of high profile expertise may partially explain the difficulty the program has had in obtaining and maintaining interest among international donors.

Staffing

One difficulty with the WIF model was that staffing needs changed greatly from the early start-up year of design, planning, and initial training to the third year and beyond after project operations were underway. Only after intervention from the three large donors did WIF shed its excess administrators and supervisors in the early 1990s.

From 1994–6, the number of beneficiaries remained quite high despite cuts in donor funds and staff levels. Nearly all central level staff, all mid-level supervisors, and half the women volunteers were dismissed. Once the WVs had established the program, project management chose the better of the two WVs hired in each union and asked her to take over the other's territory. This emergency procedure was caused by a more rapid decline in donor support than had been planned for and clearly reduced the possibility of the project to achieve sustainability after ending.

Staff reduction is painful and senior staff who were released did all they could to make life difficult for the project director and even to create public relations problems with the donors. Thus the WIF model could only work well if donor funds continued to be secured at a level adequate to allow at least senior staff always to be shifted to new districts.

Obtaining Donor Funding

NBPP and CNBPP were blessed for many years with donors who provided large grants, saving them from the disabling fate of so many NGOs, struggling to find, apply for, obtain, account for, and report on many small grants. The annual population covered, as illustrated in Figure 9.1, correlates closely with the amount of donor funds available. It can be seen that these high levels of donor funding could not be maintained in the later years. WIF's international headquarters, while stating its support for CNBPP, never translated this into financial assistance. Perhaps this is related to the functional scaling up which actually distanced CNBPP from WIF's conventional communication paradigm.

POLITICAL SCALING UP

Officially, WIF was always as averse to politics as most GRSOs in Bangladesh, and avoided being confrontational with the government at any level. The prudence of this stance became clear during a period in the late 1980s and early 1990s when the government expressed irritation that some NGOs were growing as large and powerful as its own ministries. WIF was never large or visible enough to be the target of anti-NGO action at that time.

WIF nevertheless always had a policy agenda: alleviating poverty among the poorest of the poor, a factor that enhanced program ability to reach virtually all corners of the poorer districts in which it chose to work. By the late 1980s, WIF had gained positive national attention in Bangladesh and participated in national nutrition meetings. WIF was conspicuous in avoiding the use of vitamin A capsules, even in following up tens of thousands of cases of night blindness that the WVs identified over the years. It avidly promoted the dietary approach, pointing out in its publications and in various national forums that this was the only sustainable solution for the rural poor. Gradually these efforts seemed to pay off. Though much more needs to be done, both government and donors have begun adding or increasing support to diet-based vitamin A programs. On the other hand, WIF became less dogmatic in their stance toward nutrient supplementation. CNBPP, for example, utilized iron-folate tablets along with dietary messages to prevent nutritional anemia.

LESSONS IN REPLICABILITY AND SUSTAINABILITY

The WIF approach was based on the recognition that food-based strategies do not need to achieve permanent capacity for service delivery. This point was missed for example by Greene and Kevany (1994) in their otherwise excellent discussion of sustainability in vitamin A interventions. When adequate knowledge, changes in dietary patterns and the desire to grow nutritious crops have been achieved, the people themselves, supported mainly by commercial markets (but also to some extent the educational system and agricultural extension) will sustain the necessary behaviors.

Sustainability In Gardening

From 1991, NBPP took on activities such as homestead gardening that were more complicated to sustain than communication projects. Such activities required either ongoing access to small external capital or the will and capacity to sell some produce and utilize the proceeds prudently. Most vegetables require new seed every year or two and other supplies occasionally. Without their own gardens, the poorest villagers could not afford to buy green leafy vegetables during dry seasons when they were scarce. Thus effort had to be made to find vegetables that grew round the year or at least off-season.

Review of the project in 1992 led to the realization that lack of fencing was also a threat to the sustainability of homestead gardens. A study was mounted to determine which type of live fencing would work best in the area (Andersson 1994). Since then, CNBPP has been actively promoting and assisting homestead gardeners in starting live fencing throughout its project areas.

WIF found that gardening projects with secondary schools were more sustainable than primary schools. Secondary schools, unlike primary schools, have a caretaker or other staff to attend to gardens year round, including during holiday periods when school is not in session.

Project Duration

NBPP intended to make permanent behavior changes while spending only three years in each district, without subsequent integration into any government or other long-term programs. This entailed rapid implementation followed by rapid withdrawal in district after district. In fact, in a few places the project remained for longer periods, in Dinajpur almost six years. The Gaibandah evaluation (Greiner and Mitra 1995) suggested that each project should be run for at least four or five years per district.

NBPP's large-scale three-year pilot period allowed recruitment of basic staff, development of training materials and methods, and purchase of some of the necessary infrastructure. Still, it went to a much larger scale so quickly that capacity building had to be done at management and field levels simultaneously. All of this required project start-up times longer than the span of donor patience in many cases.

Sustainability of Project Impact

The Rangpur evaluation survey was repeated in 1992, three years after project completion, in an attempt to examine the extent to which its effects were sustainable for that period of time (Hussain and Kvåle 1996). The findings were ambiguous. But the study design may have been inappropriate to judge whether the success of a project such as NBPP was sustainable on a district scale (population 3 million).

Another study (Greiner 1997) suggested that the increase in household production and consumption of high-carotene foods in Rangpur and other WIF districts appeared to be sustainable three years later. A qualitative rapid assessment based on interviews with a few local vegetable salesmen and vegetable seed salesmen was done in five towns where NBPP had been implemented. It found that sales of carotene-rich varieties and seeds for growing them were still increasing in 1992 at a faster rate than that of other types of vegetables. In discussing reasons for this uneven rate of increase, nearly all salesmen came to the conclusion that "propaganda" for vitamin A was the likely explanation. Most could remember components of NBPP, particularly the traditional folk singers.

Steps Toward Achieving Financial Sustainability

Starting in the 1990s, WIF began testing ways to earn or at least recover money from selling seeds, seedlings, iodized salt, iron tablets, and deworming medication. Profit making was against the welfare orientation of the staff, so there was resistance to this at first. But even at its most successful, the amounts that could be earned were inadequate to keep the project going on a large scale.

CONCLUSIONS

The WIF nutrition programs grew and evolved, scaled up in usually "opportunistic" ways, responding to pressures from donors and government, to the need to be competitive with other NGOs ("stealing" successful ideas from them and having their own successes replicated in this clandestine fashion), and responding to feedback from the field. Powerful projects like this one actually result in changes in society that in turn trigger changes in project functioning and priorities. Some donors were more flexible than others in allowing WIF to make changes as needed, even when this resulted in funds being spent in ways that differed from initial project plans and budgets.

This kind of dynamic project is not without a down side, and this may explain why so few like it can be found. Huge changes in the need for personnel, especially at higher levels, put enormous strains on program managers. Only when a new director came into place were changes in staffing at higher levels made on the basis of identifying dynamic, productive or highly trained personnel. If this resulted in senior staff being bypassed for promotion, they created trouble. When changes were made in the overall direction and approach, staff who had been with the project from the outset attempted to sabotage it, realizing that they would lose control.

While some of the management practices mentioned here may seem sound and undramatic within the business world, certainly in the public sector in most developing countries workers expect job security as long as funds are available no matter what their performance. WIF's managers' failure to deal successfully with the kind of resentment that arose several times in WIF's history was a major failure. But it should be kept in mind that most NGOs may deal with unproductive staff by simply keeping them as long as donor funds are available. These same management practices may be one more explanation for the surprisingly low cost per capita of the WIF approach, discussed below.

By persevering, NBPP and its successor CNBPP have provided us with rare lessons on how to solve micronutrient deficiency problems on a large scale in ways that are likely to be sustainable. One example of such a lesson is when the project changed from a pure communication approach to one that combined activities designed simultaneously to increase the supply and also demand for nutritious foods. This overcame the major problem with diet-based social marketing efforts: if demand for foods increases more than supply, there is a period when the poor are priced out of the market.

When markets are poorly responsive, this period could be so long as to have serious harmful effects on the very groups suffering most from these deficiencies. The converse occurs in gardening or other programs designed only to increase the supply of certain foods. Seasonal foods like vegetables cannot be stored and are subject to large drops in farmgate prices when sold in local markets. Gardening programs aimed at growers too small to transport produce long distances lead to great disappointment when this year's prices are far below last year's. Many small-scale growers trying a new crop for the first time quit, not having the economic means to wait for market demand to increase over a period of several years.

Another important lesson has to do with program targeting. Often tight targeting causes political difficulty as more powerful groups closer to the middle class resent being excluded. WIF's approach included only minor income transfer components, and thus exclusion of wealthier groups may not have been so controversial. Targeting the 60% who were landless or near-landless increased cost-effectiveness but still may have included enough of the community to avoid being labelled as a low-status "charity" activity. Resentment by richer excluded groups may also have been avoided by focusing on assisting households to increase production of foods of low status like green leafy vegetables.

WIF successfully walked the tightrope faced in selecting the size of pilot projects. If they are too large in scale, then the many changes required in design, training, and management result in debilitating shifts in project routines and high costs for retraining. If the scale of pilot projects is too small, then the lessons learned may not be applicable to the wider society. Lessons learned on smaller projects may be misleading because large scale implementation changes the roles and influence that highly trained and motivated managers and supervisors can have. Failure to find mid-level managers and supervisors with vision and motivation may explain the failure of most pilot projects to go to scale successfully.

WIF benefitted from the experienced technical support provided to the program from other NGOs in the field, particularly an early country director of Helen Keller International. Too often donors fail to seek ways to encourage this kind of cooperation among NGOs. Cooperation rarely emerges without positive leadership, since NGOs are always in competition for limited donor funds.

WIF's poor ability to explain the uniqueness and value of what it does in an international context may explain the program's inability to attract continued large-scale donor support. Assisted minimally by "outside" technical staff, with a stripped down management and supervisory structure and most work done by very poorly paid women volunteers, WIF reached millions of people at a per capita annual cost of US $0.13 (Greiner and Mitra 1995) a small fraction of what other programs designed to change diets have cost.

But the absence of highly trained technical staff sharply reduced the capability of WIF to communicate and interpret these successful results to government and international summit organizations. Thus one central question remains: is substantial investment in the capacity to communicate between the summit and the grassroots a necessity if NGOs are to maintain their financial viability over the long run?

NOTES

1. However, higher coverage rates were later achieved by linking vitamin A distribution to national vaccination campaigns.

2. Cited from WIF Bangladesh Newsletter, Winter 1983–84.

3. WIF focused on inexpensive sources of vitamin A in the diet, the plant source called carotene which the body converts to vitamin A. Foods of low status like green leafy vegetables were focused on, "self-targeting" to the poor.

4. This is an early sign of clinical vitamin A deficiency, sometimes designated XN. While XN is only slightly debilitating, if the deficiency gets worse, or if a serious disease like measles occurs, the child can go permanently blind and even die.

5. Sustainability of such arrangements eventually proved to be impossible to achieve. Once the gardening work improved the quality of the land, the landowners often took it back, so this approach was dropped.

6. This term was coined to cover the three nutrients vitamin A, iron and iodine, indicating that only small amounts are needed.

7. On the whole, lactation does not harm maternal iron status. Since it delays the return of menstruation, it may actually improve iron status among those women who have higher than average menstrual flows and thus are more at risk of iron deficiency. However, since breastfeeding lasts so long in Bangladesh, about 2½ years on average, substantial periods of iron tablet consumption would be achieved if women took it throughout pregnancy and lactation.

REFERENCES

Administrative Committee on Coordination-Subcommittee on Nutrition (ACC/SCN) (1993) *Second Report on the World Nutrition Situation.* Geneva: ACC/SCN.

Ali, S. M. K., Sukanta, S., Bhuyan, M. A. H., Ahmed, N., Abdullah, M., and Malek, M. A.
  (1993) "Comparative Analysis of Different Media Approaches in the Prevention of Nutritional Blindness in Selected Communities in Bangladesh." *Bangladesh Journal of Nutrition* **6**(1–2): 5–13.

Andersson, A.
  (1994) "A Study on Small-scale Vegetable Gardening with Special Focus on Live Fences." Working Paper 267. Uppsala, Sweden: Swedish University of Agricultural Sciences, International Rural Development Centre.

Bangladesh Rural Advancement Committee (BRAC)
  (1989) "Nutritional Blindness Prevention Programme Evaluation Report." Dhaka: BRAC.

Cohen, N., Measham, C., Khanum, M., and Ahmed, N.
  (1983) "Xerophthalmia in Urban Bangladesh." *Acta Paediatrica Scandinavica* **72**: 531–6.

Cohen, N. and Mitra, M.
  (1986) "Worldview International Foundation Bangladesh Media Campaign for the Prevention of Nutritional Blindness: Evaluation." Dhaka: Helen Keller International.

Cohen, N., Rahman, H., Sprague, J., Jalil, M. A., Leemhuis deRegt, E., and Mitra, M.
  (1985) "Prevalence and Determinants of Nutritional Blindness in Bangladeshi Children." *World Health Statistics Quarterly* **38**: 317–30.

Darnton-Hill, I., Sibanda, F., Mitra, M., Ali, M. M., Drexler, A. E., Rahman, H., and Samad Khan, M. A.
  (1988) "Distribution of Vitamin A Capsules for the Prevention and Control of Vitamin A Deficiency in Bangladesh." *Food and Nutrition Bulletin* **10**(3): 60–70.

Greene, J. and J. Kevany
  (1994) "Projects to Programmes: an International Perspective." *Food and Nutrition Bulletin* **15**(3): 227–32.

Greiner, T.
  (1996) "The Concept of Weaning: Definitions and Their Implications [published erratum appears in JHL 12: 220]." *Journal of Human Lactation* **12**(2): 123–28.

Greiner, T.
  (1997) "Rapid Appraisal before Impact Evaluation Studies." Letter to the editor. *World Health Forum* **18**: 66–67.

Greiner, T. and Mitra, S. N.
  (1995) "Evaluation of the Impact of a Food-based Approach to Solving Vitamin A Deficiency in Bangladesh." *Food and Nutrition Bulletin* **16**(3): 193–205.

Hassan, N., Bhuyan, M. A. H., and Jahan, K.
(1994) "Nutrition Interventions as a Strategy for Combating Nutritional Blindness in Selected Rural Locations of Bangladesh." *Bangladesh Journal of Nutrition* **7**(1–2): 5–11.

Helen Keller International and Institute of Public Health Nutrition
(1985) "Bangladesh Nutritional Blindness Study 1982-83: Key Results." *Bangladesh Journal of Child Health* **9**(4): 252–61.

Hussain, A. and Kvåle, G., Ali, K., and Bhuyan, A. H.
(1993) "Determinants of Night Blindness in Bangladesh." *International Journal of Epidemiology* **22**: 1119–26.

Hussain, A. and Kvåle, G.
(1996) "Sustainability of a Nutrition Education Programme to Prevent Nightblindness in Bangladesh." *Tropical Medicine and International Health* **1**(1): 43–53.

Karim, R., Hassan, N., and Darnton-Hill, I.
(1988) "Public Policies and Vitamin A Intake in Bangladesh." *Bangladesh Journal of Nutrition* **1**(2): 5–12.

Khan, M. R. and Nazir, F. H.
(1974) "Iron Deficiency Anaemia in Infancy and Childhood—a Review of 25 Cases." *Bangladesh Paediatrics* **1**(1): 1–5.

Korten, D.
(1990) *Getting to the 21st Century, Voluntary Action and the Global Agenda.* West Hartford, CT: Kummarian Press.

Mahalanabis, D.
(1991) "Breast Feeding and Vitamin A Deficiency among Children Attending a Diarrhoea Treatment Centre in Bangladesh: a Case Control Study." *British Medical Journal* **303**(6801): 493–6.

Pollard, R. and van der Pasch, N.
(1990) "WIF Bangladesh NBPP Final Evaluation for NOVIB." Dhaka: NOVIB.

UNICEF
(1996) *The Progress of Nations.* New York, UNICEF.

Uvin, P.
(1995) "Fighting Hunger at the Grassroots: Paths to Scaling Up." *World Development* **23**: 927–39.

Wallén, A.
(1994) "A Field Trial to Reduce the Time Required to Cure Nightblindness Due to Vitamin A Deficiency." Minor Field Study 68, Uppsala, Sweden: Unit for International Child Health, Uppsala University.

Vyas, V. S.
(1997) *Poverty Alleviation and Nutrition Enhancement in South Asia—the Missing Links.* Symposium on Nutrition and Poverty, ACC/SCN Annual Meeting, Kathmandu.

III Assessment in Partnership with the Grassroots

Community-Based Assessment of Nutritional Problems: Scaling Up Local Actions; Scaling Down Top-Down Management

Ellen Messer

Since the mid-1980s, community-based techniques for gathering ethnographic data have become a regular part of international health, nutrition, and environmental planning. Used by researchers, policy makers, and field practitioners, these qualitative data collection methods have been designed to improve program effectiveness by providing timely community-level information for project planning, implementation, and monitoring. As a supplement to quantitative survey methods, ethnographic data provide critical information on cultural beliefs and behaviors influencing nutritional health and the impacts of nutritional interventions within and among communities. The data allow development professionals to "scale down" summit-level policies to meet more appropriately the particular needs or conditions of local communities. They also suggest possibilities for "scaling-up" local community actions (see chapter by Uvin, this volume) to address development problems more widely across regions, countries, or development domains.

Additionally, the methods themselves, to the extent that they are participatory, have the potential to empower localities and leaders. The methods can be used to organize communities to respond to data collection initiatives, teach local individuals to collect and analyze data systematically, and create new communication channels between communities and sources of political or material resources.

This chapter reviews and compares the applications of these techniques— RAP (Rapid Assessment Procedures), RRA (Rapid Rural Appraisal), and PRA (Participatory Rural Appraisal)—in different nutrition-related domains (food, health, and care); in different parts of the world (Latin America, Africa, Asia); by different actors (researchers, policy makers, program practitioners). It probes especially the extent to which methods have been participatory and with what implications for community empowerment.

Nutrition problems are multisectoral, and innovative strategies for addressing them often arise when the community is consulted directly, and allowed (or encouraged) to mobilize, collect and analyze data, establish priorities, and act on and through a self-constructed plan of action, usually based on successful mobilization of resources from outside agencies. Although the origins of these techniques lie in the practical needs of program planners and decision makers (N. Scrimshaw and Gleason 1992), they demonstrate potential to set in motion community organizing for ongoing, multi-sectoral nutrition-related improvements.

THE METHODS: COMMUNITY-BASED ASSESSMENT TECHNIQUES

Community-based assessment techniques share a common objective, which is to elucidate socioeconomic conditions and nutrition-related beliefs and behaviors of the rural and urban clients nutrition programs are meant to serve. Drawing local people into the research as "experts," they employ observation, interview, and interactive techniques to explore individual and household perceptions of nutrition problems in their cultural context. Research is field-based and investigates local knowledge by means of clearly established protocols promulgated in manuals, guides, or newsletters. Findings are used to help food and nutrition programs overcome constraints in terms that ideally meet the needs of both clients and service-providers. Although the immediate goal is usually a nutrition intervention, many community-based assessment activities carry longer-term objectives of establishing the principle of community participation and the value of ethnographic data for nutrition planning.

Rapid Assessment Procedures (RAP)

RAP methodology (S. Scrimshaw and Hurtado 1987; N. Scrimshaw and Gleason 1992) originated as an anthropological research tool, designed to provide rapid but reliable sociocultural data to improve nutrition interventions. It was intended to complement more standard KAP (epidemiological knowledge, attitudes, practice) nutritional-health survey data, and so contribute to more effective nutrition, health, and family-planning programs. A long-term Institute of Nutrition for Central America and Panama (INCAP) study of health and nutrition on a Guatemalan farming estate had found conventional epidemiological survey inadequate by itself. The INCAP study integrated findings from qualitative ethnographic interviewing and observation into the interpretation of quantitative epidemiological survey data. Encouraged by these Central American results, researchers in 1982 with support from the United Nations University (UNU) designed a 16-country "pilot" comparative study of household perceptions of primary health care needs and program effectiveness (S. Scrimshaw 1992).

Each pilot study was supposed to follow a common set of procedures spelled out in a methods manual that detailed ways "focus groups" and structured question frames could be used to produce rapid but reliable and cross-culturally comparable information on household-level health-seeking behaviors. *The RAP Guidelines*, as the manual was later renamed, also suggested multiple observation and interview formats that would allow "triangulation" and verification of findings. S. Scrimshaw and Hurtado had designed and issued the protocol in 1983–84, but in its republication, the methodology was given a feisty and attractive identity ("RAP") to attract attention (S. Scrimshaw and Hurtado 1987).

The RAP concept is in essence anthropological; it focuses on the community, its social-political-economic contexts, and the cultural nutritional and health behaviors of local actors. Studies begin with background cultural and ethnographic reconnaissance. They then use direct observations, structured and open-ended interviews with individuals, especially "key informants," and "focus group" discussions to bring community members into the process of design, evaluation, and mid-course correction of health and nutrition programs (S. Scrimshaw and Hurtado 1987).

RAP departs from standard anthropological research in that field research is short-term (several weeks versus several years), focused on specific (nutrition) problems and programs rather than some larger socio-cultural domain, and is designed to involve community members (insiders) in framing issues and some data analysis. RAP derives from "applied anthropology," which also tends to be short-term, highly focused community-based research, and uses a multi-disciplinary research team approach that often formally includes one or more individuals in the group under study. It also develops training materials specifically for use by local participants, and employs multiple data collection tools to cross-check and improve reliability of information through triangulation and iterative data collection and analysis.[1] Although efforts to improve nutrition and health—and nutritional-health inventions—by more sensitive attention to social and cultural beliefs, behaviors, and contexts were not new in public health or "applied anthropology" (e.g., Richards 1939; Paul 1955; Adair and Deuschle 1970; Montgomery and Bennett 1979), the new methods offered standard research protocols and used formal methods to an unprecedented degree.

Moving beyond anthropology, RAP is also methodologically eclectic. It adds to standard ethnographic methods of direct (participant) observation and interview the tools of "formal analysis" pioneered by market researchers in the 1920s, especially "structured" or "focus" group interviews, and communications analysis. A focus group interview convenes a number of carefully selected local participants, representing desired elements of a community, to probe in greater depth cultural knowledge touching on a principal issue under investigation, such as diarrheal disease classifications (S. Scrimshaw and Hurtado 1988) or beliefs surrounding breastfeeding (Griffiths 1992). It is characterized by anthropologists "... as a complementary tool which supports data gathered by other research methods" (Khan and Manderson 1992).

Studies focusing on food preferences or illness beliefs and behaviors sometimes add other systematic data collection techniques, such as (food) pile sorts or pair comparisons, or free-association listings of concepts or attitudes associated with particular foods or illness symptoms. Studies which make extensive use of such structured data collection techniques have been labelled "focused ethnographic studies" to distinguish them from simpler RAP (e.g., Pelto and Gove 1992). "Formative research" adds techniques from communications research to construct more effective messages to improve infant feeding, micronutrient intakes, or oral rehydration. Relevant behaviors are dissected into a series of discrete steps, which indicate antecedent and consequent behaviors that upset nutrition or impair the effectiveness of interventions. Health practitioners then incorporate such understandings into messages and other interventions intended to bring about desirable behavioral changes (Creed et al. 1991). Additionally, RAP methods and manuals are increasingly aimed at non-anthropologist professional audiences, especially health-providers. This has led some anthropologists to charge that the anthropological mission of elucidating the cultural construction of health, nutrition, and the human place in the cosmos, has been so subordinated to utilitarian methods that RAP is "bereft of the theoretical and epistemological grounds from which the discipline's [anthropology] methods derive" (Good 1992).

RRA (Rapid Rural Appraisal)

RRA has distinct but overlapping origins from RAP. Like RAP, these community-based methods were a response to the perceived limitations of large-scale demographic and socioeconomic surveys and policy-makers' demands for more timely, reliable data for rural development planning. Originating in the 1970s to 1980s, RRA had as a goal to develop tools to demonstrate systematic local knowledge that might be of use for policy makers, and to introduce the concept of community participation in problem diagnosis on a range of health, economic, environmental, and nutritional issues (International Institute for Environment and Development 1988–1991). RRA extracts information on local perceptions of ecology, nutrition, and health from rural folk scheduled to be affected by a program, and offers such findings to improve programs otherwise designed from the top-down.

RRA draws on methods from rural sociology, geography, and anthropology to discern local community perceptions of ecology, social organization, natural resources, nutrition, and health. In addition to conversations, the approach employs a number of visual techniques to elicit indigenous notions and orderings of natural resources, social relations, technology, and economic conditions (Chambers 1992). Community members participate in social and natural resource mapping and modelling, data collection on transect walks, construction of seasonal food availability calendars, and analytical institutional diagrams. Researchers also use innovative oral, visual, and occasionally dramatic tools or stories to elicit information. Methodologies are tailored to exploratory, topical, monitoring, or participatory goals of specific research with the overall goal always to demonstrate systematic local knowledge that can help facilitate and improve policy interventions (Chambers 1994a).

RRA as a cost-effective and reliable source of information, pioneered especially in India, has been used widely throughout the world. Experiences were published by the London-based International Institute for Environment and Development *RRA Notes* (1988–1991) and other newsletters. A detailed discussion of RRA methodology is presented in Frankenberger's chapter (this volume).

Participatory Rural Appraisal (PRA)

PRA, the most explicitly participatory of the techniques, has been described as "a family of approaches and methods to enable rural people to share, enhance, and analyze their knowledge of life and conditions, to plan and to act" (Chambers 1994a:953). Initiated in the mid-1980s, PRA has community-centered development as its central principle and indigenous knowledge at its core. RRA moved toward "participatory" RRA at a conference in Khun Kaen, Thailand, in 1985. There were also simultaneous developments in India by the Aga Khan Rural Support Programme and the International Institute for Environment and Development. In 1988, Clark University developed a series of PRA projects and handbooks that have been used in Asia and Africa.

In PRA, researcher-practitioners begin by consulting community members on what they consider to be priorities, and develop action plans with respect to local knowledge and interests. The approach assumes villagers have valuable knowledge and information, resources, and ideas that can be mobilized to improve their lives and also to generate additional external sources of assistance (Ford et al. 1992).

Studies use a standard methodology that begins by assembling community members into groups according to gender, age, occupation, or other principle. These groups then are asked to map out spatial, temporal, and institutional frameworks significant for analyzing their social, economic, political, or health conditions. The group process leading to group product spotlight key variables and relationships that enable insiders and outsiders to identify and discuss "bottlenecks" that interfere with their well-being. The next steps are for each group to agree on certain priority needs or demands to improve their well-being, and village well-being, and to establish an action plan to remove obstacles and acquire materials or information to meet priority goals.

Drawing community toward consensus often involves considerable and delicate negotiations because interests and priorities usually differ among actors. Participatory procedures, in other words, have the potential to pit male elders against younger working females, or one occupational group against another, and to elicit evidence of intra-community differences in perceptions of resources and constraints. Well-run research exercises and projects, with good leadership, often use principles of conflict resolution to improve intergroup communications and respect for differences across groups in an atmosphere of mutual respect.

PRA's techniques have influenced or absorbed dimensions of RAP and RRA, but also trace their origins to activist participatory research, agro-ecosystem analysis, and field-based farming systems research (Chambers 1994a,b,c). From activist research, such as Freire's *Pedagogy of the Oppressed*, PRA emphasizes participant analysis of conditions and involvement in finding solutions, and creates research contexts that consciously value indigenous culture, especially technical knowledge. From agro-ecosystem analysis pioneered in Chang Mai, Thailand, are drawn expanded techniques to map resources in time and space; and from farming systems research comes a focus on successful and innovative farmers who have something to teach other farmers, close to home or across the world.

Like RAP and RRA, PRA involves principles of field-based, rapid, face-to-face learning from rural people; key informants, group interviews, and key indicators; multiple mapping, quick quantification, a variety of visual, written, and oral methods including stories as well as models and responses to questionnaires; and triangulation to cross-check information from multiple sources or methods. However, in the case of PRA in contrast to RAP or RRA, the outside investigator is more convener, catalyst, and facilitator than extractor of information and framer of programs.

Significantly the menu of methods has by now moved out of rural into urban areas, creating a misnomer leading some to delete one "R" in RRA.

APPLICATION OF RAP, RRA, AND PRA ACROSS NUTRITION DOMAINS

RAP, Nutrition, and Health

The initial set of RAP studies covered perceptions of primary health care and nutrition program effectiveness in sixteen "pilot" country studies and then were expanded into additional countries (Messer 1990, 1991). Results, methodological adaptations, and accomplishments were shared in workshops, a newsletter (*RAP News*), and monographs, which reported the ways in which RAP was being extended to address additional nutrition-related problems. Between 1985 and 1992 RAP researchers published focused protocols and findings on diarrheal disease (S. Scrimshaw and Hurtado 1988) and acute respiratory infections (Pelto and Gove 1992)—both illnesses that interact synergistically with malnutrition, especially in children. In addition, RAP methods were adopted to improve nutrition surveillance (Pelletier 1992), breast-feeding and child-feeding practices (Griffiths 1992), including appropriate child-feeding following illness (Bentley et al. 1988). Health care studies also published results, pinpointing where lack of food, time constraints, or water rather than health care resources appeared to be the central reasons for underutilization of primary health care (e.g., Novaes da Mota and Cardoso Neiva 1990; Hurtado 1990).

As RAP methodologies extended to additional countries and contexts, some researchers sought ways to introduce the utilization of RAP methods to community health care providers (Hurtado 1990), public health and medical personnel (Gittelsohn et al. 1998), and policy planners. They hoped that by involving health providers and policy makers more in health behavior studies:

> ... the problems ... would emerge from the communities and programmes themselves; information would be obtained on current conditions, not after the fact; feedback would be continuous; and the results could be applied to the programmes themselves (Hurtado 1990:310).

Although RAP, up until this point, had been aimed at social science researchers, UNICEF's Child Survival Program and then INCAP designed simplified RAP guides for health volunteers, health promoters, auxiliary nurses, and rural health technicians.

NGOs adopted a booklet entitled "What Every Health Worker Should Find Out About the Community Where He Works". The booklet suggests relevant questions for health and nutrition programs; describes techniques of observation, interview, and group discussion procedures to facilitate data collection and involve the community to obtain answers to these questions; and indicates how to use the information obtained, such as how to categorize the information into simple "positive" or "negative" health beliefs or behaviors. Health care providers also are advised to become involved in community organizations and to participate in helping to solve the problems that community members see as most urgent, many of which, such as lack of tap water or latrines, are nutrition and health-related (Hurtado 1994).

A 1990 RAP workshop, a five-year assessment of methods and impacts (N. Scrimshaw and Gleason 1992), highlighted certain dimensions of "scaling up" of RAP methods by RAP researchers, practitioners, and RAP-initiated community groups. Researchers working in Nepal and Guatemala, in two cases of "functional" scaling up, reported that community groups that had been convened in those countries around the original RAP health behavior research protocol had continued to meet to address additional concerns, especially water and hygiene (Shrestha 1992; Hurtado 1994). These case studies suggested that community focus groups that had formed around health-related RAP were "scaling up" functionally and politically to address additional (nutritional and non-nutritional) domains and reaching out to additional sources of power and material resources.

Policy makers in NGOs (Helen Keller International and Plan International) and inter-government (UNICEF and WHO) agencies also presented evidence of functional "scaling up" as they adapted RAP to address their additional micronutrient or child survival priorities and reached out to more communities on more nutrition and health issues.

Adaptations of RAP were also used by UNICEF, USAID, and partner Ministries of Health to expand and tailor growth-monitoring to local community behaviors, customs, and expectations (experiences are summarized in Griffiths, Dickin, and Favin 1996).

Unfortunately, not all that is labelled "RAP" follows RAP (or any other) standard methodology; not all "rapid" assessment is quick (there seems to be no standard time criterion or in most cases, significant measurement), and not all data produced by methods labelled "RAP" are reliable (again, there appears to be no standard or evaluation for reliability). Manderson and Aaby (1992), summarizing these faults, emphasize that only certain kinds of focused information can be collected in a short time, and that researchers or others collecting the data need considerable training to be able to frame and describe questions and answers appropriately.

An additional concern that began to be raised around this time was what would be the future role of social scientists in RAP. The value and potential contribution of anthropology to nutrition and health come from "seeing" as an anthropologist, and entail much more than mastery of a methods manual on a focused disease or nutritional problem (Manderson and Aaby 1992). Anthropologists cautioned that health personnel learning techniques to elicit relevant health beliefs and practices should not confuse themselves that they can replace social scientists, any more than anthropologists, carrying the medical manual, *Donde No Hay Doctor* ("Where there is no doctor"), should consider themselves medical experts. The same clearly applies to nutrition workers.

Simply stated, the ideal of social- and health-professionals creating effective partnerships at multiple levels with each other and with communities, is still somewhat distant. Service-providers using RAP manuals can increase their sensitivities to sociocultural factors, and such sensitivities with careful follow-up very likely can help improve design and delivery of nutritional services. One notable success story is the design of growth-monitoring tools that teach health workers how to "negotiate" with mothers to improve feeding behaviors, based on scientific nutritional recommendations and mothers' understandings and resources (Griffiths 1994).

But RAP manuals do not automatically create social contexts or dynamics for communities to become real partners in nutritional-health programs, or to take more responsibility for their own health care. Nor do RAP manuals usually prepare practitioners to intuit the most critical information on community structure or dynamics or provide guidance on how to tailor data collection to problems encountered in particular communities. Focus group methodology, after all, was designed to answer very specific questions and in many social contexts is not appropriate for identifying or resolving the underlying social structural causes of health problems (see Dawson, Manderson, and Tallo 1993).

RRA/PRA for Food Production and Environmental Protection

Although the initial focus in RRA and PRA, in contrast to RAP, was on natural resource management (watershed, forestry, fishery management), agriculture (especially farming systems), and small-scale anti-poverty programs (especially credit), the methods have been used also for food security assessment and monitoring, especially in disaster-prone areas.

Another arena for rapid assessment is emergency situations where rapid appraisal of political or ecological conditions, nutrition needs, and social capacities (including conflict potential) may make the immediate difference between life and death, and sustainable reconstruction thereafter. Agencies such as CARE are developing RRA methods to address short and medium-term needs in such settings (see Frankenberger, this volume). CARE has employed RRA to identify food-insecure groups, describe and monitor nutritionally adequate diet, and target interventions more effectively. CARE also has gone beyond a narrower concept of food security to explore "livelihood security", especially in situations where former war-torn populations are moving from reliance on relief to self-reliant development (see Frankenberger, this volume). Thus community-based rapid ethnographic methods offer great potential for a variety of nutritional ends, but have yet to be fully implemented.

Slocum et al. (1995) summarize a series of PRA projects by focal problem and country. Most focus on local resource (including food) management. They differ from more conventional participatory research and programs, such as farming systems or "farmer first" research (see Rhoades 1984), in that they focus on understanding and working through community structures and allow communities to set priorities, rather than working with individual farmers or households and having outside experts set the agenda.

An exemplary PRA series is the Ecology, Community Organization, and Gender (ECOGEN) initiative, a joint research project of Clark University and Virginia Polytechnic Institute and State University. With members of project communities, ECOGEN researchers explored alternative approaches to resource management, and also identified changing forms of community organization and clarified important gender-based factors arising in the community-level management of resources. Between 1990 and 1993 teams conducted research in Kenya, Honduras, the Philippines, the Dominican Republic, and Nepal (Thomas-Slayter et al. 1993). Significantly, given the droughts that had visited southern and eastern Africa in the mid-1980s, several African communities who used PRA identified water as the priority issue in environmental management (Ford et al. 1992); and Kenyan studies focused on gendered knowledge of critical livelihood resources, including foraged famine foods, a priority concern during the previous decade. PRA mapping exercises demonstrated, not surprisingly, that women and men, and those of older or younger age, perceive environmental resources, work loads, or social institutional structures and influences differently and have different priorities. Yet using methods of conflict resolution, researchers managed to join interests of younger women and older men into a workable plan to improve water supply.

The food domain of nutrition also raises issues of food production and environmental management. Integrated pest management (IPM), which relies very heavily on widespread community and household-level cooperation, poses a very different set of organizational issues for scientists seeking the participation of hundreds of thousands of farmers. In one outstanding case, Cornell University rural sociologists in 1991 joined forces with the Indonesian National IPM Program (INIP) to try to eliminate a plague of rice stem borers on the island of Java. Involving "farmers as experts," the program documented an immense effort to understand and encourage natural predators of the borer as the best means of pest control. In a mammoth undertaking of RRA that involved farmer participation, an INIP pilot program trained farmers to monitor insect conditions and to intervene when they noted impending infestations of rice borers. Removing egg masses was the most reliable means of thwarting the plague; farmers also set moth traps, and reared insect predators for release. The project reported successfully having mobilized 400,000 adults and children to remove egg masses, and the report (INIP 1991) celebrated the community ability to collect data, diagnose the insect problem, and organize a successful response to save the rice crop.

PRA, in contrast to RRA, usually has as an objective of community organization and participation in the project design, implementation, and evaluation process. The approach has spread laterally—country-to-country—with LDC NGOs and trainers rather than government organizations or operations taking the lead in disseminating the tools of community-based and centered analysis (Chambers 1994b,c). Practitioners describe PRA as different from RRA and RAP not only in its methods, but also in its attitude toward the community, especially its emphasis on sharing information and responsibility. In PRA the outside experts tend to be facilitators more than investigators, and the information collected tends to be owned, used, and analyzed by the local people.

PRA, which can draw on both RRA and RAP approaches, probably is the method spreading most rapidly in the 1990s because it offers a wide menu of choices for data collection, because it is adapted and spread from community-to-community, and because there is a growing emphasis among donors on self-reliant "bottom-up" development as an alternative to (flawed) "top-down" schemes. In nutritional settings, some researchers claim it is sometimes difficult to distinguish between RAP, PRA, and RRA; the goals and methods, if not the training of researchers, often are overlapping (Kashyap 1992). Others view RRA to be the more diverse methodologically and emphasize the differences (e.g., Yangyout 1992).

In all of these methods, however, few cases of impacts have been evaluated or published.

RAPID ETHNOGRAPHIC METHODS AS TOOLS FOR SCALING UP OR SCALING DOWN

Rapid ethnographic methods overall exhibit considerable potential for sparking quantitative, functional, and political scaling up by grassroots organizations. When used for operational research, they also provide critical information for scaling down large programs to better meet community conditions. RAP, RRA, and PRA all develop organizational structures and channels of communication through which communities can identify priority problems (or opportunities) and create action plans to solve them. But types of participation seem to differ by method and nutritional domain.

Scaling Up

RAP began as a tool used by researchers to analyze community response to government or other nutrition and health programs. Some communities then "scaled up" politically and functionally; they utilized the groups and dynamics assembled for purposes of nutritional-health service evaluation and reached out for sources of political and financial support to address water, food, or other development issues. Another example is the Iringa initiative in Tanzania. What began as a UNICEF child survival effort allowed the community to participate in a process of problem assessment and analysis that led to additional actions to improve nutrition, such as women's income-generating programs, cooperative child care to improve child feeding, home gardening, and the construction of pit latrines for sanitation.

Quantitative, functional, and political scaling up has occurred as RAP is funded and encouraged by UN agencies (especially UNU), NGOs (especially HKI and Plan International), international funders (especially USAID), and certain private foundations (especially the International Nutrition Foundation for Developing Countries) and applied to ever more health and nutritional issues; so many that some humorously characterize RAP as "an epidemic in the field" (Manderson and Aaby 1992).

Alternatively, there can be identified three stages of amplification or types of "scaling up." A first stage of quantitative scaling up used community-level research guides, which were designed by anthropologists to involve community members more extensively in problem identification and discussions of interventions (S. Scrimshaw and Hurtado 1987). A second stage developed illness-focused guides that addressed specific syndromes such as diarrheas (e.g., Herman and Bentley 1993). A third stage and overlapping stage addressed qualitative data collection and analysis for training of health and service-provider personnel (Dawson et al. 1993).

Notwithstanding some notable successes, such as the multiplication and local tailoring of growth-monitoring efforts (Griffiths et al. 1996), UN agencies and large nutritional donors such as the World Bank for the most part have lost a significant opportunity to develop RAP for purposes of "scaling down" programs to appropriate community dimensions. Pilot programs tested in single settings are not easily replicated and operate differently in others. RAP offers tools to analyze specific community factors that need to be taken into consideration when "scaling-up" interventions across communities. RAP data from multiple communities within a region offer insights into appropriate social or geographic scale: to identify the optimal spatial-cultural units for effective program introduction, management, and monitoring.

RAP also offers great potential for community empowerment to help scale up nutrition activities. But most RAP practitioners still operate from a top-down health provider or middle-management perspectives. A significant deterrent to their encouraging greater community control is that this threatens professional planners' and providers' roles and jobs (see Adair and Deuschle 1970, for a classic public health example). Greater community involvement in defining nutritional and health priorities, proposing and implementing solutions, and monitoring progress also raises concerns over data collection, analysis, and ownership. Local control over data and interpretation also can be viewed as threatening at higher political levels where control over information constitutes power (Messer 1991). So far there exists little information on just how threatening the true participation that RAP encourages is to service providers and planners, or politicians or military, who may find in RAP and its intended community mobilization for nutrition and health an alarming potential to usurp their own authority, raison d'etre, or political domination. A hazard of RAP or other community organizing is that national governments may see it as a threat and crack down on the now easily identified community leaders and institutions.

PRA has also been "scaling up" quantitatively, functionally, and politically, although PRA studies tend to be more in the domain of NGO than government programs. This finding is not surprising in that a rationale of PRA is to remove community reliance on government or outsiders; the community is organized to take more responsibility for themselves. PRA and RRA findings suggest that social structures, communications channels, and processes of analysis systematized for one purpose (health, environmental management, livelihood assessment, nutritional monitoring) can create social groups, dynamics, and linkages between communities and government or NGO operations that can then be used to serve other ends or goals. However, there still exists very little direct documentation describing the conditions or steps by which scaling up takes place.

Participation and Partnerships

Comparing RAP, RRA, and PRA on concepts and uses of participation, one finds RAP efforts are predominantly "top-down," PRA self-consciously "bottom-up," and RRA still framed from the top-down although the desire is to introduce more bottom-up input. RAP methods tend to be used predominantly in the health domain of nutrition, where the goal of community participation usually is to improve community conformity with programs designed largely by outside specialists and administered by outsider and insider health practitioners. Although RAP was envisioned as a tool for elucidating perspectives of policy maker (donors), service-providers, and (community) recipients, many recent RAP studies appear to be encouraging greater attention by service-providers to qualitative factors in health and nutrition rather than empowering communities to take control of their own conditions. Exceptions are a few very innovative Australian RAP initiatives, which are explicitly community-directed, e.g., aboriginal partners work with researchers to define priority problems and work toward solutions (Manderson 1996). The Indigenous Health Program in Aboriginal and Torres Strait Island communities of the Australian Centre for International and Tropical Health and Nutrition involves indigenous women in the design and implementation of research and establishment of priorities for intervention (ACITHN 1995). The Arctic Institute of North America (AINA), which launches health projects in partnership with First Nation communities is another example: research and interventions are initiated by community organizations and also funded by a variety of donor and community sources (Ryan and Robinson 1996). In addition, some RAP manuals and procedures designed by the same Australian teams are constructed in intense consultation between providers and recipients and have been successfully adapted and taken over by health workers and communities in different country contexts (Manderson 1996; Manderson et al. 1996).

By contrast, PRA natural resource (agricultural, economic, and food security) management programs appear to be more participatory. Agronomists and agricultural research institutions work directly with innovative farmers or households, although not usually with whole communities. Professionals in RRA also have a strong desire to learn from farmers, and to facilitate farmers learning from each other (e.g., Rhoades 1984). The process of participation, with the goal of "empowering communities" of course raises many questions for researchers and practitioners. Which local units to work with? How flexible should be the objectives, given intracommunity, especially gendered differences in perceptions of resources, coping mechanisms, and desires for change (e.g., Rocheleau 1992)?

One irony of PRA dynamics is that a goal (or criterion of success) in many projects is that the community is able to organize successfully to demand resources from outsiders (NGOs, IGOs, or government) to assist follow-up operations. Community "self-reliance" or action in these situations can mean organizing sufficiently to engage an external grants writer to apply for funds for additional community-owned self-reliant development projects. Across RAP, RRA, and PRA, however, the research community so far has presented very few cases which demonstrate local institutions taking over or redirecting projects and activities. RRA/PRA have been promoted as tools in farming systems research, but there are few reported cases of farmers organizing to demand additional access to research and extension as a result of their experiences with RRA/PRA. With few exceptions those participating in RAP pilot studies in the 1980s did not organize to demand better access to primary health care. RAP, RRA, and PRA all have potential to create activist social groups but so far there are few examples of where such methods moved populations or individuals toward social transformations.

Scaling Down

Complementarily, there are few studies documenting how well rapid ethnographic methods have allowed nutrition and health initiatives to scale down and better meet local community needs and build local capacities. In response to Berg's (1993) allegations of "nutrition malpractice", it was suggested that a key problem in nutrition programs launched from the "summit" is their large scale. Top-down programs need to interact better with local communities and scale down to meet local nutrition expectations (Messer 1993). But barriers to systematically integrating community knowledge in program design appear still to be formidable.

Few RAP studies reveal how the methods work or how information has been used to construct community or state-level action plans. In Australia, RAP methods have been demonstrated to have contributed to the development of better health programs, tailored to community needs (ACITHN 1995). A malaria manual (Manderson et al. 1996) employed in the Philippines, Kenya, and Ethiopia was used to collect relevant information that was then used to construct more culturally appropriate interventions. A food safety manual is under development (by WHO) to adapt commercial food safety principles to household preparations. These examples suggest that some RAP manuals are offering health providers guidance and flexibility to design appropriate interventions in consultation with communities, or in the terms of this volume, to "scale down". However, again, there has been little evaluation on the health and nutrition impacts of RAP-assisted programs, or whether communities are empowered or sustainably "partnered" through such activities.

Such issues are connected also to concerns about validity and reliability of qualitative data collected by rapid methods. Findings by rapid ethnographic methods are sometimes subject to the criticism that they cannot necessarily be validated by individuals or agencies outside the community. Therefore, there is no objective standard of "truth" to verify results as a basis for action. From a "scaling" perspective, however, the researcher might expect findings on diarrheal disease categories or ranking of foods to differ from community to community or even household to household, and between seasons or according to resource levels. The purpose of collecting data at the community level is to ascertain such community-specific beliefs and behaviors for purposes of tailoring projects and programs to their particular conditions.

RAP, RRA, and PRA capture such variation reliably to the extent that the researchers are familiar with the social and ecological terrain, its key regional and local dimensions of variation, and can anticipate and build such variations into the research design (Manderson and Aaby 1992). Rapid ethnographic assessment is reliable also only to the extent that researchers and their assistants are adequately trained, have expertise in the domain of concern, and can avoid studies that are overly rushed with inadequate field-based community contact. Many articles have been published on the need to gain a respondent sample that accurately reflects gender, age, occupational, and other differences in local knowledge (Chambers 1994c). These are also intrinsic dimensions of scaling down data collection to capture such variations.

Scaling down and community-designed studies also present challenges of cross-cultural and diachronic comparability for research and monitoring purposes. It is attractive to assert, as Chambers (1994c) does, that participatory methods are transforming development paradigms toward a greater openness to and appreciation of cultural diversity, complexity, and multiple images of what is the "good life" or desirable cultural change. But such admissions sidestep the hard questions of who will be able to use resulting data for what purposes, and whether the goal of empowering communities to make analyses leading to action in their own behalf does not present very real dangers for the community participants involved. Communities may be threatened by over-arching external political interests, who fear losing power and control, or by internal social interests, who also are threatened by proposed changes to the status quo (Messer 1991). The question whether post-Cold War democratization will change this tendency remains (see Marchione, this volume).

CONCLUSIONS

Community-based rapid ethnographic methods have as their principal aim to generate timely, valid, and cost effective qualitative data (Beebe 1995). Experiences with RAP as a tool or technique for delivery of services have been extremely variable because, as N. Scrimshaw and Gleason (1992) showed, RAP means many different things to different agencies. Although PRA, and to a lesser extent RRA and RAP, are also supposed to be participatory and generate more "bottom-up" development activities, health programs even with RAP have mostly continued to be "top down"; agricultural research institutes and extension institutes even with RRA tend not to deal with "communities" but rather with individual farmers; and those PRA programs that do involve communities more directly aim more toward self-reliance than service delivery per se. Even though qualitative methods are supposed to be part of most operational research, donors and agents of change are still not certain what "qualitative research" is good for or if it is reliable for program planning (Chung 1997). Integrating community-based knowledge and priorities into the design of large-scale nutrition programs, to scale them down to fit particular community dimensions and allow communities greater control, therefore, probably will take some time.

It is also not yet clear how communities will use rapid ethnographic assessment processes to help them scale up nutritional or other development activities. RAP probably has seen its greatest success in the design and utilization of a number of disease-specific manuals that enable health providers to tailor messages and interventions to existing community concerns and knowledge bases. Such developments empower communities or particular individuals or institutions to take action on focused health problems, but whether such disease-specific actions in health and nutrition build the community structures to take action in other domains remains to be seen.

RRA and PRA by all accounts are revolutionizing research leading to action in the development field. More than RAP, which has its origins in anthropology, these methods are elucidating "folk" perceptions of environmental resources, social rankings, and interactions and introducing them into policy and action contexts. They are also actively rather than incidentally forging community-based groups that are challenging existing decision-making and power structures (Chambers 1994c). But the dynamics of community participation carry real risks for communities and local NGOs, who may face opposition and repression from governments. The principle of participation also carries programming risks for outside experts who may lose control over priorities and the development process.

In summary, there has been little evaluation of the relative strength and ability of groups organized to solve particular problems to adapt and confront different problems. RAP, RRA, and PRA, all relatively new methodologies on the scene only since the mid-1980s, thus hold great promise to transform development research, operations, program monitoring and evaluation, and the quality of life itself if they should prove, as the promoters would have it, nothing short of revolutionary.

NOTES

1. RAP is somewhat closer to Nichter's methods of training para-professional community "social scientists" analogous to community health-promoters or health-auxiliaries (Nichter 1984), although this is not its aim. No one has followed up to see what happens to these local social (medical) scientists after the RAP project is done.

REFERENCES

Adair, J. and Deuschle, K. W.
(1970) *The People's Health*. New York: Appleton-Century-Crofts.

ACITHN (Australian Centre for International and Tropical Health and Nutrition)
(1995) *Annual Report 1995*. Queensland: University of Queensland Medical School.

Beebe, J.
(1995) "Basic Concepts and Techniques of Rapid Appraisal." *Human Organization* **54**: 42–51.

Bentley, M., Pelto, G., Strauss, W., Adegebola, O., de la Pena, E., Oni, G., Brown, K., and Huffman, S.
(1988) "Rapid Ethnographic Assessment: Application in a Diarrhea Management Program." *Social Science & Medicine* **27**: 107–16.

Berg, A.
(1993) "Sliding Toward Nutrition Malpractice: Time to Reconsider and Redeploy?" *American Journal of Clinical Nutrition* **57**(1): 3–7.

Chambers, R.
(1992) "Rapid but Relaxed and Participatory Rural Appraisal: Towards Applications in Health and Nutrition." In *RAP: Rapid Assessment Procedures*, eds. N. Scrimshaw and G. Gleason. Boston: International Nutrition Foundation for Developing Countries.

Chambers, R.
(1994a) "The Origins and Practice of Participatory Rural Appraisal." *World Development* **22**(7): 953–68.

Chambers, R.
(1994b) "Participatory Rural Appraisal (PRA): Analysis of Experience." *World Development* **22**(9): 253–68.

Chambers, R.
(1994c) "Participatory Rural Appraisal (PRA): Challenges and Potential." *World Development* **22**(10): 1437–54.

Creed, K. H., Fukumoto, M., Bentley, M. E., Jacoby, E., Verrzosa, C., and Brown, K. H.
(1991) "Use of Recipe Trials and Anthropological Techniques for the Development of Home-Prepared Weaning Food in the Central Highlands of Peru." *Journal of Nutrition Education* **23**: 30–50.

Chung, K.
(1997) "Using Qualitative Methods to Improve the Collection and Analysis of Data from LSMS Household Surveys. "In *A Manual for Designing Survey Questionnaires: Lessons from Ten Years of Experience*, ed. M. Grosh and P. Glewwe, Processed. Washington: Poverty and Human Resources Division, Policy Research Department, The World Bank.

Dawson, S., Manderson, L., and Tallo, V.
(1993)   *A Manual for the Use of Focus Groups*. Boston: International Nutrition
          Foundation for Developing Countries.

Ford, R., Kabutha, C., Mageto, N., and Manneh, K.
(1992)   *Sustaining Development Through Community Mobilization: A Case
          Study of Participatory Rural Appraisal in the Gambia*. Worcester, MA:
          Clark University.

Good, M. J. del V.
(1992)   "Local knowledge: Research Capacity Building in International
          Health." *Social Science and Medicine* **35**(11): 1359–67.

Griffiths, M.
(1992)   "Understanding Infant Feeding Practices: Qualitative Research
          Methodologies Used in the Weaning Project." In *RAP: Rapid Asses-
          sment Procedures*, eds. N. Scrimshaw and G. Gleason. Boston:
          International Nutrition Foundation for Developing Countries.

Griffiths, M.
(1994)   "Social Marketing: Achieving Changes in Nutrition Behavior, from
          Household Practices to National Policies." *Food and Nutrition Bulletin*
          15(1): 25–31.

Griffiths, M., Dickin, K., and Favin, M.
(1996)   *Promoting the Growth of Children: What Works. Rationale and
          Guidance for Programs*. Washington: World Bank, Human Develop-
          ment Department.

Gittelsohn, J., Pelto, P. J., Bently, M. E., Bhattacharyya, K., and Jenson, J.
(1998)   *Rapid Assessment Procedures (RAP): Ethnographic Methods to
          Investigate Women's Health*. Boston: International Nutrition Founda-
          tion for Developing Countries.

Herman, E. and Bentley, M.
(1993)   *Rapid Assessment Procedures (RAP): To Improve the Household
          Management of Diarrhea*. Boston: International Nutrition Foundation for
          Developing Countries.

Hurtado, E.
(1990)   "Use of Rapid Anthropological Procedures by Health Personnel in
          Central America." *Food and Nutrition Bulletin* **12**(4): 310–12.

Hurtado, E.
(1994)   "Rapid Assessment Procedures in Formative Research for a Communi-
          cation Intervention on Water-Related Hygiene Behaviours." *Food and
          Nutrition Bulletin* **15**(1): 71–76.

INIP (Indonesian National IPM Program)
(1991)   *Farmers as Experts. The Indonesian National IPM Program*. Jakarta:
          Indonesian National IPM Program.

International Institute for Environment and Development
(1988–1991) RRA Notes 1–12: (June 1988 through July 1991).

Kashyap, P.
(1992) "Rapid Rural Appraisal Methodology and Its Use in Nutrition Surveys." In RAP: Rapid Assessment Procedures, eds. N. Scrimshaw and G. Gleason. Boston: International Nutrition Foundation for Developing Countries.

Khan, M. and Manderson, L.
(1992) "Focus Groups in Rapid Assessment Procedures." Food and Nutrition Bulletin 14(2): 119–127.

Manderson, L.
(1996) "Handbooks and Manuals in Applied Research." Practicing Anthropology 18(3).

Manderson, L. and Aaby, P.
(1992) "An Epidemic in the Field? RAP and Health Research." Social Science and Medicine 35(4): 839–850.

Manderson, L., Agyepong, I., Aryee, B., and Dzikunu, H.
(1996) "Anthropological Methods for Malaria Interventions." Practicing Anthropology 18(3): 32–36.

Messer, E.
(1990) "Social Science Perspectives on Primary Health Care." Food and Nutrition Bulletin 12: 229–39.

Messer, E.
(1991) "International Conference on Rapid Assessment Methodologies for Planning and Evaluation of Health Related Programmes: Interpretative Summary." Food and Nutrition Bulletin 13(4): 287–292.

Messer, E.
(1993) "Scaling Up, Scaling Down: Increasing Effectiveness Through Community-Based Research and Action." American Journal of Clinical Nutrition 58(4): 574–75.

Montgomery, E. and Bennett, J.
(1979) "Anthropological Studies of Food and Nutrition: the 1940s and the 1970s." In The Uses of Anthropology, ed. W. Goldschmidt. Special Publication No. 11. Washington: American Anthropological Association.

Nichter, M.
(1984) "Project Community Diagnosis: Participatory Research as a First Step Toward Community Involvement in Primary Health Care." Social Science and Medicine 19: 237–252.

Novaes da Mota, C. and Cardoso Neiva, V.
(1990) "Jardim Primavera: Applications of Anthropological Procedures to the Assessment of Programmes of Nutrition and Primary Health Care in a Suburban Community of Rio de Janeiro." Food and Nutrition Bulletin 12(4): 313–317.

Paul, B., ed.
(1955) *Culture, Health, and Community*. New York: Russell Sage.

Pelletier, D.
(1992) "The Role of Qualitative Methodologies in Nutritional Surveillance." In *RAP: Rapid Assessment Procedures*, eds. N. Scrimshaw and G. Gleason. Boston: International Nutrition Foundation for Developing Countries.

Pelto, G. and Gove, S.
(1992) "Developing a Focused Ethnographic Study for the WHO Acute Respiratory Infection (ARI) Control Programme." In *RAP: Rapid Assessment Procedures*, eds. N. Scrimshaw and G. Gleason. Boston: International Nutrition Foundation for Developing Countries.

Rhoades, R.
(1984) *Breaking New Ground. Agricultural Anthropology*. Lima: International Potato Center.

Richards, A.
(1939) *Land, Labour, and Diet in Northern Rhodesia: An Economic Study of the Bemba Tribe*. London: Routledge.

Rocheleau, D.
(1992) *Gender, Ecology and Agroforestry: Science and Survival in Kathama*. Worcester, MA: Clark University.

Ryan, J. and Robinson, M.
(1996) "Community Participatory Research: Two Views from Arctic Institute Practitioners." *Practicing Anthropology* **18**(4): 7–11.

Scrimshaw, S.
(1992) "Adaptation of Anthropological Methodologies to Rapid Assessment of Nutrition and Primary Health Care." In *RAP: Rapid Assessment Procedures. Qualitative Methodologies for Planning and Evaluation of Health Related Programmes*, eds. N. Scrimshaw and G. Gleason. Boston: International Nutrition Foundation for Developing Countries.

Scrimshaw, N. and Gleason, G., eds.
(1992) *RAP. Rapid Assessment Procedures: Qualitative Methodologies for Planning and Evaluation of Health Related Programmes*. Boston: International Nutrition Foundation for Developing Countries.

Scrimshaw, S. and Hurtado, E.
(1987) *Rapid Assessment Procedures for Nutrition and Primary Health Care: Anthropological Approaches to Improving Programme Effectiveness*. Reference Series, Volume 11. Los Angeles: UCLA Latin American Center.

Scrimshaw, S. and Hurtado, E.
(1988) "Anthropological Involvement in the Central American Diarreheal Disease Control Project." *Social Science and Medicine* **27**: 97–105.

Shrestha, V. L.
(1992) "Rapid Assessment Procedures in the Context of Rural Water Supply and Sanitation Programme." In *RAP: Rapid Assessment Procedures*, eds. N. Scrimshaw and G. Gleason. Boston: International Nutrition Foundation for Developing Countries.

Slocum, R., Wichhart, L., Rocheleau, D., and Thomas-Slayter, B., eds.
(1995) *Power, Process, and Participation-Tools for Change*. London: Intermediate Technology Publications.

Thomas-Slayter, B., Esser, A. L., and Shields, M. D.
(1993) *Tools of Gender Analysis: A Guide to Field Methods for Bringing Gender into Sustainable Resource Management*. Worcester, MA: Clark University.

Yangyout, K.
(1992) "Rapid Rural Appraisal and Rapid Assessment Procedures. A Comparison." In *RAP: Rapid Assesssment Procedures*, eds. N. Scrimshaw and G. Gleason. Boston: International Nutrition Foundation for Developing Countries.

CHAPTER 11

Rapid Food and Livelihood Security Assessments: A Comprehensive Approach for Diagnosing Nutrition Insecurity

Timothy R. Frankenberger and
M. Katherine McCaston

Starting in the 1980s, rapid assessment methodology has gained increasing importance in the international development community for analyzing poverty and nutrition problems. This represents a break from the previous tendency to view diagnostic research as a largely academic and overly costly process. Mounting evidence suggests that through cross-sectoral diagnostic work the potential for positive synergistic effects and sustainability of development programs can be greatly improved. One such method, Rapid Food and Livelihood Security Assessment (RFLSA), used by CARE International in over 24 nations is proving to be a potent means of diagnosing poverty and nutrition security among the poor in developing and transition countries. As a result of the increased awareness of the value it adds to the development process, the methodology has become the cornerstone for some international non-governmental organizations (NGOs) in their efforts to move from food aid delivery to more sustainable programs for improving food and nutrition security.

The strength of the RFLSA approach lies in its ability to obtain a multi-dimensional profile of a micro-level or grassroots food and nutrition situation with strong regional and national contextualization (Frankenberger and Schaeffer 1994). Understanding the wider context allows for scaling-up interventions. It sets the stage and defines the parameters for further detailed inquiry, suggests broad program activities, and identifies potential constraints to such interventions. Importantly, the RFLSA approach can serve as a conduit for scaling up by creating a setting where communities can voice local concerns and more actively participate in the needs-identification process. By working to increase the institutional capacity of local NGOs, RFLSAs provide another potential means for scaling up. Finally, by encouraging the participation of NGO program staff, bilateral donors, and national government representatives in the assessment and needs identification process, the method provides a creative mechanism that involves key players from the development summit in the communities with the problems, or scaling down.

This chapter focuses on the work of CARE International, one of the largest and more influential NGOs working on problems of relief and development. Over the past decade, CARE has moved from being primarily a relief organization to a major implementing agency in international development. CARE's major concern for the future is the integration of its continued role in emergency and development food aid distribution with more sustainable interventions aimed towards mitigating the root causes of crises or absolute poverty, and enabling affected populations to restore their livelihoods and adequate nutritional well-being. Rapid food and livelihood security methodology can play an important role in this transition. The chapter begins by describing the origins of RFLSA in farming systems and food security studies in the late 1970s- through the 1980s, followed by a discussion of its logical connection to the livelihood security conceptual framework. This is followed by a presentation of the general steps used in applying the assessment approach.

THE ORIGIN OF RAPID FOOD AND LIVELIHOOD SECURITY ASSESSMENT

Rapid Food and Livelihood Security Assessments (RFLSA) are a type of rapid rural appraisal (RRA). RRAs employ a set of data collection techniques adapted from social science interview and survey methods, first used in farming systems research in the late 1970s and early 1980s and later in nutritional diagnostic work, for providing comprehensive sociocultural, economic, and ecological assessments of a given area for planning and project implementation (Molnar 1989). They bridge the gap between formal surveys and non-structured interviewing.

The major objective of RRAs is to gain maximum knowledge of the target area with the minimum amount of time and resources (Eklund 1990). The major advantages of RRAs are that they are: (1) rapid, with results quickly made available to decision makers; (2) interdisciplinary; (3) eclectic in techniques aimed at capturing a holistic picture of the local situation; (4) rely on more open-ended interview techniques that reduce non-sampling error; and (5) allow for valuable interaction between investigators and the target population (Molnar 1989). RRAs have been employed in food security monitoring as a way to provide a systematic overview of the diet and strategies for acquiring food in the target area, while using a minimum amount of survey time and resources (Frankenberger 1990). They help to involve local people in research and planning of program activities, and they can be used to monitor and evaluate a research and development activity or deal with conflicting differences between different groups (McCracken et al. 1988; Frankenberger and Goldstein 1992). Despite the multiple advantages of RRAs, it is important to recognize that the households assessed are not rigorously representative of wider populations. RRAs should be viewed as complementary to other research methodologies such as formal surveys and in-depth anthropological studies.

Participatory rural appraisals (PRA) also involve multidisciplinary teams that gather information in a systematic, yet semi-structured way (see Perez 1997a for a recent discussion on the origin and status of PRA methods). However, PRAs tend to focus on one village rather than a region, and community participation is considerably more active (WRI 1989). RRA and PRA should not be viewed as substitutes for each other for they serve different purposes. PRA is intended to help a community mobilize its human and natural resources to define problems, consider successes, evaluate local capacities, prioritize opportunities, prepare a systematic and site specific plan of action, and be a means of facilitating community self-help initiatives. It brings together the development needs as defined by the community with the resources and technical skills offered by the government, donor agencies, and NGOs. One drawback of PRAs is that the sample size is very small and generalizing to a broader geographic area is both difficult and risky.

Although the RRA approach used in farming systems research and for food security monitoring has been an effective diagnostic tool in many cases, household food production represents a very small portion of the income of a rural household, making the farming systems model inappropriate in explaining the socioeconomic situation of not only urban but also many rural families. Food insecurity was only one of a whole array of factors that determined why the poor take decisions and spread risk and how they finely balance competing interests in order to subsist in the short- and long-term. This called for a more comprehensive model to explain and research how poor households meet their basic needs through time. The RFLSA method was designed to address this need.

THE LIVELIHOOD SECURITY CONCEPTUAL FRAMEWORK

In the 1990s, the livelihood security conceptual framework provided CARE and other NGOs a new vision and program strategy for understanding the broader array of problems facing the poor in diverse local communities. This framework does not call for a resurrection of integrated rural development, but rather gives emphasis to identifying strong sector-specific programs (Figure 11.1). Household livelihood security is defined as adequate and sustainable access to income and other resources to enable households to meet basic needs, including adequate access to food, potable water, health facilities, educational opportunities, housing, and time for community participation and social integration (Frankenberger 1996). A livelihood comprises the capabilities, assets (stores, resources, claims, and access), and activities required for a means of living (Chambers and Conway 1992). More specifically, livelihoods can be seen to consist of a range of on-farm and off-farm activities that together provide a variety of procurement strategies for food and cash. Thus, each household can have several possible sources of entitlement which constitute its livelihood. These entitlements are based on a household's endowments, and its position in the legal, political, and social fabric of society (Drinkwater and McEwan 1992). The risk of livelihood failure determines the level of vulnerability of a household to income, food, health, and nutrition insecurity. The greater the share of resources devoted to food and health services acquisition, the higher the vulnerability of the household to food and nutrition insecurity. Therefore, livelihoods are secure when households have

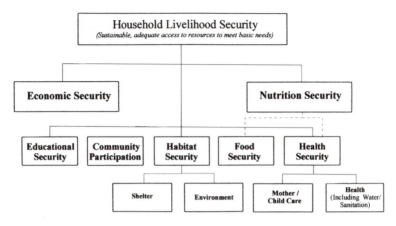

Figure 11.1. Livelihood security conceptual framework.

secure ownership of, or access to, resources and income earning activities, including reserves and assets, to off-set risks, ease shocks, and meet contingencies (Chambers 1988).

A livelihood is sustainable, according to Chambers and Conway (1992), when it "can cope with and recover from the stress and shocks, maintain its capability and assets, and provide sustainable livelihood opportunities for the next generation ..." (Frankenberger 1992). Sustainable refers to the maintenance or enhancement of resource productivity on a long-term basis (Chambers 1988). Households are not equal in their abilities to cope with stresses and shocks. Poor people balance competing needs for asset preservation, income generation, and present and future food supplies in complex ways (Maxwell and Smith 1992). People may go hungry up to a point to meet another objective. For example, de Waal (1989) found during the 1984–85 famine in Darfur, Sudan, that people chose to go hungry to preserve their assets and future livelihoods. People will tolerate a considerable degree of hunger to preserve seed for planting, cultivate their own fields, or avoid selling animals. Similarly, Corbett (1988) found that in the sequential ordering of behavioral responses employed in periods of stress in a number of African and Asian countries, preservation of assets takes priority over meeting immediate food needs until the point of destitution.

Thus, food and nutrition security are subsets of livelihood security; food needs are not necessarily more important than other basic needs or aspects of subsistence and survival within households. Food insecure households juggle among a range of requirements, including immediate consumption and future capacity to produce (Figure 11.2). A range of intervention

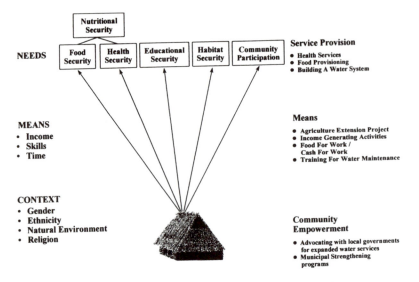

Figure 11.2. Illustration of livelihood security interventions.

options need to be available for the various circumstances that face poor populations (Frankenberger 1995). Furthermore, to enhance the livelihood security of vulnerable populations the livelihood systems approach is based on the notion that relief, rehabilitation/mitigation and development interventions are a continuum of related activities, not separate and discrete initiatives.

The practical advantages of using such a inclusive framework include: (1) the various sectors can share resources in conducting joint assessments and baselines, and measuring program impact; (2) intervention priorities can be established cross-sectorally depending upon the major constraints facing households; and (3) sector-specific programs can be targeted to the same regions to obtain a multiplier effect on the beneficiary population. Using a livelihood security framework can improve CARE's ability to target poor and vulnerable households in its programs, and ensure that the needs addressed in project activities are those that are central to households' livelihood and food security concerns. Using a common framework also helps generate coherent country office information systems.

In addition to these micro-focused interventions, Country Offices and CARE headquarters are giving increasing attention to the role of advocacy and broader development initiatives in improving the opportunities of households in meeting their basic needs. The utility of the household livelihood security concept is that basic needs can be met through improving the immediate conditions for participants and their families. However, the approach also affords opportunities to strengthen community organizations and local support networks, and/or influence national and international public policies, practices, and attitudes, thereby better confronting the basic causes of poverty and nutrition insecurity.

A HOUSEHOLD LIVELIHOOD SECURITY PROGRAMMING APPROACH

To effectively implement a household livelihood security approach, the following steps or phases have been developed to guide CARE's programming:

1. Identifying potential regions for program targeting and geographical targeting by utilizing existing secondary data to identify areas where absolute poverty is concentrated. This activity is usually done as part of the preparation of the long-range strategic planning exercise of the country office;
2. Identifying the vulnerable groups in the area to be targeted and the major livelihood constraints they face. This information is collected through a review of secondary data if they are available, or through a cross-sectoral rapid livelihood security assessment. During this phase, decisions are made on which target groups to focus on, what set of interventions are most appropriate for enhancing their livelihood security, and the minimal data set to be collected for establishing a baseline;
3. Conducting participatory community assessments (e.g., PRAs) to further design the intervention themes identified in the rapid assessment to develop programs for implementation (See Perez (1997b) for CARE's experience in agriculture projects.);
4. Collecting baseline data and identifying a set of indicators of change that will be periodically monitored;
5. Selecting the set of communities for program interventions. These communities should be chosen in such a way that they have similar characteristics to a larger group of communities in order to maximize the multiplier effect of successful interventions (scaling up);
6. Establishing a monitoring system that uses qualitative and quantitative techniques to periodically monitor program performance;
7. Measuring quantitative and qualitative changes in indicators to obtain an overall evaluation of program impacts;
8. Taking lessons learned from the evaluation and incorporating these into the next long-range strategic planning exercise.

By using such an approach to targeting and design, the opportunity for cross-sectoral integration can be enhanced. Instead of having an incremental or single-sector approach that results in widely dispersed project sites, areas of concentration can be chosen for coordinated sectoral programming with greater effect on the beneficiary population. Furthermore, household livelihood security by definition implies sustainability. CARE accords highest priority to: (1) greater focus on partnerships, institution-building, and other forms of capacity building; (2) sound natural resource management and concern for the protection of the environment; and (3) more explicit focus on issues of social equity, including gender equity.

RAPID FOOD AND LIVELIHOOD SECURITY ASSESSMENTS

Programming for livelihood security can not proceed very far without a thorough understanding of the specific livelihoods and food and nutrition security conditions in local areas. If secondary data are not adequate, rapid food and livelihood security assessment (RFLSA) provides simple methods that are quick and cost-effective (Frankenberger and Coyle 1993). They help identify: (1) the characteristics of the most food-insecure groups in an area; (2) the causes of the food insecurity situation; (3) the potential location-specific indicators for food security monitoring; and (4) the range of appropriate interventions for alleviating the food deficit problem. They also help provide an in-depth understanding of the food security context of a given area.

Rapid assessments help in the design of baseline and impact evaluation surveys through the identification of new problems and measurable location-specific indicators of them. When carried out in areas of on-going projects, they help staff to better understand the effectiveness of project targeting, and allow beneficiaries to express their perspectives regarding the program's impact on their lives. Finally, rapid assessments can provide training and capacity building for field staff in monitoring and evaluation methods, allowing them to better conceptualize the linkages between project impacts and inputs. Although not as participatory as PRAs, RFLSAs allow for more direct involvement of local communities than do formal surveys in the process of information gathering and problem analysis. They capture the general context and some detailed patterns that are found within communities and agro-ecological zones. In addition, CARE has combined this type of information with more quantitative information gathered at the household and individual level to capture inter-household variability in livelihood strategies and their outcomes. Thus, the RFLSA allows for a holistic understanding of food and livelihood security, assessing the broad contours of vulnerability, local perceptions and responses, and scope for interventions in different settings.

During the period from 1992 to 1997, CARE has carried out 24 RFLSAs in different regions of the world as one part of its strategic planning activities (Table 11.1). These countries include Ethiopia, Sudan, Somalia, Kenya, Tanzania, Mozambique, Angola, Niger, Mali, India, Sri Lanka, Cambodia, Honduras, Guatemala, Nicaragua, Haiti, Bolivia, Georgia, Azerbijan, Tajikistan, Afghanistan, Rwanda, Bangladesh, and El Salvador. A general overview of methods used in these assessments range from pre-assessment secondary data searches and institutional assessments to post-assessment program recommendations.

Pre-assessment Activities

Prior to any field activity, a review of existing secondary data and an institutional assessment of other NGOs and government agencies working in the survey area are conducted. A secondary data and literature review is conducted to assess the breadth, depth and quality of available secondary information, published and unpublished, in order to obtain a better understanding of the food and livelihood security situation, inform sample area selection, and develop survey instruments. The Institutional Assessment details all relevant institutions—government, donors, and NGOs—working in the survey area. Thus, the Institutional Assessment helps avoid duplication of effort, and provides a list of potential development partners for the assessment and future activity.

Target Area and Sample Selection

In countries where good background information already exists, such as national early warning systems or poverty profiles (e.g., crop forecasting, food balance sheets, nutrition surveillance, other background studies), information supplied by these sources can help identify the most vulnerable regions (Frankenberger 1992). These vulnerability profiles should be based upon both food security and absolute poverty indicators as much as possible to avoid designating an area as vulnerable, when it may not be. RFLSA teams are not necessarily responsible for creating these profiles. For example, consultants were contracted by CARE to prepare poverty profiles for Honduras, Guatemala, and El Salvador as part of the pre-assessment activities.

The vulnerability profiles can then be used for designating areas where more location-specific household food and livelihood security information can be gathered. It is important to consider what can be reasonably covered in the time allotted. Coverage will be influenced by such factors

Table 11.1. CARE Food and Livelihood Security Program Methods by Country

Regions Evaluation	Countries	RFLSA[a]	Staff/Counterpart	Program Design/ Training	Baseline Redesign	M & E[b] Data	LRSP[c] Systems	Impact
Asia	Afghanistan	x					x	
	Bangladesh	x	x		x	x	x	x
	Cambodia	x	x	x				
	India	x	x	x				
	Sri Lanka	x	x	x			x	
Latin America	Bolivia	x	x	x				
	Guatemala	x	x	x	x	x	x	
	Haiti	x	x	x	x	x	x	
	Honduras	x	x		x	x	x	x
	Nicaragua	x	x					x

	a	b	c
Sub-Saharan Africa			
Angola	x	x	x
Ethiopia	x	x	x
Mali	x		
Mozambique	x	x	
Rwanda	x		
Kenya	x	x	x
Somalia	x	x	
Sudan	x	x	x
Tanzania	x	x	x
Niger	x		x
Former Soviet Union			
Azerbaijan	x	x	
Georgia	x		
Tajikistan	x	x	

[a] rapid food & livelihood security assesment; [b] monitoring and evaluation systems; [c] long range strategic planning.

as environmental uniformity, technological development, socioeconomic conditions, infrastructural development, and access during the rainy season. The team should plan to spend more time in regions where the agricultural systems are more diverse and variable than in regions where they are more uniform, and they should draw up a schedule specifying the number of days to be spent in each area as well as the number of days for travel time, review, and write-up. This schedule should be flexible as time constraints may force the team to reduce the number of survey sites. Time, expense and sample coverage must be carefully balanced.

For every distinct geographical area that is targeted, it is important to have at least six randomly chosen villages. One reason for this is that a minimum of 180 cases (using a cluster sample of 30 different mothers and one of their children from each village) is needed for nutritional status measurements to be statically representative of the families with children under five years of age in the target area. In India, in the Bastar District assessment, for example, CARE used a combination of random and purposive sampling from the District's five administrative blocks. Four villages were randomly selected from a comprehensive list of all villages located in each of the five blocks (the fourth village was selected in each block in case substitution was necessary). Fifteen households from each village were purposively selected for the household interviews—using local definitions of livelihood status to select five households from each of the different strata—for a total of 225 household interviews. These household interviews were considered intensive case studies. A separate random sample was made of families with children under five years of age to collect nutrition and health information on 30 children in each village, for a total of 600 cases.

Development of Primary Data Gathering Methods

Starting with secondary information available on the target areas and villages, a number of methods must be employed for directly gathering information on their livelihood systems, the constraints to livelihood improvement, and the possible program opportunities that could alleviate constraints. The four principal methods include group interviews, focus groups, household interviews, and nutrition and health assessments.

Group interviews, using a topical outline rather than a questionnaire format, are conducted with the whole community to understand the villages' access to infrastructure, common property resources, land, markets, schools, health facilities, and other services. In addition, general characterizations of livelihood activities operating in the village, seasonal coping strategies, consumption patterns, participation in food aid programs, and community perceptions of problems and solutions are solicited in community-level meetings. Group meetings are held separately with men and women to allow the women to speak freely about these issues to avoid gender bias and to obtain both perspectives. Information is recorded in notebooks and then transferred to matrices the following day, raising considerably the value of information obtained from individual households later (Eklund 1990; Frankenberger et al. 1987).

The group meeting aids the team to organize small *focus groups* based on primary livelihoods. The interviewing format is similar to that followed in group interviews; however, the size of the group is usually limited to six to ten people. Their smaller size allows richer and more intensive communication and dialogue than the larger group interviews, and they provide a channel for sub-sectors of communities to participate in the needs assessment. For example in the Tanzania assessment, focus groups were conducted with food vendors, petty traders, unemployed youth, female-headed households, shop owners, water vendors, prostitutes, households workers that had lost their jobs (retrenched), primary school teachers, government employees, tailors, and carpenters. Focus groups are generally differentiated on this basis of primary production or livelihood system. However, in situations where the livelihood systems are not differentiated, wealth differences can define the different groups. Emphasis is always placed on conducting some focus group discussions with women participating in different livelihood systems as well as other women's activities (e.g., in Tanzania, one group focused on women's time-allocation). Selecting focus groups this way provides detailed systematic information regarding the constraints facing people in a particular livelihood, their relative vulnerability compared to other livelihoods, and the means by which they cope with hardships (i.e., their coping strategies).

In addition to collecting this community-level information, the team identifies and selects an opportunistic sample of households in each livelihood category for intensive *household interviews*. At this point the data collection objective shifts from describing general patterns to describing variation between households within particular categories or livelihoods. In these interviews it is important not to assume that one member of the household can speak for all the rest, because information about livelihood details is usually partitioned within the family, particularly along gender lines (Molnar 1989). Interviewed households are described in intensive case studies of particular livelihood systems over decades and in the course of the annual cycle. The purpose is to analyze individual households of both similar and different livelihood system sets. Regular patterns of differences in coping strategies can be documented for households in the same livelihood set. For example women in stressed farm families who must cut, headload, and sell firewood in towns might be compared with patterns employed by women in households engaged in different livelihood systems, such as cattle herding households or merchants. In this way, intra-community variation in livelihood and coping strategies that may be more or less successful are systematically documented and analyzed. Such a procedure greatly aids targeting community development intervention priorities across sectors.

The types of information collected from households, both male- and female-headed, includes: (1) household demography; (2) household assets and resources; (3) primary livelihood activities; (4) secondary livelihood activities; (5) seasonality of production; (6) months of self-provisioning; (7) proportion of income spent on food per year; (8) time/season of stress; (9) coping strategies identified and ranked by respondent; (10) health problems; and (11) perceptions of production and food security constraints. This information is recorded in questionnaire format constructed on a simple spreadsheet or register on paper. This information is subsequently transferred to computer data files for analysis with standard analysis packages. While this survey method does not achieve a statistically representative sample about the village, bundles of assets, resources, strategies, and constraints can easily be compared among and between households to help identify possible sectoral intervention priorities.

The fourth type of data collection in this assessment is a parallel *nutrition and health assessment*, using a larger and representative sample of households with children under five in each village. This information includes nutritional status assessment (anthropometric measurements of child growth), dietary recalls, immunization records, history of child illness (diarrhoeal episodes and acute respiratory problems), and household criteria so that comparisons across livelihoods or household type can be made, e.g., female versus male-headed households. Child nutritional status is one of the best indicators of livelihood security because it represents a composite measure of access to food, health facilities and practices, clean water, education, and related conditions of well-being. In many ways these aspects of livelihood are the same as those used in the UNICEF conceptual framework for diagnosing nutrition problems (see Ch. 13 by Beaudry). This information can be generalized to the assessment area because usually more than 400 children and their mothers are surveyed.

Selecting the Survey Team

The survey team for a country can range in number from six to 35 individuals, coming from various disciplinary backgrounds and organizations, and normally male and female researchers are equally represented. Multi-disciplinary and gender-balanced teams strengthen the diagnostic process and encourage cross-fertilization of ideas, which is particularly useful during problem analysis. The country team is broken into smaller teams every day during the survey period, ideally with social scientists and physical/biological scientists in each. The disciplines represented in RFLSAs vary across surveys and are best shaped according to the anticipated development problems in the target areas. For example, in the Kenya assessment the following specialties were represented: sociology, agronomy, nutrition, economics, business, health and population, nursing, forestry, anthropology, agricultural economics, civil engineering, and community development. In some instances translators from the target areas are part of the team, providing not only translation, but useful information to the team about the target area during training and entry to the target communities. Usually, a nutritional assessment sub-team of six to eight nutritionally trained individuals is also created from within the country team. Where members of the nutrition team are not already expert at methods used, a brief training is conducted.

Each team, including members of the nutrition sub-team, visits a different village in the same agro-ecological zone in the same day, taking not more than one day per village. Each team, ideally, has two people focusing on nutrition and health data, and four to six people collecting group, focus group, and household data. Team members work in pairs rotating periodically to give each team member a chance to work with all other team members and share ideas and skills (Hildebrand 1981).

The size of the team will vary. Large teams are used in countries where there is a strong desire to build local capacity in such data collection techniques, helping local organizations to scale up. CARE has also placed considerable emphasis on carefully composing teams to encourage cross-organizational sharing and learning. Local and national government agencies as well as local and international NGOs are invited, encouraging participation from a diverse group of knowledgeable and skilled individuals and institutions that work in the development field. For example, in the Tanzania RFLSA 15 team members were representatives from government ministries, four were representatives from local NGOs, and one was a representative from an international NGO. This type of group is a unique creation in field assessments that enables people from the grassroots community to interact directly with representatives from the local and national government as well as local and international NGOs. RFSLA teams become an ideal medium where the grassroots organizations meet the representatives of summit organizations to understand development problems and create solutions.

Training the Team

Prior to going to the field, the team participates in a four to five day work-shop. This workshop introduces the team members to each other and to the concepts that form the basis of the data collection procedure, the cultural nuances of the target area, and to the data collection tools they are about to use. The training exercise is very participatory with the various people from all levels of society and organizational affiliation involved in influencing the data collection instruments. Team members try out and partici-pate in the review of data collection forms to insure that appropriate topics are being addressed in the most appropriate ways for the cultures in the local areas. It is a mutual learning process as well as a capacity building exercise for local institutions where the best local knowledge and expertise is mobilized in refining the CARE survey, while encouraging commitment to the assessment and program follow-on from various organizations par-ticipating. In addition to CARE country office personnel, government min-istries and local NGOs are also represented. For example, in the India RFLSA, representatives from three CARE Country Offices (India, Nepal and Bangladesh), three Government Ministries and three local NGOs par-ticipated in the assessment along with tribal translators from the target areas. Training in this way not only helps insure that the best available data is obtained, but leaves behind a number of people able to carry out this type of research in the future without relying on external consultants.

An additional training exercise is conducted with the nutritional assess-ment sub-team. Team members are trained or refreshed in anthropometric weight, height and age determinations to ensure that measurement tech-niques are valid and consistent across the team. Team members practice taking the measurements on each other. Members of the nutrition sub-team also review the nutrition data collection form to determine if the health and diet sections of the instrument are complete and to ensure that any loca-tion-specific considerations are properly covered. The team then conducts a field test near the training site and adjustments are made, if necessary. Testing the instrument also helps to ensure that all team members are skilled not only in anthropometry but also in conducting interviews, such as diet recalls and health histories.

Conducting the Field Survey and the Analysis

The field survey and the primary data analysis is normally conducted over a two to four week period, alternating village surveys with a day of analy-sis (Frankenberger and Lichte 1985). This procedure is followed to insure that the survey process is iterative, such that the team uses the previous day's information collected to form hypothesis about constraints that could be further investigated in the following set of villages. At the end of the survey, two days are spent analyzing the constraints and formulating preliminary recommendations. In Kenya, India, and Sri Lanka, a problem analysis approach was used to determine the key priority constraints. The nutrition and health data are coded and analyzed at the same time.

After interviews are completed for a selected village, the next day the team members get together to analyze the data and formulate hypotheses about the food and livelihood security situation that characterizes that region. It is important to remember that at least as much time is needed to review and evaluate the content of the interviews as to conduct them. This procedure helps summarize the important attributes, constraints, and opportunities characterizing the food and livelihood security situation and provides a basis for comparison when the survey work is started in other villages. These reviews will help revise topical outlines for further interviews. This process can be a crucial team-building exercise.

The analysis involves tabulating the qualitative data obtained from the group and focus group interviews into matrices that can be compared across villages. In addition to these matrices, the nutrition and health data are tabulated and graphically represented, and the household data are summarized into cross-tabs. In many instances, survey teams will have gathered enough information to construct annual calenders of cropping patterns, labor access, food procurement strategies, diet, heath problems, and major expenditure patterns and prices, or may have used other methods (Chambers 1985). The rich mix of qualitative and quantitative data are then used by the team to identify the key constraints affecting the livelihood systems in the survey area, the most vulnerable groups, and the potential solutions that could be considered for addressing the constraints. If more than one team is collecting data, then each team presents its information to the other teams. Such village comparisons help the teams determine which constraints are recurring across villages and which are unique to certain villages.

Problem Analysis, Program Recommendations, and Write-up

At the end of the survey the information is reviewed by the team to determine the key constraints across villages or relevant to particular agro-ecological zones. A problem analysis approach is usually used for this process. Once the problems are prioritized, intervention themes are identified using multiple criteria analysis. Interventions will be aimed at helping people sustain their livelihoods. This may be achieved through: (1) a focus on retaining or expanding productive assets at the household level; (2) expanding alternative economic activities through capacity building or sustained improvement in access to services (health, education, water, etc.); (3) protecting livelihood systems through food-for-work or cash-for-work programs; (3) stabilizing markets during food shortages; and (4) devising appropriate interventions in conflict situations (Caldwell 1992).

Team consensus is sought on all constraints and recommendations proposed. The following questions are often posed to help determine the most appropriate recommendations for follow-up to the RFLSA from the team.

1. What population groups in the targeted areas are most in need and what constraints to livelihood improvement do they face?
2. What priority program activities provide the greatest leverage points for improving the food and livelihood security of the local populations? Do these vary by region or vulnerable group? To what degree are the local communities, local NGOs, and government aware and seeking solutions themselves? Should CARE develop a new program, or should collaborative links be established with other partners that do specialize in these interventions? Can CARE serve to mentor and assist to scale up local organizations that are already working on the solution?
3. If a new program is needed, how do the recommendations fit in with existing CARE programs? Will adjustments have to be made in ongoing programs (e.g., targeting, cross-project coordination), or do new initiatives have to be pursued? If new initiatives are recommended, does CARE presently have the skilled staff to take on such initiatives? If not, where will the staff and resources come from? Is there a development niche that is not presently being filled for which CARE can obtain donor funding? Does this activity fit in with CARE's strategic plan for the country? Does it fit in with the government's overall development strategy? How does it fit in with donors' strategies?
4. When considering a recommended food aid action, have the disincentive effects or changes on local production, marketing, and consumption been taken into account in the recommendation? Has consideration been given to ration size and quality, as well as timing? In addition, how is targeting information being used in the selection of project interventions and determination of wage rates? What is the government's role in the intervention? Has a plan been considered on how to phase out of the food distribution activity or other program activity? How will project benefits be sustained?
5. Have partners been identified to implement the project activities? How were these partners selected? What additional institutional capacity

building is necessary to scale up partner organizations and their performance? What are the constraints to successful partnerships?

6. What is the influence of government and donor macro policy on the success of the interventions proposed? Is there a potential advocacy role for CARE and its partners?

7. What are the steps that need to be taken into account to set up monitoring and evaluation systems for proposed project activities? What resources and technical assistance are needed for establishing baselines and monitoring and evaluation systems?

The results of the rapid food and livelihood security assessment are written up in a time-effective manner. To facilitate this write-up, the team leaders assign each member a portion of the report to be written. (Table 11.2 is an sample set of recommendations and indicators for a program in Kenya from a RFSLA.)

CONCLUSION

CARE has conducted over twenty rapid food and livelihood security assessments (RFLSAs) throughout the world since 1993. The overall message from the field has been that rapid assessments are very valuable to its country office operations, particularly for project design and multi-sector programming. These assessments have resulted in major changes in the ways that country offices partner with local NGOs and government agencies, and in the ways country offices measure impact. It is one of the most comprehensive tools currently being used to identify the factors that determine the nutritional status of a target population.

The methodology of RFLSAs is evolving and being refined, building on the lessons derived from accumulated experience and CARE is sharing this methodology with other organizations. From CARE's perspective, it is one of the most important diagnostic tools in use for making strategic decisions for development programming across sectors. Most importantly, however, RFLSAs provide a valuable mechanism for scaling up local development efforts. Local communities, CARE, other NGOs, and governments which participate in this type of needs assessment will find it sufficiently broad to allow the design of programming strategies that not only affect the communities that participated but also the much wider neighboring areas that were sampled. RFLSA is also specially suited for scaling down. It provides both an assessment tool for gathering good data and a strong mechanism for social interaction across the divide between the development summit and the grassroots community. By employing RFLSA,

Table 11.2. Sample Results of Rapid Food and Livelihood Security Assessment in Kenya

Recommended Program Elements	Indicators
Improved Agricultural Productivity	
extension/adaptive research	yield/acre
(land-use practices, soil	reduction in non-sustainable
conservation, soil fertility)	coping strategies
agro-forestry	number of months self-provisioning
drought resistant crops	
storage	
veterinary services	
Credit	
non-specific but used for	repayment rate
inputs, traction animals	increased area under production
range of products to meet	number of months of self-provisioning
varying demands i.e. group	participating female household heads
lending, linkage with banks	
Water and Sanitation	
de-siltation of dams/pans	availability
wells	accessibility
roof catchment	quality
hygiene education	affordability
(including latrines)	
supplementary feeding in	
hungry months	
AIDS Awareness	
education focussing on	community support
knowledge re-transmission,	mechanisms in place
prevention and control	
counseling	
community support mechanisms	
for care of AIDS victims and orphans	

an international NGO at the development summit can help people working in summit organizations to hear the people in the communities of the developing world, see problems from their viewpoint, and work with them to find sustainable solutions to their poverty, food insecurity, and nutrition insecurity. The livelihood security concept offers the promise of a new configuration of resource allocation, decision-making, and action responsibility between CARE, its local partners, and beneficiary households. If realized in practice, it could represent a breakthrough in bringing about secure livelihoods and nutrition security in the world's poorest communities.

REFERENCES

Caldwell, R.
(1992) *AgPaks as a Famine Mitigation Intervention*. Tucson, AZ: University of Arizona, Office of Arid Lands Studies.

Chambers, R.
(1985) "Shortcut Methods of Gathering Social Information for Rural Development Projects." In *Putting People First: Sociological Variables in Rural Development*, ed. M. Cernea. London: Oxford University Press.

Chambers, R.
(1988) "Sustainable Rural Livelihoods: a Key for People, Environment and Development." In *The Greening of Aid*, eds. C. Conroy and M. Litvinoff. London: Earthscan.

Chambers, R. and Conway, G.
(1992) "Sustainable Rural Livelihoods: Practical Concepts for the 21st Century." Institute of Development Studies Discussion Paper 296. (Cited in Drinkwater 1992.) Brighton, UK: IDS.

Corbett, J.
(1988) "Famine and Household Coping Strategies." *World Development* **16**: 1099–1112.

de Waal, A.
(1989a) *Famine that Kills: Darfur, Sudan, 1984–1985*. Oxford: Clarendon Press.

Drinkwater, M. and McEwan, M.
(1992) "Household Food Security and Environmental Sustainability in Farming Systems Research: Developing Sustainable Livelihoods." Paper presented to the Adaptive Planning Research Team (APRT) Biannual Review Meeting, Mangu, Zambia, 13–16 April.

Eklund, P.
(1990) *Rapid Rural Assessments for Sub-Saharan Africa: Two Case Studies*. Washington, D.C.: The Economic Development Institute of the World Bank.

Frankenberger, T. R.
(1990) "Production-consumption linkages and coping strategies at the household level." Paper presented at the Agriculture-Nutrition Linkages Workshop, Bureau of Science and Technology. Washington, D.C.: USAID.

Frankenberger, T. R.
(1992) "Indicators and Data Collection Methods for Assessing Household Food Security." In *Household Food Security: Concepts, Indicators, Measurements. A Technical Review*, eds. S. Maxwell and T. R. Frankenberger. New York and Rome: UNICEF and IFAD.

Frankenberger, T. R.
(1995)   Household Food Security: a Unifying Conceptual Framework for Care
         Programming. Atlanta: CARE.

Frankenberger, T. R.
(1996)   Measuring Household Livelihood Security: An Approach for Reducing
         Absolute Poverty. *Food Forum* **39**.

Frankenberger, T. R. and Lichte, J.
(1985)   A Methodology for Conducting Reconnaissance Surveys in Africa.
         Farming Systems Support Project Networking Paper #10. Gainesville,
         FL: University of Florida.

Frankenberger, T. R., Franzel, S., Odell, M., Odell, M., and Walecka, L. (eds.)
(1987)   *Diagnosis in Farming Systems Research and Extension*, Vol. 1. Farming
         Systems Support Project Training Units Series. Gainesville, FL: Uni-
         versity of Florida, Institute of Food and Agricultural Sciences.

Frankenberger, T. R. and Coyle, P. E.
(1993)   "Integrating household food security into farming systems research and
         extension." *Journal for Farming Systems Research-Extension* **4**(1):
         35–66.

Frankenberger, T. R. and Goldstein, D. M.
(1992)   "The Long and the Short of It: Relationships Between Coping
         Strategies, Food Security and Environmental Degradation in Africa."
         In *Growing Our Future*, ed. K. Smith. New York: Kumarian Press.

Frankenberger, T. R. and Schaeffer, C.
(1994)   CARE Rapid Food Security Assessments/Impact Evaluations: Lessons
         Learned. Memorandum. Atlanta: CARE.

Gross, R., Altfelder, S. and Koch, E.
(1995)   "To reduce poverty." Mimeo. Jarkarta, Indonesia: GTZ.

Hildebrand, P.
(1981)   "Combining Disciplines in Rapid Appraisal: the Sondeo Approach."
         Agricultural Administration **8**(6): 423–432.

McCracken, J. A., Pretty, J. N., and Conway, G. R.
(1988)   *An Introduction to Rapid Rural Appraisal for Agricultural Develop-
         ment*. London: International Institute for Environment and Develop-
         ment (IIED).

Maxwell, S. and Smith, M.
(1992)   "Household Food Security: a Conceptual Review." Mimeo. Sussex,
         UK: Institute of Development Studies, University of Sussex.

Molnar, A.
(1989)   *Community Forestry: Rapid Appraisal*. Rome: FAO.

Perez, C.
(1997a) "Participatory Research: Implication for Applied Anthropology."
         Practicing Anthropology **19**(3): 2–8.

Perez, C.
(1997b) "Negotiating Beneficiary Involvement in Agricultural Development Projects: Experiences from CARE." *Practicing Anthropology* **19**(3): 31–36.
WRI (World Resources Institute), Center for International Development and Environment
(1989) *Participatory Rural Appraisal Handbook: Conducting PRAs in Kenya.* Washington, DC: WRI.

CHAPTER 12

Nutrition Capacity Building: Reflections on an Application of the Nutrition Program Constraints Assessment in South Africa

Milla McLachlan and F. James Levinson

The nutrition program constraints assessment (PCA) is an analytical tool designed to improve program effectiveness, which reflects both the concepts of scaling down and scaling up. Its development was prompted by international recognition that despite ambitious goals and important scientific advances, existing approaches to combating malnutrition are not leading to a significant reduction in the prevalence of global malnutrition. It appears that translation of knowledge and experience into effective programs has been inadequate (see Ch. 3). This chapter describes the events leading up to the development of new approaches, including the PCA methodology, and presents a case study of the application of this methodology in Gauteng Province, South Africa.

"NUTRITION MALPRACTICE" AND THE PCA APPROACH

In June 1991, Alan Berg, senior nutrition advisor of the World Bank, presented, as the annual Martin Forman Memorial Lecture, a paper titled "Sliding toward nutrition malpractice: Time to reconsider and redeploy" (Berg 1991).[1] The paper described graphically the gap existing between malnutrition problems in low-income countries and efforts by the international nutrition community to address them. Berg lamented the lack of training and research efforts, particularly by academic institutions in industrialized countries, which explicitly address operationally-oriented malnutrition problem solving in developing nations.

Berg provided data indicating that the large majority of malnutrition research studies are concerned with the "why," "who," "where," and, to some extent "what" questions, as opposed to the "how" questions which Berg identified as most immediately impeding progress in the development of effective programs.

In terms of training, Berg cited the small number of individuals trained and oriented to design and manage nutrition programs. In many cases, Berg argued, the misdirected research and lack of appropriately trained personnel stem from an "academic culture and reward system (which) leads in other directions."

> "What we need," Berg argued, "are students trained in economics and administration and logistics and planning and budgeting and the dozen other necessary skills in addition to nutrition. People who will feel at home in both the scientific and bureaucratic worlds. People who can do nuts and bolts work in getting projects going in specific country situations month after month.

Berg affixed the label "nutrition engineer" to this needed cadre of professionals, defining engineer, as does Webster, as "a person who carries through an enterprise and brings about a result." "Unlike many other fields," Berg continued, "nutrition doesn't have the equivalent of engineers—we have the equivalent of physicists, but not of engineers—and we need them."

Berg's paper, subsequently published by the *American Journal of Clinical Nutrition*, elicited considerable controversy and debate—and more letters to the editor than any article in the history of the *AJCN*. Perhaps predictably, responses from the academic community were somewhat defensive while officials of governments, donor agencies and NGOs responded positively. Clearly the paper had both struck responsive chords and hit upon raw nerves.[2]

While the debate continued in the letters columns and in the classroom, the Berg thesis moved ahead, fueled in part by pent up government and donor frustration with journal article-driven nutrition research and theory-based nutrition training often far removed from policy and program realities.

The next step in the progression was a feasibility study commissioned by the Rockefeller Foundation in 1992 on means of operationalizing the Berg thesis (Levinson 1993). This study enlarged on Berg's research and training discussions, provided definitions and examples of the types of research and training needed, and presented several structural alternatives:

1. An International Center for Nutrition Research and Training with its own highly qualified staff capable of providing technical assistance and developing partnership relationships with national and regional institutions interested in such program-driven efforts;
2. An International Nutrition Research and Training Fund with a small secretariat housed at the headquarters of an international agency which would provide funding, on the basis of proposals, for high quality, operationally-oriented research and training in well specified categories; and
3. Regional initiatives designed to stimulate and manage such research and training.[3]

The Rockefeller Foundation subsequently agreed to follow up the study with a conference on the subject at its conference and study center in Bellagio Italy. The conference, held in October–November 1994, brought together officials of governments, international and bilateral assistance agencies, NGOs and academic institutions to examine the Berg thesis, consider the need for international action, and discuss options offered in the feasibility study.

The conference reaffirmed the importance of program-driven research and training, opted for the regional action alternative, adopted a "Bellagio Declaration" of principles, and appointed an interim steering committee to help stimulate regional activity. Such a high level international adoption of principles clearly represented a "summit." The challenge now was to "scale down" these investments in program-driven research and training to appropriate levels so that groups and individuals could scale up their capacities to address these needs. (See the Preface for definitions of scaling up and scaling down and Chs. 5 and 13 for related discussion of scaling down the development summit.)

It was suggested that countries or subnational administrations interested in participating in regional applied research and training initiatives, might wish to carry out what came to be known as "program constraints assessments" (PCA). Such assessments would seek to identify systematically all major constraints to existing nutrition-related programs, and then determine the subset of these constraints that could be addressed by policy reformulations, by operationally-oriented research, or by training. Appropriate research and training would be specified and costed.

The PCA approach was recognized as offering an alternative, and possibly complementary, approach to that recommended for national governments at the 1993 International Conference on Nutrition (ICN). The ICN recommended that countries develop national nutrition plans or strategies which define national level governmental responsibilities for addressing nutrition needs. The national nutrition strategy approach is being pursued, often with FAO, WHO or UNICEF assistance, by a large number of developing countries which participated in the ICN.

A national nutrition strategy is sometimes formulated as if a blank slate were available on which a rational and coherent strategy can be specified on the basis of identified problems and available resources. Such a blank slate is rarely available. In addition, such strategy exercises may underestimate the time and effort required for genuine consensus building, not simply on goals, priorities and strategy content, but even on the nature of problems faced. In a context of limited resources and political pressures, changing existing programs from the top down in line with a new strategy may not be realistic in the short or medium term.

The PCA approach may offer a more organic process by beginning with what is already in operation and with the preexisting operational context. Through analysis of constraints impeding effectiveness in these programs, a set of program-driven policy, research and training needs emerges, permitting gradual movement towards more effective programs, and in a way which elicits full participation by the primary stakeholders.

The national nutrition strategy and PCA approaches need not be mutually exclusive, and, ideally, should be complementary. Because the PCA is, by definition, limited to programs which already exist, it may not alert policy makers quickly to priority problems which are unattended and may require new initiatives.

It should be clear that the PCA does not represent a policy and program panacea, but rather deals with a critically important component: the need for program-driven policy, research and training agendas designed to address constraints which impede the effectiveness of existing programs. In the long run, effective programs are likely to result from the creative interface of (1) such program-driven policy change, research and training; (2) more basic research and related training which move our conceptual understanding forward; and (3) the consensus building process itself.

APPLICATION IN SOUTH AFRICA: THE PROGRAM CONSTRAINTS ASSESSMENT

After the Bellagio Conference in 1994, various follow-up initiatives were taken in Africa, Asia and Latin America. UNICEF promoted several initiatives in South and Southeast Asia, and was involved, for example, in establishing the South-East Asia Nutrition Research-cum-Action Network. The World Bank and USAID together with UNICEF assisted efforts by the Network of African Public Health Institutes (NAPHI) and the Commonwealth Health Secretariat for Eastern, Central and Southern Africa (ECSA).

Complementing these regional activities were efforts at a national level. South Africa and a subnational government, the Gauteng Provincial Administration, offer a case example of these national efforts to scale down the Bellagio principles to appropriate levels, and then scale up capacity to meet a highly specific and unique set of needs.

South African Context

After years of violent conflict over apartheid and exclusion of Blacks from the electoral process in South Africa, the early 1990s ushered in a period of negotiations. Both the National Party government and the Congress Alliance led by the African National Congress were prepared to make compromises to achieve the goal of a non-racial democracy. By 1994, the first democratically elected government was formed. The first step in the country's critical transition was achieved, and South Africa found itself embarked on the long road toward equity, reconciliation and broad-based economic growth.

The political commitment to negotiation and consultation beginning in the early 1990s also created a context for development-related discussions among a broad array of public interest groups, service organizations, community-based organizations, academics and, increasingly, public servants. Among the topics negotiated was nutrition.

Initially, the specific context of nutrition-related discussions was the devastating drought of 1992. A Nutrition Task Force (NTF) was established under the auspices of the National Consultative Forum on Drought, but with a mandate to initiate public discussion and debate on national nutrition programs more broadly. A critical focus of these early discussions was the controversial National Nutrition and Social Development Program, established by the National Party administration to address poverty—but also to protect needy individuals who would be adversely affected by its proposed value added tax on basic foods. The Nutrition

Task Force made a major effort to build consensus among a range of interest groups on issues relating to this and other existing programs, and, more broadly, on the nature of malnutrition problems facing the country.

Soon after the elections, the new Government of National Unity announced a comprehensive reconstruction and development program which committed the government to poverty alleviation and recognized the importance of addressing hunger and malnutrition. Among its lead projects was the Primary School Nutrition Program, discussed in detail below. Although the South African nutrition community was divided on the choice of program, it readily acknowledged the symbolic significance of a high profile nutrition program announced personally by President Mandela.

Meanwhile a high level committee proposed the development of a nutrition strategy for the country.[4] As a direct outcome of its recommendations, a Nutrition Directorate was established by the Ministry of Health with a mandate to restructure the existing fragmented and vertical programs into an integrated program. Implementation of that plan, however, as dictated by the interim national constitution, would be the responsibility of provincial rather than national structures.

It quickly became apparent that devolution of this responsibility in South Africa would have to be done with considerable care, given the uneven capacities of provincial administrations in health and nutrition. Discussion papers prepared at this time reflect a keen awareness of the need for capacity building particularly, but not exclusively, at the provincial level, and also for an openness to learn from past experiences and experiment with new approaches.

In July, 1995, the still active Nutrition Task Force, in collaboration with the Development Bank of Southern Africa (DBSA), organized a workshop on "Research and Training in Support of Nutrition Programs." The workshop called together many of the leading nutrition training and research professionals in the country plus representatives of major governmental and NGO nutrition programs. The workshop identified constraints facing national nutrition programs and research and training activities which might address these constraints. Importantly, the workshop also informed the South African nutrition community about the Bellagio Conference, and initiated discussions on related activities which could be carried out in the country.

One of these subsequent activities was the Gauteng Program Constraints Assessment described in detail below. Other relevant initiatives include (1) development of a national nutrition surveillance system based on a pilot effort developed in one of the provinces; (2) implementation of comprehensive research on the Primary School Nutrition Program; and

(3) design of a modular in-service training program to support community-based nutrition projects.

Overall, the critical prerequisites for effective scaling in both directions appear to be present in South Africa. The policy environment is receptive to new strategies and willing to adapt and redesign existing programs on the basis of appropriate studies. In addition, a high premium has been placed by the new government on capacity building both within the government and at the community level. Finally, there is recognition, particularly among key support organizations, of the need to foster a culture of inquiry among all groups involved in nutrition-related activities.

The Gauteng Program Constraints Assessment

Nutritional data for South Africa as a whole reveal both undernutrition and chronic dietary-related diseases. An estimated 30% of South African children under the age of six are stunted, and data on caloric intakes among children in some rural areas are as low as 60% of recommended daily allowances (Vorster et al. 1997). At the same time, cholesterol intake figures are high, particularly for White and Mixed Race populations (over 330 mg/day). Infant mortality rates range from seven per 1000 live births to estimates of as high as 10 times that for Blacks. Gauteng, with a more urbanized population, has lower rates of stunting (an estimated 11%) but probably a higher prevalence of chronic dietary-based diseases than the national average (SAVACG 1995).

The 1995 Workshop on Training and Research in Support of Nutrition Programs, discussed above, also led to discussion between the Development Bank of Southern Africa and Tufts University on the feasibility of conducting in one South African province the program constraints analysis tool recommended at the Bellagio Conference. The question was which province.

Although Gauteng, being highly urbanized, is not representative of South Africa, a decision was made to carry out the assessment in that province. The Gauteng Provincial Administration already had initiated a nutrition program review and its director of Mother and Child Health and Nutrition expressed interest in using the results of the study during the program review process. Furthermore, there were logistical advantages to doing the first assessment in a centrally located province, with the clear understanding that the methodology and results would be shared with other provinces.

The assessment methodology and results are fully presented in the constraints assessment report (Levinson et al. 1995). The pages that follow summarize key elements of the assessment methodology and then present illustrative results.

Assessment Methodology

In Central America and Mexico, a related exercise utilized a highly structured questionnaire and a relatively large number of enumerators. Results of that assessment indicated that the highly structured format may be inadequate, given the frequent need for follow-up questions to elicit and elucidate responses (Rivera Dommarco et al. 1996).

In Gauteng the assessment team consisted of two international nutrition researchers and two national counterparts. The skills and experience represented by team members included knowledge of international nutrition programs, semi-structured interviewing techniques, local policy understanding, policy analysis experience, and necessary language skills, all of which proved important in the assessment. The use of a single team (as opposed to large numbers of enumerators) for information collection and synthesis and the utilization of a semi-structured interview format (as opposed to formal questionnaires) proved highly successful.

Although the program constraints assessment is geared primarily to professionals with design and decision making responsibilities, the assessment team found it necessary to interview a broader spectrum of people to elicit a more complete picture of programs and the constraints they face.

The interviews were conducted to elicit detailed information on: (1) the purposes, scope and nature of specific program activities; (2) the numbers of professional staff involved, the nature of their design and decision making responsibilities, and the minimum requirements for these positions; (3) an assessment of program effectiveness; (4) identification of constraints of any kind believed by respondents to be inhibiting program effectiveness; (5) enumeration of specific training and research activities which, according to respondents, might have the potential to address the constraints identified; and (6) identification of previous training and specific future training which respondents believe might assist them in better carrying out their responsibilities.

The interviews and site visits were carried out over a period of eight days after which the team worked together for another three days in consolidating and organizing the information. During this period, the constraints were organized into five categories: (1) political viability and vested interests; (2) problem definition and program thrust; (3) target group definition and targeting; (4) program implementation; and (5) monitoring and evaluation.

Included at the request of the Gauteng Provincial Administration was an identification of policy issues emerging from examination of the constraints. The Provincial Administration, actively moving towards an integrated nutrition strategy, recognized that a portion of the constraints identified lent themselves to policy resolution rather than to research or training, per se, and that the very identification of program constraints might shed light on these policy issues.

The nutrition-related activities included in the constraints assessment were the following: (1) school nutrition and health; (2) nutrition through primary health care; (3) nutrition-related poverty alleviation; and (4) behavioral change. In this chapter, for purposes of presenting an example we will limit discussion to the first of these, school nutrition and health.

Application to School Nutrition and Health Example

Although sporadic school feeding projects had been implemented in Gauteng, broad-based attention to school nutrition and health is a recent phenomenon, emerging from President Mandela's announcement of a Primary School Nutrition Program (PSNP) at the opening of the first democratic parliament in May 1994.

The PSNP, established as a nationwide "Presidential Lead Project," was to be implemented nationwide in 100 days in all schools "where need was established." The program received an allocation of nearly R.500 million (US $140 million) for the first year of its operation under the national Reconstruction and Development Program (RDP) Fund, and was, arguably, the RDP's most visible early success.

Nonetheless, given severe budgetary constraints and pressing needs in all sectors, continued large scale national government support for the program was not assured at the time of the assessment. While some insisted that school feeding is a basic right which should be made available to all school children, others argued that greater needs existed among younger children. In the second year, funds for the program were reduced by 35%.

The PSNP reached roughly 13,000 schools and an estimated 5.5 million children, or over half of the primary school children in the country in 1995. (An estimated 85% of school age children attend at least the lower grades of primary school.)

In Gauteng, the program operated in 296 of the 5400 primary schools or roughly 5.5%. This smaller percentage coverage in Gauteng related not to financial constraints but rather to PSNP provincial staff's uncertainty at the inception of the program regarding the targeting of schools and the targeting of children within schools. The PSNP within Gauteng opted to limit the program initially to "farm schools," because rural areas were identified as the neediest in the province.

Food provided in the schools supplied roughly 22% of Recommended Dietary Allowances for calories. The food, usually provided as an early morning supplement,[5] consisted generally of a peanut butter sandwich and milk.

In most of the schools, food was procured under the "tender system," meaning that procurement and delivery to the schools was arranged by the provincial government on the basis of tenders received. Tenders were awarded, in most cases, to large, well-established private sector distributors who delivered supplies to schools and were directly reimbursed by the Department of Health. A smaller number of schools operated under the "quotation system" in which school project committees were responsible for contracting with food suppliers and were reimbursed by the government.

Once the program was initiated in Gauteng and the other provinces, attention of responsible staff expanded in several directions, including:

(a) means of increasing community participation in school feeding programs, and making such feeding sustainable at the local level;
(b) means of contributing more broadly to the learning capacity of pupils through nutrition and health inputs beyond the food itself, leading to consideration of micronutrient provision, deworming and nutrition education;
(c) means of improving food supply processes for the feeding programs, while placing higher emphasis on local supply and income generation.

At the same time, staff found it difficult to function effectively in a programmatic climate of high uncertainty.

Constraints Identified

Analysis of interview data led to the identification of twelve nutrition program constraints which were organized into five categories:

Political Viability and Vested Interests

(1) An overriding constraint identified was the uncertainty regarding resource allocation and the future of the program. Staff indicated morale problems and a difficulty in generating cooperation from local counterparts in light of such uncertainty.
(2) Major food suppliers, relied upon heavily in initiating the program within the 100 day deadline, represented a powerful vested interest in

the program, even as the province and local communities were looking for ways to supply more of the food locally through vendors and the development of cottage industries.

Problem Definition and Program Thrust

(3) There was a lack of consensus at all levels about the problem being addressed. Was it hunger (and, if so, weren't there hungrier people in the province)? Was it malnutrition (and, if so, wasn't it more important to reach younger children)? Was it learning capacity (and, if so, where was the evidence that it would make a difference in South Africa)?

(4) There was a general lack of understanding of linkages between nutrition and learning, particularly on the part of education professionals.

(5) There was uncertainty about scope. Should the activity be limited to food provision, or should a broader-based school nutrition and health initiative include micronutrient provision, deworming and nutrition education? If so, on what basis (e.g., survey data, cost-effectiveness data from pilot projects) could these added inputs be considered?

Target Group Definition and Targeting

(6) Given the likelihood that stricter targeting would be needed because of budgetary constraints, there was an acknowledged lack of understanding of the relative effectiveness, administrative feasibility, and political acceptability of alternative targeting approaches (i.e., targeting of schools by geographic area, or of pupils by age group, economic status, or anthropometry).

(7) Among those professionals who considered the school nutrition and health vehicle an appropriate mechanism for at least the procurement of food for pre-school programs and creches, there was no information on which to base such consideration.

Implementation

(8) Professional staff at the provincial level expressed considerable discomfort and uncertainty about food supply procedures and about the cost-efficiency of provisions currently in place. Among the primary issues: (a) relative effectiveness of the tender and the quotation system; and (b) a perceived imbalance between external procurement from large food supply firms and local procurement from vendors and other community food production and processing groups.

(9) There was a shortage of provincial level personnel to manage the food supply.

(10) There was a lack of adequate management skills both on the part of government and local project committee personnel.

Monitoring and Evaluation

(11) A management information system for monitoring purposes (in a program already constrained by the lack of clear objectives and targets) was not yet functioning for the province, although this need was being addressed.

(12) Evaluation was not yet an accepted component of the program, and government staff felt neither empowered nor professionally prepared to carry out systematic data collection and analysis for this purpose. There was a clearly articulated need among government staff for increased computer literacy.

Policy issues requiring attention as well as research and training needs were formulated on the basis of the identified constraints. Resource requirements necessary to carry out these activities were also estimated in the report. The combined cost of all the proposed research and training activities totaled approximately 1% of the provincial nutrition budget, far short of the 2% figure recommended in 1987 by the International Commission on Health Research for research alone.

Research emerging from the identified constraints in the area of school nutrition and health covered a broad spectrum of activity. A study to measure the effects of school feeding and school-based micronutrient, deworming and nutrition education interventions on learning capacity was considered important to address constraints related to problem definition and problem thrust. To address issues relating to targeting, program professionals identified the need to design and test alternative options for community-based targeting. A study of food procurement procedures was identified, consisting both of a management review of existing practices and a feasibility study of alternative means of generating more efficient local food provision. Finally, a suggested study to consider linkages between the Primary School Nutrition Program and existing pre-school and creche programs emerged from concerns about these other priority target groups.

The training agenda emerging from the constraints assessment related to needs for increased understanding of nutrition problems and their determinants; program-related management skills; community-related communication, facilitation and advocacy skills; and, for some staff, training skills.

Utilization of the Assessment Results and Lessons Learned

An important conceptual strength of the PCA approach is that it permits the identification of a set of research and training needs not by the research and training communities per se (although both are essential partners in the process) but by program professionals and service providers directly engaged in service delivery programs and most sensitive to constraints inhibiting those programs. Program professionals fully involved in a PCA also will be more committed to research and the training emerging from it.

In the Gauteng assessment, the professionals who were interviewed valued the opportunity to discuss constraints and offer opinions on related research and training needs. While it is still too early to assess the full benefits of their involvement, it appears that further participation in the assessment itself, particularly in discussing findings, would assure a sense of ownership of the results.

Because the constraints assessment was carried out in Gauteng at the beginning of its Mother and Child Health and Nutrition program transformation process, it has served as an important input throughout that process. A collaborative project between the Gauteng Department of Health and the Development Bank of Southern Africa, which extensively utilized the PCA and other information sources, was also important in facilitating the transformation process and actually initiating specific identified research and training activities. (By 1997, an estimated 80% of the recommended research and training activities had been initiated.) In addition, the PCA results were utilized in the national level dialogue on a range of nutrition program areas.

The Gauteng PCA experience underlined the importance of a skilled, reasonably senior team for information collection and analysis. At the same time, the PCA could itself be utilized for capacity building purposes by including on the team a few more junior professionals who are likely to increase significantly their understanding of policy and program issues as a result.

More broadly, the Gauteng experience suggests that, to be effective, a PCA requires an enabling policy environment. It is unlikely to yield practical insights and action in an environment not open to discussion and debate about its nutrition problems and program effectiveness, or one unwilling to engage seriously in a process of program-driven research and training. In the absence of such receptivity, a PCA may unfairly raise expectations among program staff and intended beneficiaries who will then be frustrated by the lack of responsive action. A prior commitment to serious policy review of assessment results and an assurance of technical and financial support to permit implementation of acceptable research and training agendas may, accordingly, be appropriate prerequisites for a PCA.

Finally the Gauteng experience indicates that a program constraints assessment can both contribute importantly to the establishment of a culture of inquiry in nutrition programs and to concrete, affordable and appropriate actions designed to improve program effectiveness.

NOTES

1. Dr. Martin Forman had served for nearly 20 years as Director of the Office of Nutrition of the U.S. Agency for International Development in Washington.

2. Criticisms of the Berg thesis centered on three recurring points:

   (1) Rather than "nutrition engineers," effective nutrition work requires teams of professionals, each well grounded in particular complementary disciplines.

   (2) The lack of adequate operationally-oriented research and training in international nutrition is more a problem of inadequate funds than the lack of will.

   (3) Problems of malnutrition relate more to structural constraints embedded in the political economies of developing countries and to the lack of empowerment than to "technical" or "reductionist" issues relating to research and training (Csete 1993; Carpenter 1993; Brown and Dewey 1993; Jonsson 1993).

3. The third alternative emerged from subsequent discussions and developments and is not contained in the feasibility study document itself.

4. The process had actually been initiated earlier by a Working Group on Nutrition, one of many such fora established to initiate formal consultations and encourage joint decision making among representative groups as elections approached.

5. The purpose of providing an early morning supplement is to alleviate problems of temporary hunger (and the resultant learning constraint) for children, many of whom eat no food before coming to school. During the first year of operation, however, it became evident that some portion of the pupils were coming to school only for the snack and then leaving. This has led to consideration of a smaller early morning supplement followed by a school lunch later in the day.

REFERENCES

Berg, A.
  (1991) "Sliding Toward Nutrition Malpractice: Time to Reconsider and Redeploy." Martin J. Forman Memorial Lecture. Reprinted in *Annual Review of Nutrition*, **13**, 1993.
Brown, K. and Dewey, K.
  (1993) "Slipping to Scapegoating in International Nutrition." Letter to the Editor, *American Journal of Clinical Nutrition* **57**: 1.

Carpenter, K.
(1993) "Nutritional Science and the Third World." Letter to the Editor, *American Journal of Clinical Nutrition* **57**: 1.

Csete, J.
(1993) "Malnutrition and 'Nutrition Engineering' in Low-Income Countries: A Comment on Alan Berg's Vision of the Nutrition Track Record." *International Journal of Health Services* **23**: 3.

Jonsson, U.
(1993) "The Global Embarrassment of Malnutrition and the Role of Nutrition Engineers." Letter to the Editor, *American Journal of Clinical Nutrition* **58**: 4.

Levinson, F. J.
(1993) "Addressing Nutrition Malpractice: Feasibility Study of an International Center or Fund to Facilitate Applied Research and Training in International Nutrition." New York: The Rockefeller Foundation.

Levinson, F. J., Dladla, C., McLachlan, M., and Olivar, M.
(1995) "Nutrition Program Constraints Assessment: Gauteng Province, South Africa," Medford, MA: International Food and Nutrition Center.

Rivera Dommarco, J., Flores, R., Levinson, F. J., and Remancus, S. M.
(1996) "Neighbors Nutrition Programs: Training Needs Assessment (Phase A) for Mexico and Central America." Medford, MA: International Food and Nutrition Center.

SAVACG (South African Vitamin A Consultative Group)
(1995) "Children Aged 6–71 months in South Africa, 1994: Their Anthropometric, Vitamin A, Iron, and Immunization Coverage Status." Unpublished.

Scrimshaw, N. S. and Altschul, A. M.
(1971) *Amino Acid Fortification of Protein Foods*. Cambridge: MIT Press.

Vorster, H. H., Oosthuizen, W., Jerling, J. C., Veldman, F. J., and Burger, H. M.
(1997) *The Nutritional Status of South Africans: A Review of the Literature from 1975–1996*. Durban: Health Systems Trust.

IV Scaling Down the Summit

CHAPTER 13

Opportunities for the Summit: Improving the Practice of Public Nutrition

Micheline Beaudry[1]

"Public nutrition" deals with the nutrition problems of populations and the public policies and programs to address them (Mason et al. 1996; Eide and Oshaug 1997; Rogers and Schlossman 1997). This chapter suggests opportunities for practitioners working on public nutrition issues from their positions at the development summit.[2] These opportunities are inspired by an interpretation of the different analyses of conditions associated with success in improving nutrition (Miller and Drake 1980; UNICEF 1990; Jennings et al. 1991; Jonsson 1995; Gillespie et al. 1996) in light of the author's experience both at the United Nations Children's Fund (UNICEF) and in the debate on the needs of nutrition research and training which followed a related conference held in Bellagio, Italy, in 1994.

The example of UNICEF is particularly relevant because of its recognized leadership role in attempting to better the lives of children. Such leading international agencies, exert considerable influence over choices made for nutrition around the world, and so do academic institutions, albeit via different paths. While both have contributed substantially to existing improvements, important opportunities remain for more effective scaling down to facilitate necessary changes in the policies and strategies of governments to trigger the emergence, and scaling up, of relevant and effective community-based and community-focused nutrition programs that could accelerate the reduction of malnutrition,

PROGRAMMING

From the mid-1970s to 1995 important progress in reducing the prevalence of underweight[3] in young children has been observed in countries from different regions (see Ch. 1). An analysis of this progress reveals the expected broad relation between a country's economic situation and its nutrition situation (Gillespie et al. 1996). It also strongly suggests that an equitable economic growth strategy—rather than poverty-alleviation programs—accelerates nutrition improvement. So do strategies which include: (1) ample social sector financing that effectively reaches the poor and malnourished, (2) building and sustaining institutions for problem analysis and monitoring, and (3) facilitating community-based programming. Among the latter, it has repeatedly been shown that direct nutrition programs that are strongly rooted at the community level tend to be more successful and more sustainable, and that decentralized decision-making power—not just responsibility—is crucial. However, the global rate of progress is still less than one-fifth of that necessary to reach the goal of halving the prevalence between 1990–2000 (ACC/SCN 1996).

Given the limited global progress, even in several countries that have witnessed economic growth, one might conclude that efforts to scale up successful local programs have generally failed. Following a rapid appraisal commissioned by UNICEF of 23 successful community-based programs in South Asia, Jonsson (1995) proposed that simply scaling up quantitatively or going to scale may be the wrong concept. He suggested that in cases where successful community-based nutrition projects have accelerated nation-wide, the government has changed its policies and strategies and these changes have triggered the emergence of many similar community-based initiatives. He proposed four steps that seem important in this transformation:

—governments and their advisors need to know, understand and accept the conclusions from their own community-based projects;
—governments need to develop and implement economic and other policies (e.g., health, education, water, sanitation) that create local environments that are conducive for the contextual success-factors to emerge and operate;

—planners, designers and implementers of nutrition-oriented programs and projects need to use the conclusions from these studies;
—multi-lateral and bi-lateral agencies, international and national NGOs and others need to promote the preparation and implementation of programs and projects based on these principles (Jonsson 1995).

Jonsson also suggests Thailand as the best example of a country where the experience from community-based nutrition programs and projects was used to change national policies and strategies along these lines. (See Tontsirin et al. 1995 for a summary of their experience.) Jonsson's suggestions parallel those of Uvin in Ch. 5 regarding the need to create interactions between the grassroots and the summit in ways that are beneficial to local communities and poor people. Two processes would be necessary: scaling up[4] or the process by which grassroots organizations expand their impact and enter into relations with the summit, and scaling down, the complementary process by which the summit adopts modes of functioning that allow for meaningful interactions with the grassroots and strengthen their capacity for scaling up.

In an agency such as UNICEF, several forces have competed since the early 1990s to influence programming and the allocation of resources. They include: (1) the goals approved at the World Summit for Children (WSC) (UN 1990); (2) the Convention on the Rights of the Child (CRC), now ratified by all but two countries, which broadened the mandate of UNICEF to include all aspects of the human development of children; (3) the end of the Cold War and the opening up of Eastern Europe; (4) the increasing number of emergency situations around the world for women and children; and (5) the results of the multi-donor evaluation of UNICEF which reflected the increasing global concern for sustainability (Engbert-Pedersen et al. 1992). Trying to respond effectively within a near stable resource base has reinforced the relevance of the UNICEF Nutrition Strategy (UNICEF 1990) approved in 1990 and highlights opportunities to facilitate its broader implementation in the current context. Key elements of the UNICEF nutrition strategy include:

—Recognition that poor people are knowledgeable about their world and that in general they adapt to their situation in a sophisticated way;
—A theoretical framework on the likely causality of malnutrition (Figure 13.1);
—An understanding that decisions are made in a cyclical way based on the information available for the assessment and analysis of a situation leading to action, reassessment, reanalysis and revised actions.

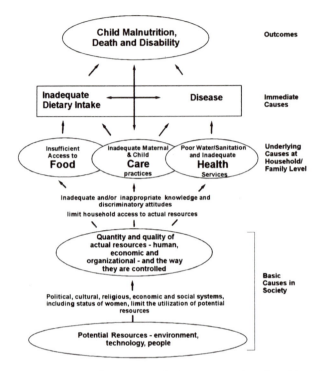

Figure 13.1. Conceptual framework of the causes of malnutrition (source: UNICEF 1997:24).

UNICEF's nutrition activities over the years have included most of those seen in many countries and across continents (Gillespie and Mason 1991): the promotion of breastfeeding and good complementary feeding practices; monitoring and promotion of child growth; encouragement of the production of nutritious food; provision of complementary feeding and specific nutrients to combat deficiency diseases; promotion of nutrition education and training; and development of national food and nutrition policies. However, there are no pre-defined technical packages, and programs must be flexible enough to adapt to the results of the local assessment and analysis and to evolving situations (i.e., be context specific while also being biologically/scientifically appropriate). Local involvement in both planning and implementation, as well as in evaluation, is considered essential to success. Thus simple scaling up is likely to be ineffective and

UNICEF recognizes that what matters at all levels is not only the choice of activities, but *mainly* how these activities are selected:

—Do the activities selected respond to an assessment and analysis of the situation within an explicitly formulated framework that considers the social causes of the problem as well as the biological ones?
—Who participates in the assessment and analysis leading to the choice of actions: are all stakeholders, including those most affected by the problem, involved in related decisions?
—Do the activities selected make an explicit attempt to address underlying and basic causes of the problem, not only immediate causes?

It is through opportunities to more broadly facilitate the implementation of this approach in practice that the summit could help trigger the emergence of many more successful community-based nutrition programs.

Making Explicit Our Understanding of the Causes of Malnutrition

The framework of the causes of malnutrition that was adapted by UNICEF (1990) from the successful experience of Tanzania has now been adopted by a number of country programs as well as by other agencies (Figure 13.1). Its use facilitates the exploration of the major causes of malnutrition, and the priorization for action of the key constraints to implementing the right to *food*, to adequate *health* services and a healthy environment, and to appropriate *caring* practices, the necessary conditions for implementing the right to adequate nutrition.

While adopting such a framework is an important step, the objective is to actually use it to guide the assessment of the situation and the analysis of its causes in a given context. Yet, from our experience, this step remains absent in too many of the country program proposals received from country offices. The country program is the core of UNICEF's programming and is intended to be the instrument for priority-setting and for the choice of appropriate strategies. In the five year programming cycle, every country program is approved by the Executive Board in year one, undergoes a mid-course evaluation in years two to three, leading to corrections if necessary in years three to four and to a renewed "situation analysis" around year four, leading to the preparation and submission of a new proposal in year five, and so on. Several reviews occur throughout the process. Yet in many countries the situation analysis is done as a separate exercise, often by outside consultants, and often without an explicit conceptual framework to guide them. It is frequently another group, the program people, who then begin the brain-storming that leads to programming, often building more on their former program experience than on the situation analysis just carried out, but also often without an explicit conceptual framework to guide the analysis of their experience.

Even fewer countries have devised their own conceptual framework linking the situation specific information to what is scientifically known about the problems, although some have done it masterfully, such as Indonesia, Cambodia, and Uganda. Through an elaborate intersectoral participatory process and with initial guidance from the UNICEF framework on the causes of malnutrition, theirs has become not only more context specific, but also more alive and relevant as participants own it, see its usefulness, and can take action upon it. Equally important is the fact that their framework is used to guide not only programming for nutrition but actually all of the country's programming to improve the well-being of children (Gautam 1995). They recognize that nutritional status of young children is an outcome of processes in different sectors and an indicator of their effectiveness in overall efforts to improve children's well-being.

Using an explicit and well-understood conceptual framework makes it easier to confront one's work with what is scientifically known and ethically appropriate, to make sure that one's assessment and analysis of the situation start from a valid standpoint. It is also an important element of communication between institutions and also between levels in each institution, thus facilitating participation at all levels. Its role was particularly evidenced in Tanzania (Pelletier 1991). Making more explicit what guides the local assessment and analysis of the causes of malnutrition needs to be more widely facilitated and supported by the summit.

Planning with Community Understanding and Participation

It is generally accepted that actions or solutions that draw on existing local knowledge and that enhance existing behavioral strategies by which people maintain their nutrition have more chances of reaching families and communities than trying to introduce de novo solutions or to compete with existing ones. This requires an understanding of how people's strategies and coping mechanisms work in practice, recognizing that they are often quite complex. If those affected by the problem participate in the assessment of the situation and analysis of its causes, together with other key stakeholders in the existing situation, including people technically trained in the area, it is more likely that actual strategies or coping mechanisms will be identified, as well as ways to enhance them.

To assess and analyze the role of participation in government food and nutrition programs, Shrimpton (1995) proposed an analytical framework of different aspects of participation related to needs assessment, organization, leadership, training, resource mobilization, management, orientation of actions and monitoring, evaluation, and information exchange. He applied it to four government programs that have claimed to be effective and to have community participation as an important part of their strategies (Tamil Nadu Integrated Nutrition Project, India; Iringa Nutrition Program, Tanzania; National Growth Monitoring Program, Thailand; Family Nutrition Improvement Program, Indonesia). The results indicate that even limited community participation was both possible and beneficial in government food and nutrition programs.

In the analysis of national case studies referred to concerning progress in reducing malnutrition (Gillespie et al. 1996), the more effective programs all seem to have achieved genuine involvement in decision-making in the initial assessment of the problem as well is in the analysis of its causes and in the choice of relevant activities to incorporate in program design. While some of these programs may have scored low initially on community participation, they appeared to have evolved in that direction over the years. The case studies did not include enough information to be able to assess the different aspects of participation proposed by Shrimpton (1995).

Such processes of genuine community participation also need to be facilitated and supported by the summit and are likely facilitated when the management of the institution is itself participatory and empowering (see for example Holcombe 1995). How to ensure such conditions is now becoming an important challenge in many agencies and efforts in this direction need to be pursued and analyzed. It may be especially challenging from an agency's perspective to effectively promote participation regarding the more complex processes in families and communities associated with issues such as good growth of young children (as opposed to repaying loans or consuming iodized salt or nutrient supplements for example). In many cases, communities, as well as agencies, are also exhausted from participation that was not always well-managed or effective. More efforts are needed to identify from the perspective of summit agencies what works regarding participation of communities in nutrition-relevant actions from an agency's perspective. Perhaps we need studies for nutrition such as the Holcombe (1995) study for the Grameen Bank! The analysis provided by Shrimpton (1995) stands out among the few of the studies on participation that actually focus on the effectiveness of nutrition programs. Yet the centrality of nutrition issues to the well-being of communities, the intersectoral nature of nutrition problems, and the need to combine scientifically relevant action with appropriate social processes may pose different challenges to the implementation of participatory processes and to their study.

Addressing Underlying and Basic Causes: Capacity-Building and Empowerment

Let us reiterate that our major concern here is with young child malnutrition, generally reflected by poor child growth, more than with specific micronutrient deficiencies. An adequate intake of micronutrients (e.g. iodine, vitamin A, iron), which can be enhanced by the delivery of nutrient supplements, the appropriate fortification of foods, or the diversification of food intake, is essential and even critical for adequate child health and development. However, it will not compensate for the deficiencies in *macro*nutrients in a young child who is fed only two or three times a day a diet of insufficient nutrient density. The latter also requires strategies that lead to the daily deliberate actions (appropriate caring practices) that must be undertaken by caretakers, generally mothers, to achieve adequate and timely dietary intake by the young child as well as protection from illness (see Engle 1995; Engle et al. 1997; Kumar-Range et al. 1997). Such strategies generally need to also address the constraints of caretakers and of communities so they can take these actions. Because they are more situation specific, such actions are less amenable to the effective use of top-down approaches. Fostering capacity-building and empowerment of families and of communities is essential. Admittedly, such approaches are more labor intensive and require personnel who can be secure walking into a community without knowing all the answers and yet still be responsive.

Finding and fostering the appropriate mixture of strategies in a given situation is an important challenge for the summit and was the object of one of the major recommendations of the multi-donor evaluation of UNICEF mentioned earlier (Engbert-Pedersen et al. 1992). UNICEF has been particularly successful at promoting several important service-delivery strategies. During the 1980s its support for the rapid achievement of Universal Child Immunization by 1990 contributed to the successful launch of the WSC. Its masterful use of strategies of advocacy, of information, education, communication, and of alliance-building to mobilize efforts and resources were applied quite successfully to reach goals related to immunization, oral rehydration, and salt iodization. Though the goals of the WSC address a broad spectrum of issues in child health, those initially addressed more energetically by UNICEF focused mainly on service-delivery strategies. To successfully address young child malnutrition via this route is more difficult given the need for individual caretakers to undertake daily deliberate actions to change the situation in a sustainable way. Also, as the world becomes more successful in addressing the problems that can be affected by service delivery strategies (e.g., immunization and nutrient supplements) further progress in child health/growth will increasingly come from addressing the more complex underlying causes, for example why don't children have adequate dietary intake, or why are they not immunized?

To give fish to someone in need is service delivery, to teach him/her how to fish is capacity-building, to ensure access to a river or lake is empowerment. All three are probably necessary at different times, or may be needed simultaneously at times, but capacity-building and empowerment must be included to achieve sustainability.

Three issues discussed below point to avenues to facilitate reaching this appropriate mixture of strategies and their effective scaling down:

Dilemma of "Objective" Monitoring and "Local Empowerment"

The legitimate need to show results at the agency level has generally favored initially addressing goals that could be achieved through service-delivery strategies. To that effect, an institution's headquarters sometimes by-passes the country program, using more of a "top-down" approach, to raise awareness and drive the program. This was likely necessary to set up the first rounds of immunizations, or of vitamin A supplements in several countries, so as to show the feasibility and benefits of such activities and to gain the support of all stakeholders. It is in fact easier (though not necessarily easy) to monitor the number of immunizations carried out or of vitamin A supplements distributed, than the number of infants who receive adequate and sufficient complementary foods. Yet, the process often takes on a life of its own and the theoretical preference to set up sustainable processes for identifying locally appropriate and sustainable targets and solutions is frequently forgotten. While the two are not necessarily mutually exclusive and could well be very complementary, in practice it is necessary to balance the need for an agency (whether international such as UNICEF, a government agency, or other) to show results at the agency level, and to show a responsive contribution to sustainable nutrition progress in the population being served.

Complementary Intersectoral Programming

If the underlying causes of malnutrition relate to access to food, to adequate health services and a healthy environment as well as to appropriate caring practices, these in turn result from actions in different sectors, such as health services, agriculture, social services, water supplies, education. Households and communities integrate access to food, to health services and to care; children live in families and families live in communities, not at the national level. Governments however, are organized in sectors: ministries of health, agriculture, environment, education, and so forth. Governments are the major programming counterpart of agencies such as UNICEF. UNICEF also is organized in sectors: within the Program Division at headquarters, there are sections of Health, Water and Environmental Sanitation, Education, Nutrition and others. Country offices tend to replicate this pattern. But if nutrition is an outcome of development strategies, a measure of equity in a society, nutrition also needs to be a preoccupation of health, of water and environmental sanitation, of education, and other sectors. How can programming for nutrition be integrated in other sectors so as to become complementary and synergetic without losing its unifying specificity and disappearing through integration? Just as integrating considerations of micronutrients with those of macronutrients would be more effective for child growth than either alone, integrating considerations of nutrition into health, education, water, agriculture and other programming could have a greater and a synergetic impact on child growth.

Nutrition of Adolescent Girls and Young Women

If women enter pregnancy with better nutritional status and can maintain it, several benefits are apparent: reduced complications of pregnancy including less nutritional anemia and maternal mortality, improved birth weight, lactation performance, child growth and development, as well as improved birth weight of the girl child's children, thus beginning to break the intergenerational cycle of small mothers giving birth to small babies. But such results do not show up after two years; they result from deliberate long term programming, and also require an intersectoral approach in addressing immediate as well as underlying and basic causes of malnutrition in young girls and women. Increased attention to the status of women, and their opportunities for education is as important as targeting for nutrition monitoring and appropriate food and nutrient supplements (see Walker 1997). Because so many adolescent girls bear the double burden of their own unfinished growth in addition to that of pregnancy, to target their nutrition should be a priority investment. Yet, effectively reaching them is a challenge when the most vulnerable are probably not in school!

Awareness of the need for and potential of improving the nutrition of adolescent girls and young women must also be raised. Most maternal health specialists are very concerned about maternal mortality but don't see that nutrition can help. We need to make the problem and the solutions more visible, to stimulate better analysis and action. A recently produced UNICEF working paper should contribute to such efforts (Gillespie 1997). As long as an important proportion of births are of low birth weight, the problem keeps being compounded! The cycle needs to be broken at some point—why not now?

Many of the avenues suggested above have been the object of former recommendations and internal analysis. Several country offices in UNICEF have tried to implement them. Some have even embarked on complementary intersectoral programming for better child health/growth, largely those that have developed their own conceptual frameworks of the causes of the problem to guide their programming. Summit agencies need to facilitate such developments as well as to provide a supportive administrative structure at all levels, not only through training, but also in aspects as varied as budgeting and evaluation of personnel. UNICEF nutrition advisors identified several administrative processes that were considered constraints to wider implementation of the Nutrition Strategy. Effectively addressing these in view of the needs of better programming was clearly identified as a priority (Gautam 1995).

RESEARCH AND TRAINING

Much of our existing knowledge is not widely translated into practice, a function frequently associated with training. Understanding why this is so is a function of research. Much of the leadership in research and training traditionally rests with academic institutions. In studying the various ways information is used to improve nutrition, Pelletier (1995) concluded that the biggest single need was for training (at all levels) and institution building. Alan Berg (1991, 1993) of the World Bank proposed that our approaches to research and training were a more important constraint to progress in reducing malnutrition than were more commonly cited reasons. He tried to demonstrate that academics and operations people did not work well together, that academics emphasized the wrong research issues, and that they had been negligent in preparing nutritionists to work operationally in this field doing little either to apply new knowledge to the actual solution of nutrition problems, to identify the obstacles to its application or to seek new knowledge to facilitate its application.

Berg proposed that if we think of nutrition knowledge as arising from a chain of research questions that must be addressed to bring about large-scale improvements in nutrition, we might divide the work into several reasonably distinct categories, starting with "why" a nutrition problem occurs (generally understood as the physiologic or metabolic explanation), to "who" has the problem or is vulnerable, "where" those people are, "what" to do about the problem and finally "how" to do it (which includes understanding the constraints to changes in practices and how they can be overcome). He then tried to demonstrate that most of our efforts in research and training remained concentrated towards the "why" end of the chain while more progress would be expected from concentrating on the "how" end given the amount of existing knowledge not widely applied. While recognizing that further knowledge on the "why" side was sometimes still necessary, he advocated for a better balance in efforts between the "how" and other components of the chain. This suggested shifting towards the "how".

Berg's analysis raised many concerns (see American Journal of Clinical Nutrition 1993; Csete 1993; Berg 1993b) that led to the Bellagio Conference, "Addressing the 'How' Questions in Nutrition: Unmet Training and Research Needs" (IDRC-ACC/SCN 1994). At this conference, 22 international nutrition specialists from both the North and the South and from a mix of experiences in research, training and operations, focused specifically on the need for more responsive program-related training and research efforts. They identified a two-fold challenge:

—how to utilize existing knowledge in programs that affect communities and individuals, and
—how to generate additional knowledge that can improve the impact of such programs.

The Conference clarified that the focus of both research and training should be on the spectrum of knowledge and skills needed to address the actual obstacles to program success in a given situation. The identification of such obstacles was considered a critical step in designing appropriate and relevant training and research, and one too frequently neglected. Given the existing balance, many more training and research programs needed to concentrate on questions to address specifically the processes associated with, or leading to, the "how" question. In the final report of the Conference, key characteristics of the proposed approach to research and training were specified and are summarized here.

First and foremost, the proposed training approach focusses on developing a culture of inquiry while applying and improving appropriate skills for those responsible for the design, implementation, management and evaluation of nutrition interventions. Its design and content, and the selection of trainees involve an iterative process based on assessment and analysis of community and program needs, and of obstacles to program success. Such training builds on what is already known and emphasizes factors that have been shown to influence program success. This includes a focus on animating community processes and engaging communities and households as participants in the program process. It recognizes that adequate nutrition is a human right internationally recognized in several fora. Finally, it seeks to resolve problems that emerge from the use of the three-fold nutrition causality and intervention framework where access to food, access to adequate health services and a healthy environment and the capacity of families to provide adequate care to vulnerable groups are recognized as necessary conditions to ensure adequate nutrition.

For maximum impact on program success, training will generally concentrate initially on government and NGO nutrition workers at different levels and then expand to other actors depending on the needs assessment in each country and region. It will foster the development of a new cadre of trainers to support the human elements of programming, bringing together considerations of ethics and science (the heart and the mind) in theory and practice. It will also utilize a variety of methods, including new technologies, and methods which are iterative with practice (supervision and training) for confidence building among the trainees.

Relevant research, more responsive to program needs, aims to improve the design, implementation, management, and evaluation of nutrition programs. At program level, operational research can improve effectiveness by identifying key knowledge gaps which must be addressed to improve the effectiveness of existing efforts. It also requires tools designed to augment the problem-solving capacity of communities while, at the same time, providing training in relevant research skills, some of this through on the job training and mentoring. More specifically, it requires improved capacities to assess and analyze nutrition problems and their causes in order to stimulate questions at each level: community, program, and policy. In other words, training and research needs are highly interactive with program operations (see Figure 13.2):

(1) successful program experience is promoted by operationally-oriented research;
(2) priority research questions are identified by program experience;
(3) program effectiveness is promoted by relevant training;
(4) the nature and content of training is informed by program experience;
(5) research results inform the content of the training;
(6) operationally-oriented training will promote the "culture of inquiry" and skills needed to conduct relevant research.

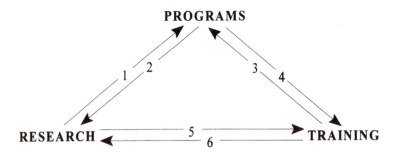

Figure 13.2. Interactions of programs, research and training.

Networks for Research and Training to Improve Nutrition Programs

To lead to significant changes in program effectiveness, and to accelerate progress in reducing malnutrition, field-driven training and research need to be fostered and multiplied. What will be learned from these experiences needs to be shared at regional and national levels—hence the promotion of networks to foster this approach. An Interim Steering Committee was formed at the Bellagio Conference (IDRC-ACC/SCN 1994) including different stakeholders (a developing country government representative— Zimbabwe; a developing country NGO—the Bangladesh Rural Action Committee (BRAC); an international professional association of nutrition- ists—the International Union of Nutritional Sciences (IUNS); a UN agency—UNICEF; a bilateral donor—USAID). With the administrative support of the International Development Research Center (IDRC) and of the UN Administrative Committee on Coordination/Sub-Committee on Nutrition (ACC/SCN), the committee has since tried to encourage and facilitate the development and operation of "Networks for Research and Training to Improve Nutrition Programs." These networks would link pro- gram managers, training and research institutions and other concerned organizations to (1) carry out their own regional needs assessment regard- ing obstacles to program effectiveness and to (2) respond considering new or expanded training, operationally-oriented research, and resource and experience exchanges. Progress is described in a first "Newsletter of the Networks" (Anon 1996). Interest in the process and the issues raised is evi- denced by over 500 replies to the announcement of the initiative received from around the world, the number of regional workshops held on the sub- ject (over a dozen that we know of in several regions), and the support of important donors (mainly USAID-Africa Bureau, UNICEF, and IDRC).

Yet progress in further *joint* activities between program managers, training and research institutions remains slow. On the one hand, the cultures of program managers and that of training and research institutions are very different. On the other hand, debate is ongoing about the priority of fundamental research over applied research, about training for science or for problem solving, and about the more traditional approach of northern-based "centers of excellence" as heads of networks or an approach that is more clearly driven by what happens in communities. Briefly, advocates of the more traditional approach consider that it has learned from past errors and is now more clearly based on the problems and realities of communities (see Anon 1997), although it appears more centrally driven. Advocates of the networks argue that training and research must be more clearly driven by the needs of community programs to become more effective and hence must be decentralized so as to be planned with community understanding and participation. In practice both approaches are complementary and should probably develop in synergy. How to strengthen a central facilitating mechanism to stimulate the development of truly decentralized and community-responsive field-driven training and research is a key part of the challenge. Currently the traditional approach remains the dominant model. There is little demonstrable evidence of any change in the focus of research and training around the world.

Focus of Research and Training in Nutrition among Leading Academic Institutions

While not all training and research take place in academic institutions, few would dispute academia's important influence in defining major approaches, or the approaches most widely applied, in training and research for nutrition. A picture of the current nutrition research focus in major academic institutions can be drawn from the work of their students.

Full-time graduate students from developing countries had been invited to apply for a "young investigator travel grant" to the International Congress of Nutrition (Montreal, July 1997) by submitting a research abstract.[5] Given the importance of research in the training of graduate students, we assumed that the most promising students would submit abstracts, and that these would be a fair representation of priorities in the field. The abstracts were analyzed with regard to the focus of nutrition interests. Main results are summarized in Tables 13.1 through 13.4.

A total of 143 applications for 20 grants were received from graduate students from non-industrialized countries who were conducting their research in non-industrialized countries. They were generally divided by region as would be expected from the population distribution, with nearly half coming from Asia (Table 13.1). Following the areas of concentration proposed by Kazarinoff and Habicht (1991), over half addressed nutrition issues in populations (52%), the rest being divided among those focusing on organs and organisms (22%), on intracellular nutrition processes (12%) and on foods or food systems (14%). The majority of projects were carried out with humans (68%), the remainder being almost evenly divided between animals and foods or plants.

The nutrition problems addressed are listed in Table 13.2. Ten percent (10%) focused on problems generally associated with young children (other than those related to micronutrients), 23% on micronutrients, and 21% on chronic diseases. Globally, around 27% of the problems addressed were those mainly prevalent in developing countries and associated with young child malnutrition (39% if one includes those related to food security and to general malnutrition in adults).

The distribution of the 97 projects carried out on humans was further examined (Tables 13.3 and 13.4) in light of the chain of questions proposed

Table 13.1. Selected Characteristics of Abstracts Submitted (N = 143)

Region of Study	%	Area of Concentration	%	Species Studied	%
Asia	43	Populations	52	Humans	68
Sub-Saharan Africa	17	Organs/organisms	22	Animals	17
N. Africa/M.-East	17	Intracellular processes	12	Food/plants	15
L. African/Caribbean	15	Foods/food systems	14		
East Europe	8				

Table 13.2. Nutrition Problems Addressed in Abstracts Submitted (N = 143)

Children	%	Micronutrients	%	Chronic Diseases	%	Miscellaneous	%
PEM	6	Iron	8	Cancer	3	Food security[a]	9
Breastfeeding		Iodine	1	Cardio-		Pro-energy adult	3
& lactation	3	Vitamin A	5	vascul.	6	Energy metabol.	3
Diarrhea	1	Zinc	3	Diabetes	6	Lipid metabolism	6
		Other micronutr.	6	Obesity	6	Other[b]	23

[a] Includes food safety, street foods and non-traditional foods.
[b] Includes methodological aspects of asessing dietary intake, metabolic aspects of fiber and of alcohol, treatment of renal dialysis, etc.

Table 13.3. Comparison between stages of the 'triple A' process (UNICEF 1990) being addressed, and of the 'Why' to 'How' chain (Berg 1991, 1993): distribution of abstracts dealing with projects on humans (N = 97)

	Pre-Why %	Why %	Who %	What %	How %	Total N	Total %
Assessment	62	9	67	3	—	28	29
Analysis	38	91	33	61	—	56	58
Action	—	—	—	36	—	13	13
Total	38	22	3	37	—	97	100

Table 13.4. Distribution of abstracts dealing with projects on humans by the stage of the "triple A" process and the level of the conceptual framework of the causes of malnutrition being addressed (UNICEF 1990) (N = 97)

	Assessment %	Analysis %	Action %	Total N	Total %
Manifestations or Consequences	50	18	0	(24)	25
Immediate causes	46	52	77	(52)	54
Diet intake	(13)[a]	(26)	(9)		
Disease	(0)	(3)	(1)		
Underlying Causes	0	14	23	(11)	11
Food			(1)		
Health					
Care			(1)		
Mixed		(8)			
Unspecified			(1)		
Basic causes	4	16	0	(10)	10
Total	29	58	13	(97)	100

[a] Numbers in parentheses refer to absolute number of cases.

by Berg (1991, 1993), the stages of the 'triple A' process (UNICEF 1990), and the levels of the conceptual framework of the causes of malnutrition (Figure 13.1).

Concerning Berg's chain of research questions (Table 13.3), over a third (38%) were clearly on the left end of the chain, addressing whether or not there was a problem and what the problem was, while 22% addressed the "why", 3% the "who", 37% "what" to do to solve and none addressed the "how". The distribution is not very different from that reported by Berg (1993) concerning funds obligated by US government agencies for international nutrition research in the mid 1970s (67% on "why", 20% on "who" and "where", about 11% on "what" and less than 2% on "how"). An analysis of funds disbursed in Canada for nutrition research in 1991–92 suggests similar trends (Anon 1995).

Concerning the stages of the "triple A" process, 29% of abstracts focused on an "assessment" of the situation, whether of manifestations, consequences, or causes of a problem (i.e. describe a situation without analyzing relationships); over one half (58%) referred to an analysis of relationships between either causes or associated factors and manifestations or consequences of a problem; while 13% focused on actions or the processes used to address causes or consequences of a problem. Comparing these two distributions, the majority of abstracts focusing on the assessment stages focused on the "pre-why" end of the chain and on "who", whereas the majority of those focusing on the analysis stage dealt with the "why" or "what" questions; those focusing on the action stage all dealt with "what", but none with "how".

Regarding the levels of the conceptual framework being addressed (Table 13.4), overall 25% of abstracts (whether assessment, analysis or action) focused on manifestations or consequences of a problem, 54% on immediate causes, 11% on underlying and 10% on basic causes. Assessment itself was divided evenly between the level of manifestations (50%) and that of immediate causes (46%); analysis focused on manifestations in 18% of cases, on immediate causes in 52%, on underlying causes for 14% and on basic causes for 16%; only 13 abstracts focused on actions, ten on immediate causes and three on underlying causes.

As stated earlier, to improve the effectiveness of nutrition programming, summit institutions must learn how to facilitate and support better situation analysis: making explicit one's interpretation of the causes of the problem, gradually moving towards a better analysis of underlying and basic causes and their constraints, then identifying and implementing effective and sustainable actions, including at each step the participation of all key stakeholders.

While over half of the 143 research abstracts addressed nutrition issues in populations and some 68% described research carried out on humans, just over half of those focused on analysis and only 13% focused on actions. All the projects classified as assessment focused either on the manifestations or on immediate causes of a problem, and so did nearly 70% of those classified as analysis. Projects focusing on underlying and basic causes were a minority (11% and 10% each). If underlying or basic causes are not assessed nor analyzed, they have less chances of being understood and acted upon effectively. In total, only 9% of the abstracts on humans focused on actions, and most of those focused on immediate causes and none on the process itself, or the "how" question. None of the abstracts referred to any participation of stakeholders or "partners" other than academic institutions and the subjects, or rather the "objects," of the research. In short, few links with actual community based programs, their managers or their preoccupations were evident.

The results suggest that the balance currently fostered is still too tilted towards the left end of the chain, and towards assessment and analysis of immediate causes of malnutrition. This finding is contrary to the priorities suggested by Berg (1991, 1993), by the Bellagio Conference (IDRC-ACC/SCN 1994) or by the Networks for Research and Training to Improve Nutrition Programs (Anon 1996). It is perhaps not surprising that little progress is apparent in the translation of existing knowledge and experience into effective programs.

WHERE DO WE GO FROM HERE?

Opportunities for scaling down to help accelerate progress in reducing malnutrition are apparent for several institutions of the summit, including governments, international agencies, and academic institutions. Accelerating progress is usually an explicit or accepted objective of the former two. For academic institutions, the high proportion of research actually carried out on humans and on population-based issues and the problems described, suggest that the majority do want to see improvements in the situation of communities and of individuals. Yet, this summary assessment of their apparent research and training priorities suggests the need for many changes if effective scaling down is to take place, if the considerations for successful programming discussed earlier are to be more widely shared, analyzed, evaluated, and implemented by their graduates, the future advisers and leaders of the summit.

More research as well as training likely needs to focus on underlying and basic causes of malnutrition, and this at each of the stages of assessment, analysis, and action, but with the explicit intent of moving towards the action stage. While there is probably much that still needs to be researched on the biological mechanisms that lead to malnutrition and its consequences, much of the currently existing knowledge at that level is still not widely applied, and related constraints remain poorly understood. Addressing such issues requires a good presence in the field, and good contacts with program managers, community workers, as well as community representatives. Unless there is free and responsive and credible communication between these groups, research projects, and hence much of training, will continue to focus on the more obvious: manifestations, consequences and immediate causes. At the same time, the increasing demands from the grassroots for their needs to be addressed, along with the increasing economic constraints faced by most community-based programs and their managers, push the latter to look for ways to increase their effectiveness. This could actually be an opportunity for developing more and better links between field programs, research programs and training programs.

Many program managers think of those in academic institutions as isolated in their ivory tower and not understanding their reality and constraints, and vice-versa. They often mutually feel misunderstood and misused. Links between them will thus not likely develop spontaneously. Efforts need to be made by academic institutions themselves, but also by governments, multilateral and bilateral agencies, to foster and support the development of more joint activities between program managers and those in training and research institutions, and especially more joint activities led by the quest to actually reach children, families and communities to improve their nutrition.

Efforts to recognize the value of such work on par with the more traditional activities in academic institutions need to be strengthened: e.g. revision of criteria for promotion, for publishing, for research grants. The low recognition given to research activities that are considered "soft" by the more traditional "scientific" community has often negatively influenced progress. Increased attention should also be given to the dissemination of knowledge which emerges from program-driven research and training as well as from program evaluations. It has been proposed that instead of the "science of nutrition" we should refer to the "science of nutrition problems in society" (Jonsson 1996), or as mentioned earlier to "public nutrition." If public nutrition is to become an increasing concern of at least some academic institutions, communication also has to be fostered between these different groups (operations, research, and training). This could be facilitated by the regional Networks for Research and Training proposed earlier.

Several additional suggestions for academic institutions also merit serious consideration such as those of Eide et al. (1996) in the context of promoting nutrition rights and their actualization, or those of Pelletier (1997) in the context of institution building for research and advanced training. The emphasis here has been on advocating for this new role of research and training in view of some current constraints to more effective scaling down.

While this is definitely not advocating that research, training, and program management be brought under the same roof, it is advocating for more partnerships, towards more joint activity between related institutions. Such joint, complementary activity can lead to a synergy, to new knowledge, and to a better application of existing knowledge, towards better processes of scaling down so as to nurture and complement local grassroots development, and achieve and sustain accelerated progress in reducing malnutrition.

NOTES

1. I would like to thank Hélène Delisle, Suzanne Gervais, Thomas Marchione, Michael Latham and Andrée Roberge for their valuable comments on earlier drafts of this paper. This paper represents the views of the author and not the official position of the groups or agencies mentioned.

2. These terms are defined in this book's "Preface." Derived from Uvin, the "summit" is composed of central governments, international organizations, first-world universities, large international nongovernmental organizations, transnational enterprises, and bilateral donor agencies, whereas the grassroots is composed of households, community organizations, and local government functioning close to local populations where nutrition problems result in the malnutrition of individuals. Scaling up and scaling down are the means by which the Summit and grassroots interact in a constructive and creative way.

3. Underweight is generally used as an indicator of global malnutrition (undernutrition). Because of its prevalence in young children as well as of its drastic and lifelong consequences on their physical, intellectual and social development, the level of malnutrition among them is commonly used as an indicator of progress in nutrition.

4. Before Uvin's analysis (1995), "scaling up" was generally thought of as a more simple replication or extension in size of existing activities.

5. A committee of nutrition specialists with experience in international nutrition to recommend candidates for these grants was formed by Dr. Hélène Delisle (Université do Montréal). Dr. Réjeanne Gougeon (McGill University) and the author participated. Content analysis was then carried out by the latter and discussed with the Chair for the purposes described here.

REFERENCES

ACC/SCN
(1996) *Update on the Nutrition Situation 1996. Summary of results for the Third Report on the World Nutrition Situation.* Geneva: ACC/SCN.

American Journal of Clinical Nutrition
(1993) "Letters to the Editor." *American Journal of Clinical Nutrition* **57**: 86–87, 89–90; and **58**: 571–581.

Anon
  (1995)   "Nutrition research funding in Canada—A snapshot of 1991–1992."
           National Institute of Nutrition. *Rapport* **10**(1): 7.

Anon
  (1996)   Networks for Research and Training to Improve Nutrition Programmes.
           Newsletter 1, June.

Anon
  (1997)   Special Issue on Institution-Building for Research and Advanced
           Training in Food and Nutrition in Developing Countries. Based on a
           Workshop held by the United Nations University and the International
           Union of Nutritional Sciences in Manila, Philippines, 18–23 August
           1996. *Food and Nutrition Bulletin* **18**: 103–178.

Berg, A.
  (1991)   "Sliding toward Nutritional Malpractice: Time to Reconsider and
           Redeploy." Martin J. Forman Memorial Lecture. Washington, D.C.:
           Helen Keller International.

Berg, A.
  (1993)   "Sliding toward Nutrition Malpractice: Time to Reconsider and
           Redeploy." *American Journal of Clinical Nutrition* **57**: 3–7.

Berg, A.
  (1993b) "Malnutrition and 'Nutrition Engineering' in Low-Income Countries: a
           Rejoinder." *International Journal of Health Services* **23**: 615–619.

Csete, J.
  (1993)   "Malnutrition and 'Nutrition Engineering' in Low-Income Countries:
           A Comment on Alan Berg's Vision of the Nutrition Track Record."
           International Journal of Health Services **23**: 607–614 (and reply to
           Alan Berg, pp. 621–623).

Eide, W. B., Alfredsson G., and Oshaug, A.
  (1996)   "Human resource building for the promotion of nutrition rights." *Food
           Policy* **21**: 139–152.

Eide, W. B. and Oshaug, A.
  (1997)   "Community, public and global nutrition." *American Journal of
           Clinical Nutrition* **66**: 197–198.

Engbert-Pedersen, P., Faure, S. D., and Freeman, T.
  (1992)   *Strategic Choices for UNICEF: Evaluation of UNICEF—Synthesis Report.*
           Australia International Development Assistance Bureau, Canadian
           International Development Agency, Danish International Development
           Agency, and Swiss Development Cooperation.

Engle, P. L.
  (1995)   "Child Caregiving and Infant and Preschool Nutrition." In *Child
           Growth and Nutrition in Developing Countries: Priorities for Action.*

ed. Pinstrup-Andersen, P., D. Pelletier and H. Alderman. Ithaca, NY and London: Cornell University Press.

Engle, P., Lhotska, L., and Armstrong, H.
(1997) *The Care Initiative—Assessment, Analysis and Action to Improve Care for Nutrition.* New York, NY: Nutrition Section, UNICEF.

Gautam, K. C.
(1995) *Final report, Meeting of regional advisers/focal points in nutrition:* September 25–29, 1995. CF/PROG/IC/95–011. New York, NY: UNICEF.

Gillespie, S.
(1997) *Improving Adolescent and Maternal Nutrition: An Overview of Benefits and Options.* UNICEF Staff Working Paper Nutrition Series No 97–002. New York, NY: UNICEF.

Gillespie, S. and Mason, J. B.
(1991) *Nutrition-Relevant Actions: Some Experiences from the Eighties and Lessons for the Nineties,* State-of-the-Art Series, Nutrition Policy Discussion Paper No. 10. Geneva: ACC/SCN.

Gillespie, S., Mason, J. B., and Martorell, R.
(1996) *How nutrition improves.* State-of-the-Art Series, Nutrition Policy Discussion Paper No. 15. Geneva: ACC/SCN.

Holcombe, S. H.
(1995) *Managing to Empower. The Grameen Bank's Experience of Poverty Alleviation.* Dhaka: University Press Limited; London: Zed Books.

IDRC-ACC/SCN
(1994) *Training and Research Needs in Nutrition. Summary of Proceedings of a Bellagio Conference on "Addressing the 'How' Questions in Nutrition: Unmet Training and Research Needs"* Bellagio, Italy: Rockefeller Foundation Study and Conference Center.

Jennings, J., Gillespie, S., Mason, J., Lofti, M., and Scialfa, T. (eds.)
(1991) Managing Successful Nutrition Programmes. State-of-the-Art Series, Nutrition Policy Discussion Paper No. 8. Geneva: ACC/SCN.

Jonsson, U.
(1995) "Success Factors in Community-based Nutrition-oriented Programmes and Projects." Paper presented at the ICN Follow-up Meeting. New Delhi: UNICEF.

Jonsson, U.
(1996) "Nutrition and the Convention on the Rights of the Child." *Food Policy* **21**: 41–55.

Kazarinoff, M. and Habicht, J.-P.
(1991) "Future Directions for the American Institute of Nutrition." *Journal of Nutrition* **121**: 1498–1499.

Kumar-Range, S. K., Naved R., and Bhattarai, S.
   (1997) "Child Care Practices Associated with Positive and Negative Nutri-
           tional Outcomes for Children in Bangladesh: a Descriptive Analysis."
           Discussion Paper No. 24. Food Consumption and Nutrition Division.
           Washington, D.C.: International Food Policy Research Institute.

Mason, J. B., Habicht, J.-P., Greaves, J. P., Jonsson, U., Kevany, J., Martorell, R.,
and Rogers, B.
   (1996) "Public Nutrition"—Letter to the Editor. *American Journal of Clinical
           Nutrition* **63**: 399–400.

Miller, R. L. and Drake, W. D.
   (1980) *Final Report: Analysis of Community Level Nutrition Programmes.*
           Washington D.C.: USAID and Community Systems Foundation.

Pelletier, D. L.
   (1991) The Uses and Limitations of Information in the Iringa Nutrition
           Program, Tanzania. Cornell Food and Nutrition Policy Program, Work-
           ing Paper No. 5. Ithaca, N.Y.: Cornell University.

Pelletier, D. L.
   (1995) "The Role of Information in Enhancing Child Growth and Improved
           Nutrition: A Synthesis." In *Child Growth and Nutrition in Developing
           Countries; Priorities for Action*, eds. Pinstrup-Andersen, P., D. Pelletier,
           and H. Alderman. Ithaca, NY and London: Cornell University Press.

Pelletier, D. L.
   (1997) "Advanced Training in Food and Nutrition: Disciplinary, Inter-
           disciplinary and Problem-oriented Approaches." *Food and Nutrition
           Bulletin* **18**: 134–150.

Rogers, B. and Schlossman, N.
   (1997) "Public Nutrition: the Need for Cross-disciplinary Breadth in the
           Education of Applied Nutrition Professionals." *Food and Nutrition
           Bulletin* **18**: 120–133.

Shrimpton, R.
   (1995) "Community Participation in Food and Nutrition Programs: An Analysis
           of Recent Governmental Experiences." In *Child Growth and Nutrition
           in Developing Countries*, eds. Pinstrup-Andersen, P., D. Pelletier, and H.
           Alderman. Ithaca, NY and London: Cornell University Press.

Tontisirin, K., Attig, G. A., and Winichagoon, P.
   (1995) "An Eight-Stage Process for National Nutrition Improvement." *Food
           and Nutrition Bulletin* **16**: 8–16.

United Nations
   (1990) *World Declaration and Plan of Action. World Summit for Children.*
           New York, NY: United Nations.

UNICEF
  (1990)   *Strategy for Improved Nutrition of Children and Women in Developing Countries. A UNICEF Policy Review.* New York, NY: UNICEF.

UNICEF
  (1997)   The State of the World's Children 1998. Oxford and New York: Oxford University Press.

Walker, S. P.
  (1997)   "Nutritional Issues for Women in Developing Countries." *Proceedings of the Nutrition Society* **56**: 345–356.

CHAPTER 14

Overcoming Malnutrition in a New Era: Conclusions and Lessons

Thomas J. Marchione

As the twentieth century comes to a close, more than two billion people (approximately one-third of human society) suffer from various forms of malnutrition, especially in developing countries in Asia and Sub-Saharan Africa. Laudable international goals and human rights promoted in the later part of the century would, if reached, significantly reduce this number. Sadly, the world is falling far short of reaching these aspirations. Uvin's analysis in Ch. 1 of the food supply situation is valuable background: although concerns for the future are justified for Sub-Saharan Africa, the continuing problem of malnutrition is not likely to be the result of the collapse of the global food supply. In the main, the larger problems of malnutrition are not explained as the direct result of national food shortages or famines, natural or manmade, although these events occupy the public's attention. The larger problem is chronic malnutrition, or more exactly undernutrition, the result of persistent income and asset poverty and poor governance that underlies household food insecurity, poor health, and lack of capacity for good quality interpersonal care within households.

The authors in this volume analyze both scaling up the strength of the grassroots community while scaling down the power of the development summit. However, their conclusions and lessons are most pointedly directed to the summit. In general terms, the authors conclude that scaling down entails increasing the accountability of the summit to the grassroots and not the other way around. The summit becomes one end of a creative and innovative development partnership; scaling down does not mean the withdrawal of technical or resource assistance, leaving development responsibility to those too weak to carry it out.

This chapter summarizes the challenge that malnutrition poses and how, within a newly emergent development era, practitioners and researchers at the summit can better carry out their responsibilities to meet the challenge of sustainably reducing malnutrition throughout the world.

THE CHALLENGE

The challenge accepted by the authors in this volume is to reduce the malnutrition of nearly one-third of the world's children under five years (0–60 months) of age (an estimated 160–180 million in 1995) who suffer from underweight-for-age, indicating protein energy malnutrition or general malnutrition. In Sub-Saharan Africa, the number of malnourished children under five is increasing and is projected to be 40 million in 2020. But the numbers are highest in south Asia; although their percentages are declining, nearly 100 million malnourished children can be found there. Given no dramatic improvement of program and policy action, and no sustained increase in civil conflict, by the year 2020, 150 million of the world's children under five will still be seriously underweight in the developing world (IFPRI 1997). These children will be subject to higher risk of death from infectious diseases because of preventable malnutrition.

Out of nearly 12 million child deaths each year in the 1990s, UNICEF estimates six and one-half million children died because of the association of malnutrition with increased risk of death from infectious disease. Millions more were left mentally and physically disabled for life (UNICEF 1997). This conclusion rests on one of the most profound technical discoveries of the twentieth century about the epidemiology of young child health and nutrition: good nutrition is the *master* key to child survival. By the 1960s, basic biological research by Nevin Scrimshaw and others showed that the combination of malnutrition and infection posed a potent synergistic danger to children under five.

Pelletier, in Ch. 2, brings together over two decades of subsequent public nutrition research in a meta-analysis of 28 studies from 10 countries.

He demonstrates convincingly that even modest improvements in the general nutritional status of children can have dramatic effects on the quality and length of their lives. Eight times more children die each year from risks caused by moderate and mild underweight (60–80% of standard weight for age) compared to those who succumb due to the increased risk associated with severe malnutrition (<60% of weight for age).

Furthermore, because improved nutrition simultaneously reduces the risk of mortality for a spectrum of infectious diseases (e.g., diarrhea, measles, acute respiratory infections, malaria, among others) addressing general malnutrition must now be considered in any cost calculation of targeted approaches to a series of specific disease-focused interventions. Such interventions may be keys to reducing deaths from specific infections, but improved nutrition is the master key. This result implies a very high payoff for programs directed to reduction of general malnutrition of individuals and nutrition insecurity of households, a phenomenon tied through epidemiological research to a complex of underlying and basic causes which are summed up briefly in Ch. 13 and the livelihood security model in Ch. 11.

A NEW ERA

Those taking on this challenge face very different conditions and institutions than existed thirty years earlier. Marchione (Ch. 4) claims these changes to be profound enough to constitute a new development era, which provides a new array of opportunities and constraints for addressing the world's nutrition problems. Of overarching significance is that the end of Cold War competition has largely removed socialist and non-aligned economic alternatives, and reduced the size and breadth of economic assistance to governments for strategic, geopolitical reasons. This new global, trade-focused economy, combined with the internal pressures within Third World countries for greater freedoms and the rapid growth of telecommunications and computer technology, will shape nutrition and food programming in the coming period.

The following trends in the development environment that have taken shape in the last quarter-century are discussed in chapters by Uvin and in greater detail in Ch. 4 by Marchione:

- Offering most hope is that nutrition progress is not only the outcome of basic economic and social developmental processes, but is the realization of international norms of human decency. In the latter half of the twentieth century, the world community shaped a formal body of interrelated international law on economic and political rights addressed to nutrition security: economic rights to food and freedom from hunger; the civil rights of women and children; and the political rights of communities to participate in shaping the policies and programs affecting them.

- Another hopeful trend is that citizens in Third World countries, left and right on the political spectrum, are breaking the grip of repressive, corrupt and controlling central governments. Although overcoming fifty years of Cold War policies will not happen overnight, evidence from the early 1990s reveals unprecedented progress, especially in Latin American and to a lesser degree in southeast Asia and Africa south of the Sahara. However, this transition has a downside: many governments have been weakened and delegitimized, crippling their abilities to maintain some of the valuable functions of the state (see also World Bank 1997).

- Connected to this political liberalization, is the rising importance of civil society as a force for development, particularly the active role played by non-governmental organizations, both international and local, which have increased in number and power throughout many parts of the developing world since the 1970s. The chapters in this book written by persons working in international NGOs such as CARE (Ch. 11) and Save the Children (Ch. 6) attest to the interest of this growing third sector.

- In apparent conflict with growing acceptance that the state should better guarantee basic economic rights is the liberalization and globalization of economies. Since 1980, in many Third World countries the romance with socialism and trade protection has been replaced with a romance with neo-liberal economic policies and free trade regimes. Countries have privatized state enterprises, removed producer and consumer food subsidies, shrunk government spending, opened borders to imports and volatile prices, while opening economies to outside investment and monetary volatility. Will this ultimately strengthen the capacity of the state to respond? What part of the summit's responsibility will the third sector and the private sector assume in the realization of such rights in grassroots communities? These are questions this book raises, but only more experience may answer.

- Troubling is the probability that private investors will find little incentive to compensate for the post-Cold War erosion of official development resources to the poorest countries. Of special concern is the decline in food assistance to developing countries by approximately 50% in the first half of the 1990s. While food aid's actual value for overcoming chronic malnutrition can be legitimately questioned, this precipitous drop conveys a message of falling commitment of rich developed countries to the food security of developing countries. The least developed countries have both looming food deficits and high rates of malnutrition. Food is less available for targeted feeding, more scarce foreign exchange must be spent for food imports, and government revenues from donated food sales evaporate. Genuine government attempts to maintain growing economies and vigorous development budgets, while lowering real food prices to the poor, are undermined.

Most troubling is the possibility that a post-Cold War trend of increasing civil conflicts and complex emergencies could continue. If so, increasing millions of people affected by conflict will demand a greater and greater portion of shrinking foreign assistance resources. Too often institutional stability needed for development will be absent (see the review in Ch. 1). Our hope is that this and the demands for assistance from the new states of Eastern Europe and the former Soviet Union are temporary post-Cold War transition problems. (There are no chapters on emergency food programs in this book; these are problems that merit a book complementary to this one.)

NEW ROLES AND CAPACITIES

Given the continuing challenge and the new conditions of this era of development, what is the summit to do? Returning to the questions with which this book began: What types of information are needed? What roles must partners play and what capacities must they have? What is the mix of skills and concerns that produces practitioners who can plan and implement successful nutrition security programs?

What Types of Information Are Needed?

Little new biological and food science information is needed to overcome the undernutrition problem in developing countries. Better understanding of some relationships, such as the intergenerational factors influencing the high rates of child stunting and its consequences, especially in south and southeast Asia, might be helpful. However, the quantity of knowledge about nutrition in the human organism has probably reached a critical mass, and what is sorely lacking is its application.

Similarly, more theoretical analysis and conceptual work on causes of general malnutrition and food insecurity are not needed. This has been valuable work, but the current frameworks are sufficiently clear and convergent to move on to more practical matters. By the same token, work describing and developing new general indicators of hunger or malnutrition should take much lower priority than more and better use of those indicators we have. If there is a generic need for information, it is to make plain how successful programs come into being, scale-up through local participation, and are sustained. Information is needed from careful program evaluation studies such as those outlined in part II of this book. One might also ask: Are there limits to devolution of responsibility to communities? What responsibilities can local and international NGOs be expected to assume? Some of this is discussed later under roles and needs of specific players.

However, the greatest information needs are more specific to actual programs, their target groups and their social, institutional and physical environments, such as: How to mobilize local financial resources? How local ethnic, economic, and political dynamics improve or constrain poor households' chances to achieve food and nutritional security? What strengths exist in the indigenous culture for maintaining and improving nutrition? Methods for gathering such information are presented in part III of this volume. In part IV, using UNICEF's conceptual model, Beaudry calls for better "situation analyses" of the basic causes affecting malnutrition and the programs designed to address them. There is a strong tendency among nutrition practitioners, even in this volume, to accept and leave unanalyzed the societal and development conditions affecting their programs; these are presented merely as background.

However, these basic causes are increasingly important considerations as the liberalization of economies and political systems make societies change and become more changeable. It is always important to know how local program structures and program results are being influenced by factors such as lack of legal human rights protections of vulnerable groups, policies constraining organizational development, and the interplay of powerful local actors.

What Roles Must Partners Play and What Capacities Must They Have?

Overcoming malnutrition will be a joint effort, a creative and innovative partnership between the grassroots and the summit. An important lesson of the last fifty years is that policies and programs based solely on First World patronage or Third World isolationism will not solve the problem. Although the grassroots has the energy and ingenuity to solve its nutrition problems, these efforts almost always involve outside resources and summit organizations. The question is, how can the development summit scale down to help local programs scale up? What new capacities are required of traditional players: central governments in developing countries, bilateral aid organizations, international organizations, academic institutions and large-scale private enterprise based in the First World? And what capacities are required of newer entrants: the international NGOs and the universities in the developing world. In the programming relationship, these institutions take on a set of overlapping functions for overcoming malnutrition: (1) *program management*; (2) *applied research and training*; (3) *policy-making and advocacy*; and (4) *donor funding*.

Program Management

The most important information for program planners and implementors is knowing how to encourage and manage scaling up. This book puts to rest the notion that scaling up a nutrition program is only a matter of increasing the size and participation in a program. Over time many programs increase in size, but also in sensitivity to local conditions, complexity, sustainability, and power. NGO and government program managers, whether building from the top-down or from the bottom-up, will arrive at various summit-grassroots partnerships, and should know how to mobilize preexisting strengths of sub-national communities, cultures, and institutions. Mobilizing such participation is an essential component of successful and sustainable nutrition improvement for a number of reasons connected to scaling up.

First of all, participation taps a stock of indigenous knowledge, social organization, and communication skills which may be appropriate solutions to nutrition problems or project management. When good food, health, or caring practices are "culturally scaled up" from a few households to many, or when scientific nutrition is "grafted" to local practice, they become inherently sustainable; cultural behaviors are related to the identity of the group, they become tied to values and unifying symbols, and are passed on from generation to generation.

As both the Bangladesh vitamin A program (Ch. 9) and the Haiti and Vietnam Hearth programs (Ch. 6 and Ch. 7) demonstrate, reliance on local social and cultural resources is a very cost-effective means of scaling up. In Vietnam and Haiti, Hearth programs helped identify and spread the most successful feeding practices used by positive deviant mothers who, though poor, were successful at raising healthy children, coping under the most adverse economic and physical shocks. In Bangladesh, women volunteers were involved in promoting consumption and production of low status, vitamin-A rich foods through familiar cultural media, having lasting effects on demand for these foods years after the program began. In Togo, the traditional dowry system was used to symbolically connect contributions to the health center operating funds to community ownership of the center.

Second, when managers open programs to participation and ownership the programs become more multi-functional and sectorally integrated. These programs require more attention to the underlying and basic causes of malnutrition that households and communities face. Nutrition-related programs in Bangladesh, Haiti, Togo, and Vietnam began with a careful focus on the immediate causes of malnutrition, insufficient consumption, and infection, and two of the three underlying causes of malnutrition: poor nutrition care and inadequate primary health care. Attention to household food security, the third underlying cause of malnutrition, evolved later. The World Hunger Program award-winners (see Ch. 5), which grew from local NGO initiatives in response to the felt needs of grassroots communities, rarely began with services for nutrition improvement, although they have functionally scaled up to include attention to underlying causes such as agricultural production and other credit and income generating activities.

Only deliberate external restraints imposed by summit agencies have prevented nutrition programs from becoming increasingly like community development programs and only local training and promotion can make community-controlled programs see the value of nutrition promotion. A dilemma for the manager is finding the balance of local empowerment and response to felt needs of communities versus the requirements for results that external donors find credible. The most nutritionally focused program presented in this book, the Hearth Program in Haiti, is the one with the least control by local communities and local governmental authorities. Vietnam's Hearth program was also limited in scope, though it was more under district governmental control. These limitations enabled the two programs to demonstrate their nutrition effectiveness to the outside world. Each demonstrated an impact on the nutritional status of children under five: dramatic across the board improvements in Vietnam and mild and moderate improvements in Haiti—very important results in light of the renewed and better understood connection between malnutrition and mortality. The other program, limited by its parent NGO, the Bangladesh Comprehensive Nutrition and Blindness Prevention Program, also had valuable evaluation data.

Third is the question of how program managers can preserve quality while quantitatively scaling up. Larger size seems to be intimately connected with cost-effectiveness; evidence of economies of scale was presented for the micronutrient program in Bangladesh and in Haiti's Hearth program. However, programmers should not expect that small programs suitable to one community or area will be suitable for all. The programs that were most clearly cost-effective were models found to work in small settings that were replicated by governments and NGOs with careful consideration of the particularities of new coverage areas. For example, Vietnam's Living University was showcased for outsiders who carried and applied the message to their own communes in their own ways. The program did scale up with quality intact.

Fourth, political content is perhaps the most difficult to build and manage from the grassroots without losing program support or bringing on suspicion from government officials. What a local program *is not permitted* to do may be most important to nutrition improvement. And what it *is permitted* to do may have little effect on sustainably reducing malnutrition. Hopefully, the new era of democratization will change this Cold War pattern. Uvin's description of some NGOs judged by the World Hunger Program to be most effective at combating hunger were combatants against the basic causes of hunger and malnutrition, advocating for political freedoms and economic rights of the poor (Haiti's Papaye Peasant Movement, Gram Vikas in the Indian state of Orissa, CORDES in El Salvador, and the National Farmers Association in Zimbabwe). He gives none of these programs high marks for addressing or affecting nutrition problems as such.

Finally, critical to all scaling up is how to make a grassroots nutrition organization financially sustainable. All the programs described here, whether initiated from grassroots or by a summit organization, were dependent to some degree on outside donor funding. Given the scarcity of resources, managers must become ever more adept at project self-financing and competition for scarce donor funding. Food and nutrition program managers might take note of the analysis of the revitalization of the Government of Togo's primary health centers in one region using district official and community contributions through user fees (Ch. 8). Kasa Pangu and coauthors make a convincing case that, if given a chance, local communities can support a fee system and control services they need without sacrificing equitable access to the services. In contrast to the Togo program, in Bangladesh managers were unable to overcome the local staff's ideological opposition to financing through sales or fees.

In the case of Vietnam, sustainability was a matter of government asset management. The government invited the international NGO Save the Children to develop the program and then supported it through community endowments by provincial communes. In northern Bangladesh, Greiner and Mannon (Ch. 9) relate program growth to increased donor funding. However, more donors led to struggles for control of program priorities, and increased funding became more a matter of international image management at the summit than actual results at the grassroots.

Scaling up and scaling down require scientific assessment of the biological nutrition problem combined with assessment of the constraints of diverse physical and social environments and organizational strengths of beneficiary communities. Nutrition programs well-adapted to local realities and with good chances of being sustained are often small and variable to begin with, and, some say, should stay that way. In any case, the most important information is local information on basic and underlying social, economic, and political causes and capacities. An important lesson is that participation is not enough; all "local" staff are not expert on the particularities of all areas, especially in large diverse countries. To the advantage of food and nutrition programmer managers is the development and widespread adoption since the latter 1980s of rapid, cost-effective community assessment tools derived from anthropology and social science disciplines; these are presented both by Messer and by Frankenberger and McCaston in part III.

Operational Research and Training

The best nutrition programs will occur where researchers, in cooperation with program managers, develop what McLachlan and Levinson in Ch. 12, and Beaudry in Ch. 13, call a "culture of inquiry." Program constraints assessment (PCA) reshapes nutrition programs through methods for assessing the institutions surrounding programs and applying operational research suited specifically to sub-national institutional environments. The method, applied in this case to school feeding in Gauteng Province in South Africa, demonstrates how detailed assessment of program functioning leads to relevant inquiries. It also serves as a medium for training and building local capacities of district level staff.

To meet the need, research and training at major academic "centers of excellence" in nutrition must shift away from research for generating new biological knowledge toward knowledge on how to apply existing knowledge to human populations. This shift involves new attitudes, new networks, and implies new curricula. These are in direct response to Alan Berg's disturbing accusation in 1993 that academic institutions at the summit have been too absorbed by the consequences and manifestations of malnutrition rather than the reasons the problems persist and how to solve them. Support for the Berg thesis is examined in Chs. 12 and 13. Micheline

Beaudry analyzes the research abstracts of applications for funding by students from non-industrialized countries for research in nonindustrialized countries to the 1997 Conference of the International Union of Nutritional Sciences in Montreal, finding only 10% focused on basic causes and 10% on underlying causes, and the rest on immediate biological causes and manifestation and consequences (Ch. 13).

Changing this picture will require simultaneous change in attitudes in leading academic institutions that attribute softness to studies of public nutrition (nutritional problems in society) and program managers' attitudes that studies are relevant only in ivory tower debates. The solution is that action institutions and research institutions must develop a culture of inquiry into the dynamics of societal causes and the mechanics of programming. This can be facilitated by better collaboration of action and research institutions through regional networks, pairing action organizations with academic institutions and fostering free and credible communications and interaction within and between these networks, promoting a synergy which will improve training, research, and programming.

Marchione, in Ch. 4, proposes a shift in the professional culture of public nutrition to make it more suitable to the new era of development, a shift that involves training the next generation of nutritionists differently. He argues for more attention in research and training to the human rights dimensions underlying nutrition security, investigating the normative aspects of nutrition in international law and local culture. He sees a need for better research on the social and political causes basic to the social systems and policies which enable or constrain overcoming malnutrition. Finally, he urges the use of tools to tap stocks of indigenous/local knowledge relevant in different settings, seeking practical lessons from this broader set of empirical knowledge of foods and their effects on the body and strategies by which local people cope and grow under different social, institutional, and natural environments.

Government Policy-Making, Advocacy, and Funding

This book does not review policy options, yet recognizes their importance for facilitating community-based programs. Although the era of the "nutriocentric" view of the government policy is behind us, central governments should ideally have food and nutrition sector programs and strategies, as recommended by the International Nutrition Conference, including sensitivity to the nutritional consequences of policies in health, agriculture, water and sanitation, education, and other sectors. Furthermore, governments and their international and bilateral advisors should seek rights-based policies and governance strategies that enable local programs at district levels and in grassroots communities to succeed. Beaudry, looks back on her leadership role in UNICEF and cites Urban Jonsson's and other colleagues' call for governments to improve their knowledge and acceptance of community realities, and track particular policies and investments, economic and social, that are associated with program success. Evaluations, reviewed by the UN Sub-Committee on Nutrition, show programs can succeed even within countries that have unfavorable development and economic performance. But chances of success are much greater when the national policy environment is favorable. The authors in this volume do not broaden their analyses very much on this point, but I suspect that the economic and national policy changes during the life of the programs in Bangladesh and Vietnam have made measurable contributions to success in those countries particularly, compared to the more modest results in Haiti.

The flip side of policy-making is advocacy, a needed shift along the scientific to normative scale of public nutrition practice according to Marchione. Uvin (Ch. 5) stresses the increasing use, and misuse, of NGOs to implement donor food and development programs, and their increasing access to the corridors of power in donor agencies and international organizations. This becomes a unique way international NGOs can "scale up" politically. In the 1990s, 40% of World Bank programs had NGO involvement. UNHCR, WFP, UNICEF, UNFPA, USAID and others have developed consultative mechanisms that increasingly involve Third World NGOs. International NGOs are urged to represent the interests of the grassroots community with large donors such as the World Bank, deflecting possible harm from large lending programs and advocating for policy change, transparency, and resources. They call for greater access to self help financial (credit) and appropriate technical assistance for local organizations and local government to help them build up their capacities.

Donor Funding

Perhaps the most important conclusions of this book are directed to the changing role of funding agencies, particularly large bilateral donors in developed countries, the development banks and the international organizations. Two conclusions stand out: one related to problem identification and implementation, and one relating to performance monitoring and evaluation.

First, the summit's public or private donors must learn to accept that building and maintaining good nutrition is not limited to the goal of enhancing human capital for better economic growth or the goal of mitigating food and famine emergencies, though these are certainly important benefits of food and nutrition programming. The end to chronic malnutrition is part of the vision of a decent world for the twenty-first century that we want for the bodies of the malnourished children and their families and the spirits of the well-nourished children and their families. When given the facts and a choice, few would want a poor child to suffer. On that score, the people of the world are ahead of the donors and governments in recognizing the universal right to food.

Second, donors should use their resources and position of power at the summit to foster local participation, respect for, understanding of, and inclusion of local realities in programming and policy reform (on issues of macro-level policy reform, see Cornia, Jolly, and Stewart 1987). This means recognition of the relevance of ethnic and cultural variety. Many of the most egregious development errors of the last half of this century are the result of operating as if the world was culturally uniform and poor communities basically the same. It also means avoiding facile notions of local participation that Levinson and McLachlan warn are too often elitist, disinclined toward projects geared to its disadvantaged population groups and poorly informed about models from elsewhere (Ch. 3).

This means investing in social assessment and training, helping the international NGOs make good on their promise of local community participation. In sector policy reform, donors should provide more support for building local government capacity (World Bank 1997). This includes proper training and use of the assessment tools described in part III, not just paying them lip service. It means finding funds for operational research as part of program funding and for building the networks of training, research, and programming discussed in Ch. 13. Funding for assessments of local livelihoods, the local culture, and the environment should not always be under pressure to be the fastest and most cost effective element in the nutrition program plan. Studying the shape and dimensions of good programs would not be considered irrelevant by programmers if donors accepted their value; the academy will find a way to join if useful and careful studies are to be done.

The third point is the need for enough patience to allow grassroots capacity and sustainability to grow. Donors should not demand results too quickly, but should not lose sight of them. Demanding results too quickly drives out sustainable capacity building. In an era of scarce funding, the emphasis is on tangible impacts on nutrition outcomes visible to the political and popular constituencies of the donor and international program agencies. "Quick wins," using the engine of high profile, vertical service interventions (e.g., vitamin A supplementation or oral rehydration) may generate visibility and financial support while leaving the more complex, locally appropriate, and sustainable programming starved of support.

This requires taking the time to know the organizations being funded and what they are doing, knowing how to separate image from reality, and to separate endless process activity from process that leads to nutrition results, results not only valuable to donors but valuable to the grassroots community and that malnourished child we are all supposedly concerned about.

What is the Mix of Skills and Concerns that Produces Practitioners Who Can Plan and Implement Successful Nutrition Security Programs?

This begins by hiring and training practitioners who are respectful and responsive to the needs of the poor. Furthermore, the practitioner of public nutrition problems must come equipped to constructively incorporate ethical considerations. The international nutrition of the past was never an engineering science, nor is the public nutrition of the future likely to become one. It is more appropriately a social science and a normative pursuit with firm footing in biological science. Coherent expressions of rights related to nutrition problems have become universally recognized and many constraints to realizing these rights locally have been removed with the end of the Cold War. Pertinent international rights need to be known by professionals and practitioners at every level and used in complement with scientific understanding of nutrition.

The ability to understand nutrition problems and solutions can no longer be isolated from an understanding of national and global economic forces. Basic causes of nutrition problems that shape the more proximate underlying causes will increasingly originate far from the community, linked to volatile international food prices, global labor markets, and trade and monetary policy. To understand these links, professional nutritionists and food and nutrition program planners in governments and NGOs must be better equipped to use economics not as context but as content. As resources for amply funded government safety nets are weakened and funding for the social sector programs are forced to become more cost-effective, economists must be made sensitive to the consequences of macro-policies for household nutrition and livelihoods at the grassroots.

Practitioners must more readily incorporate "indigenous" understandings and perceptions of food and nutrition problems and how to solve them. Greater human rights recognition and enforcement will demand that ethnic and gender perspectives be part of nutrition situation analysis.

Armed with these increased analytical capabilities, the practitioner will be able to carry a culture of inquiry into programming. Process-centered programming requires respect for local cultures and organizations, capacities for working with mothers and both genders of local leadership, and employing and teaching the methods of rapid, low cost, community-based assessment. In program situations, the practitioner should be eager for opportunities to gain local knowledge and seek interaction with people at the grassroots on an equal footing.

Process planners should not simply expand participation and empowerment of the grassroots in community-based programs, but should be skilled at joining with them to politically scale up, advocating for interventions, resources and enabling policies from governments, the private sector, and international organizations. This requires an understanding of the dynamics of local political systems.

Opening participation to communities will lead to programming that crosses the spectrum of basic rights and human needs. The felt needs of the community when mobilized will require nutrition generalists with organizing skills. Summit practitioners must be trained to address nutrition programs that are more like community development programs, with wide variation from situation to situation. An appropriate focus on scientific assessment of nutrition status, though difficult to maintain, must not be lost as programs scale up functionally to other sectors. Collaborative skills will also be required on the part of agents of the nonprofit sector, the private sector, and local government.

Within the environment of development resource scarcity, nutrition practitioners must learn to scale down to better target their limited resources to produce sustainable and demonstrable results. Traditionally, the culture of nutrition practice had its conceptual origins in western universities and its practice rooted in the world's summit development organizations. Increasingly, in the last quarter of the twentieth century, the loci of cultural change are passing to persons and institutions based in developing countries. This trend is not only economically efficient, but is essential if the summit is to scale down effectively. The summit organizations must help facilitate this shift while becoming adept at assisting community-based efforts to scale up organizationally, generate resources locally, and compete effectively for scarce international grant funds. Ultimately, the success of nutrition programming in the new development era will depend on the summit scaling down as people at the grassroots become the custodians of their nutrition security and their own futures.

REFERENCES

Cornia, G. A., Jolly, R., and Stewart, F. eds.
    (1987) *Adjustment with a Human Face: Protecting the Vulnerable and Promoting Growth*. Oxford: Clarendon Press.

IFPRI (International Food Policy Research Institute)
  (1997)   *The World Food Situation: Recent Developments, Emerging Issues, and Long-Term Prospects*. Washington: IFPRI.

UNICEF (United National Children's Fund)
  (1997)   *The State of the World's Children-1998*. Oxford: Oxford University Press.

World Bank
  (1997)   *World Development Report 1997*. Chapter 7, "Bringing the State Closer to the People." Oxford: Oxford University Press.

INDEX